THE ROUGH GUIDE TO

Economics

Andrew Mell & Oliver Walker

A catalogue record for this book is available from the British Library

Credits

The Rough Guide to Economics

Editing & picture research: Andrew Lockett
Typesetting/Diagrams: Tom Cabot
Proofreading: Jason Freeman
Production: Luca Frassinetti & Charlotte Cade

Rough Guides

Publisher: Joanna Kirby

Publishing Information

Published March 2014 by
Rough Guides Ltd, 80 Strand, London WC2R 0RL
345 Hudson St, 4th Floor, New York 10014, USA
Email: mail@roughguides.com

Distributed by Penguin Random House:
Penguin Books Ltd, 80 Strand, London WC2R 0RL
Penguin Group (USA), 345 Hudson Street, NY 10014, USA
Penguin Group (Australia), 250 Camberwell Road, Camberwell, Victoria 3124, Australia
Penguin Group (New Zealand), 67 Apollo Drive, Rosedale, Auckland 0632, New Zealand

Rough Guides is represented in Canada by Tourmaline Editions Inc.,
662 King Street West, Suite 304, Toronto, Ontario, M5V 1M7

Printed in Singapore by Toppan Security Printing Pte. Ltd.

368 pages; includes index

A catalogue record for this book is available from the British Library

ISBN: 978-1-40936-397-2

3 5 7 9 8 6 4 2

www.roughguides.com

Contents

Part Five: Macroeconomics –"the economy"

Part Six: Hot topics

Part Seven: Resources

Preface

One of the main concerns of economics is how best to allocate scarce resources. This preface aims to help allocate scarce copies of this book to the right readers, and guide different readers through various ways of using it.

Who should read this book and in what order?

This *Rough Guide* has been designed as a (relatively) painless introduction to economics for the uninitiated, non-technical reader. Our intention is that anyone should be able to read through it and, with a little perseverance, understand all of its contents. We hope it will be useful for people who want to learn about economics for their work or studies, or who simply seek to understand how markets and governments affect prosperity in a digestible, self-contained guide. For these readers, we recommend starting with **Chapter 1** and pressing on to the end – although, for a bare bones treatment, **Chapter 2** and **Parts Four** and **Six** could be skipped.

Another group of readers we hope will benefit from the book are students and professionals who may have studied the topics we cover in the past, but who may be a bit "rusty" in certain areas. We hope these readers will be able to treat the guide as a reference, dipping into the relevant chapters for a straightforward refresher as and when the need arises.

How this book works

This book presents, in an intuitive way with minimal use of mathematics, much of the material usually taught to first- and second-year undergraduates at several leading universities (where it is approached in a more technical manner).

Part One of the book introduces the science of economics and the idiosyncratic approach economists take to solving problems. In particular, it provides an outline of the model of "rational" human decision-making used by economists to explain things, and gives a survey of the evidence gathered by behavioural economists who challenge this paradigm. **Parts Two to Four** then turn to the area known as microeconomics, looking at how consumers and producers interact in markets. It considers the famous "invisible hand" argument that ideal markets can produce the best of all social outcomes, before examining the real-world market imperfections that can obstruct the invisible hand and the remedies available to the government when markets do fail. However, economists always caution that governments might well fail just as markets do.

Part Five of the book moves on to macroeconomics, starting by asking how we should measure "economic performance", before going on to consider rival theories of what determines economic performance in the long run. It then turns to shorter-term theories of the economy – including the question of if and how governments can manage it to control unemployment and inflation – setting out ideas from John Maynard Keynes and Milton Friedman along the way.

Part Six concludes the book with some hotly debated topics that bring micro- and macroeconomics together. These include globalization and free trade, global poverty, and the causes and consequences of the financial crisis of 2007–8. **Part Seven** contains recommendations for further reading and further materials, both online and in book format.

Acknowledgements

Both of us have been hugely fortunate to learn from some wonderful teachers over the years, and we'd like to pay special tribute to Professors Sujoy Mukerji and Peyton Young, and Dr. Meg Meyer at the University of Oxford for inspiring us to follow careers in economics. In drafting this book, we are indebted to editorial assistance from Andrew Lockett at Rough Guides, and for perspicacious comments and criticisms from Mark Vandevelde, Alex Harris, Maria Brooks, Avin Rabheru, Nick Ames, Joe Walker, Jackie and Terry Foote, David and Ellen Mell, and Elizabeth Foote.

This book is dedicated to our delightful wives, Elizabeth and Lucy, who made the economically questionable decision to marry us while it was being written.

Andrew Méll and Oliver Walker, 2014

PART ONE:

The basics

This part of the book offers an introduction to:

▶ **what economics is and what economists do; and**
▶ **the mindset of an economist or how economists think.**

Chapter 1 discusses what economists do and the different kinds of economist that there are and how they differ in terms of the questions they are interested in answering. There is also a broad introduction to the way in which economists think in terms of the use of **models**. Never afraid of a dodgy pun, it's an approach economists sometimes summarise with the saying "Economists do it with models".

The point of an abstract model to an economist is not to sell clothes, but to strip a problem down to its bare minimum of moving parts, making it easier to solve. This necessitates making **assumptions** which sometimes seem distorting, but help to get rid of extraneous details and focus on the key elements of a problem.

This chapter also introduces economists' fondness for **graphs**, and the use of **marginal analysis** to solve problems. Marginal analysis means looking at how some of the key variables in economic models (such as profit and cost) vary as the quantity produced or consumed is changed. Economists are especially interested in scrutinizing changes on **the margin**.

Chapter 2 introduces the way in which economists think about people, the model of so-called **homo economicus**. The chapter will examine how *homo economicus* behaves and what is really meant by his characterization as a **utility maximizer**. It then considers criticisms of this model from the field of **behavioural economics**, including work carried out jointly by economists, psychologists, and neuroscientists.

Chapter 1
What is economics?

The *Oxford English Dictionary* defines economics as follows:

> The branch of knowledge (now regarded as one of the social sciences) that deals with the production, distribution, consumption, and transfer of wealth; the application of this discipline to a particular sphere; (also) the condition of a state, etc., as regards material prosperity; the financial considerations attaching to a particular activity, commodity, etc.

Which is a bit of a mouthful! What most people think of when they hear the word economics are the statistics that get a lot of coverage in the news: the daily movements of the stock market; the interest rate; unemployment; and inflation. Part of the problem with defining economics is that one particular branch of the subject, the branch dealing with widely reported statistics such as Gross Domestic Product (GDP), tends to attract much more attention than the rest. So it might be best to outline some of the different types of economist and what they do before answering the question: what is economics?

> Gross Domestic Product is the total value of all goods and services produced in an economy.

Types of economist

Broadly speaking, there are two kinds of economist:

- ► **microeconomists**
- ► **macroeconomists**

The difference between the two could be summarized as concerning the *level of analysis*. Microeconomists are concerned with analysing individual markets and the relationships between different markets.

Macroeconomists are concerned with analysing whole economies and, sometimes, the impact of one economy on another. An "economy" here should be understood as a reference to the total value of everything produced within a particular geographical area.

However, some economists and some economic issues will have one foot in either camp.

Microeconomics

Microeconomics is concerned with the behaviour of economic actors such as consumers, households, or firms within individual markets. The level of analysis relates to particular markets. Questions asked might include:

▶ **Why are some goods expensive and some goods cheap?**
▶ **Who should produce particular goods and services – the government or private individuals?**
▶ **How will a worker respond to a change in their wages?**

Macroeconomics

Macroeconomics is concerned with the performance of whole economies: whether they are the economy of a particular region (e.g. the Northeast of England); the economy of an entire country (e.g. the USA); or the economy of a supra-national bloc of countries (e.g. the EU). The sorts of questions asked in macroeconomics include:

▶ **Why are some countries rich and other countries poor?**
▶ **What happens when the government "stimulates the economy"?**
▶ **What causes inflation?**

So most – but by no means all – of the economics that makes it into the news concerns macro- rather than microeconomics.

Whilst they differ in terms of the level of analysis, both micro- and macroeconomics are seeking to answer questions about people's decisions regarding how much of which goods and services to produce and consume. They also share a common approach to answering these questions through the use of models, which emphasize the **incentives** that give rise to these decisions. These will be discussed in more detail below.

Positive and normative economics

Naturally, making forecasts is a risky business. Economists do not always get it right, but some economists would go even further than simply making predictions and would go so far as to make **prescriptions**.

This is the difference between **positive economics** and **normative economics**. A positive economist would confine themselves to statements such as : "If a tax is imposed on cigarettes, the price of cigarettes will rise; smokers will smoke fewer cigarettes and some may give up the habit completely." Such a statement makes no comment about the desirability of the effects of a cigarette tax; it simply aims to inform as to what those effects would be.

A normative economist might say something a bit different, such as: "Smoking should be reduced so that people are healthier. Therefore a tax should be imposed on cigarettes to reduce smoking." A normative economist will subscribe to a goal and then consider which economic tools will best achieve that goal.

This doesn't mean that a positive economist would never dispense policy advice, but it would always be of the form: "If your goal is x then you should do y". Whereas advice from a normative economist would sound like: "Your goal should be x, and so you should do y".

Thinking like an economist

The real world is vast and complicated with a huge number of things going on all at once. Imagine trying to answer a simple economic question, such as "what determines the price of a PC?" or "will GDP increase or decrease this year?" In this environment, it is virtually impossible to take all the relevant variables into account.

Models and assumptions

The solution of an economist is to simplify the problem. Imagining how the world would work if it were simpler is rather like a thought-experiment. The aim of simplifying the world is to ignore the factors at play in the real world that will have no impact or very little impact on the solution. These factors might tend to confuse the important issues so we assume them away. This procedure is actually rather similar to the way in which a physicist, thinking about the path of a ball thrown from one person to another, might build a model in which they imagine that the ball is a particle. The ball isn't really a particle; it is simply that a ball would be subject to air resistance whereas a particle would not be subject to any forces other than gravity. Imagining the ball as a particle allows the physicist to ignore the relatively unimportant force of air resistance and concentrate on the more important force of gravity. Simplifications like this often allow both physical and social scientists to come to an approximate solution with dramatically less calculation, but with very little shortfall in accuracy.

So in the example of the price of PCs mentioned above, economists would start with a simplification. They might imagine that the demand for PCs depends only on the price, with more PCs being demanded the lower the price. They might also assume that the supply of PCs depends only on the price, with the number of PCs firms are willing to supply being greater at higher prices, and then imagine that the price will adjust until it is at a level where suppliers are willing to supply to the market exactly the same number of PCs as consumers are willing to buy. Economists call this an **equilibrium** price and quantity. It is an equilibrium because none of the agents involved have an incentive to change their behaviour. At this point, it is unlikely any of the agents will want to move away from it. This is the famous economic model of supply and demand. If the price were higher than this equilibrium price, more PCs would be built by suppliers than consumers were willing to purchase, so sellers would lower the price in order to reduce their unwanted surplus stock. If the price were below this equilibrium price, consumers would be trying to buy more PCs than the producers were manufacturing. So sellers would be taking calls from potential purchasers and having to explain that their stocks had been depleted. It would not take them long to realize there was room for them to raise the price.

A good economist will then go back to the initial assumptions and question how the results of a model change if the assumptions change.

A good economist will go back to initial assumptions and question how the results of a model change if the assumptions change.

Supply and demand

To economists, demand is defined as the quantity of goods (or services) consumers are willing to buy at the prevailing price over a given period of time. Economists define supply in a similar way as the quantity of goods (or services) that producers are willing to sell at a given price over a given period of time.

To assume makes an ASS of U and ME

Economists' fondness for simplifying assumptions has been mercilessly parodied by others. One such parody involves a chemist, a physicist and an economist stranded on a desert island with only canned food to survive. They start discussing how to open the cans. The chemist suggests they leave the cans in a shallow lagoon and wait for the saltwater to corrode the cans to make it easy to open them. The physicist and the economist point out they will have starved to death by the time the cans corrode sufficiently. The physicist suggests building a fire and heating the cans; the air inside will heat and expand until the cans explode open. The chemist and economist protest that the risk of being hit by exploding can shrapnel is too great. Frustrated, the physicist and chemist turn on the economist and ask how he would suggest opening the cans. The economist thinks for a minute and then says: "Assume we have a can opener..."

Whilst economists can appreciate the humour, this offers a neat illustration of a bad assumption for an economic model. The assumption assumes away the very problem the model is trying to solve: namely, how to open cans without a can opener. A good assumption would instead leave the main features of the problem and assume away the extraneous details that are making it difficult to see the solution.

The key question in the case of the model of supply and demand is this: what would happen if factors *other than the price* could affect the quantity of PCs that consumers would demand and producers would supply? For example, what would be the influence of the price of Apple Macintosh computers? Apple provides a similar product to a PC, so if they drop their price, a decrease in demand for PCs at all price levels might be expected. This could be incorporated into the model of supply and demand with demand shifting whenever Apple change their prices.

The key to a good model is to make broadly accurate assumptions, which reduce the number of factors involved. Such assumptions might sound cavalier from time to time, but they serve a useful purpose in allowing economists to think clearly about the things that really matter. Economists will, wherever possible, go back and look at their original assumptions and check how changes in those assumptions would change the results of the model.

Testing models and assumptions

To economists, the thought-experiments described above are only half the job. For most economists, economics is not purely an armchair activity: rather, once a model has been built and conclusions drawn, economists want the model to be tested as much as possible. This is where economists are at a grave disadvantage compared to physical scientists.

A physicist, interested in the path of a ball thrown through the air, can set up an experiment to test their model of a thrown ball as a particle, with an initial speed and trajectory, being acted on by the force of gravity. They will be able to set up their experiment so that only one variable is altered at a time and the influence of each can be isolated.

For the most part, such experiments are not available to economists. An economist, interested in the impact of a minimum wage on employment decisions in the UK, cannot make ten "copies" of the UK economy and examine outcomes in the employment market when the minimum wage is £0 per hour, £1 per hour, £2 per hour... and so on. Economists must instead rely on observations of the real world. A large amount of effort is put into thinking what predictions an economic model makes that could be observed in gatherable data. If such predictions are not observed, the model is rejected and a new one sought.

While economists, for the most part, cannot conduct controlled experiments, some have been innovating in this area. **Experimental economics** is now a field in its own right with economists such as Ernst Fehr and Colin Camerer being particular proponents. In economic experiments, participants are typically recruited in much the same way as they are in psychology experiments. The experiment then consists of a "game" (see **Chapter 8**) in the laboratory, which is supposed to simulate a real economic situation.

Theory and practice in economics

As with other sciences, there is naturally some division of labour within economics. Some economists are primarily theorists who conduct the thought-experiment stage of building an economic model. Other economists are primarily applied economists who test the new theories that theorists have put forward. Naturally this is not a cut-and-dried distinction and some economists will straddle both categories.

There is a third category, sometimes called an econometrician. Econometricians study economic datasets and think about the difficulties inherent in inferring relationships from the data. Their work concerns looking at the typical difficulties that emerge when dealing with economic datasets and using advanced statistical techniques to ensure that estimates derived from those datasets represent real economic relationships rather than being tricks of randomness. While the work of econometricians is very important for economists, there is relatively little discussion of it in this book. Such discussion would require readers to have a significant background knowledge of statistics, and would simply make this book too long. Readers interested in an introduction to econometrics should consult the **"Resources"** chapter at the end of the book.

The way the participants play the game is then compared to the predictions of economic models.

For example, Ernst Fehr and his colleagues Georg Kirchstciger and Arno Riedl published an article in the *Quarterly Journal of Economics* in 1993. They reported the results of a laboratory experiment they had conducted. Participants were randomly assigned to being workers or employers. The researchers ensured there were more workers than employers – economic theory would then suggest that competition among the workers for jobs would drive down wages to the lowest that workers would accept. In fact this didn't happen and wages higher than the minimum were observed. Furthermore, the higher the wage, the more "effort" a worker would expend, even though effort choices were made *after* the wage had been agreed and so could have no effect on the wage! Evidence like this is often portrayed as undermining economics. It doesn't, though it may undermine some economic theories, in this case the theory that people behave in a self-interested way in the labour market. This work is thought to confirm an alternative hypothesis that **gift exchange** is important in labour markets. The idea is that workers reciprocate the "gift" of a higher than required wage with a "gift" of higher effort.

However a note of caution should be sounded. Economists are interested in how people respond to incentives in the real world. Even the most carefully designed laboratory experiment cannot compensate for the fact that the participants are in a laboratory rather than in the field, which changes the nature of the incentives they face. It would be wrong to underestimate the importance of familiarity with a situation. The situation of bargaining over wages and then working is a familiar one. The situation of being in a laboratory, haggling over a number that someone has called a wage, and then choosing another number that someone has said represents effort, is not familiar. In the jargon, this is a criticism that experiments in the lab lack **external validity**, and tell us nothing about human behaviour outside the lab.

The work done by John List has shown that some of the strange results found in laboratory experiments almost completely disappear, or are short-lived when the experiments are conducted in the field instead. List and his colleague Uri Gneezy conducted field experiments in which participants were given an actual job to do. Whilst the gift exchange effect was present initially, it tended to die away quite quickly. Their results were published in the journal *Econometrica* in 2006. This provides an example of the caution that should be attached to lab experiments; the results are not meaningless, but economists need to be cautious about extrapolating from lab settings to the real-world equivalent they are trying to emulate.

The use of graphs and diagrams

Even when they are not looking directly at data, but are thinking through a problem, economists make a great deal of use of graphs and diagrams. A graph provides a clear way to think through a problem and often a concise way to describe it.

Graphs have two **axes**, one vertical and the other horizontal. In an economic diagram, these axes are assigned to variables of interest, such as price or quantity for a particular good, or the level of GDP and the interest rate. Lines can then be drawn on the graphs to show the combinations of the two variables that are consistent with some agent's objectives or with some proposed economic relationship.

The **slope** of such a line shows how much the parameter on the vertical axis must change in response to a one-unit change in the parameter on the horizontal axis. For example, how much the price must change in order for the quantity demanded to increase by one unit. Where one of the parameters decreases as the other increases the line will slope downwards, while if both parameters increase or decrease together the line slopes upwards. The magnitude of the slope of any line – how steep or shallow it is – is given by the ratio of a change in the parameter on the vertical axis and the resulting change in the parameter on the horizontal axis.

For example, return to the description above of how supply and demand determines the price and quantity of PCs. This started by describing a relationship between the price of PCs and the quantity of PCs consumers will demand. As the price decreased, consumers demanded more PCs. This is a relationship that can be drawn on a graph where the quantity of PCs is on the horizontal axis and the price of PCs is on the vertical axis. The relationship can then be represented by a downward sloping line, known as the **demand curve**. The slope of the line tells us how far the price of PCs has to fall in order to ensure consumers will buy an extra PC.

The supply of PCs has been described as a relationship between the price of PCs and the number of PCs firms would be willing to produce and sell. This can be represented as a line on the same set of axes, but which will slope upwards – the **supply curve**. Both of these lines have been shown in figure 1.1.

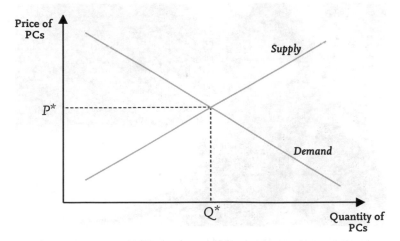

Figure 1.1: The famous supply and demand diagram. At any price greater than the equilibrium price of P*, the amount of the good supplied would exceed that demanded. In order to sell their excess stock, firms lower prices until they reach the equilibrium. At any price lower than the equilibrium price of P*, more of the good is demanded than firms are willing to supply. So consumers will bid the price up until they reach the equilibrium.

Figure 1.1 also shows what is meant by an **equilibrium**. There is only one price and quantity at which supply and demand coincide: P* and Q*. So there is only one price and quantity where firms would want to supply the same number of units as consumers want to consume. At this point nobody wants to change what they're doing – hence the name "equilibrium".

By contrast, at any price higher than P*, the amount supplied is greater than that demanded. This is a **disequilibrium** because there is a tendency for people to change what they are doing. At the higher price a number of businesses won't be able to sell their products, so they'll have to lower prices in order to shift everything. Similarly, at any price lower than P*, demand outstrips supply, meaning many consumers will risk coming away disappointed unless they "bid" against each other, raising the price.

Marginal analysis

Economists are always interested in *maximizing* various kinds of variables, and understanding how to read and interpret graphs can help to understand how economists go about maximizing various things like welfare

Desert island economics. The so-called Robinson Crusoe economy has a long pedigree in the subject, acting as a simplified economic model. It assumes one individual acting as producer and consumer. See p.11–15 on marginal analysis.

or profit. One of the key ways in which economists do this is through **marginal analysis.**

Marginal analysis is a very important tool for economists and provides them with a useful way of thinking about decisions. To illustrate marginal analysis, imagine a castaway on a deserted island. In a stunning display of a lack of imagination, economists often call the hypothetical castaway Robinson Crusoe.

Robinson is on a deserted island and must make the best possible use of his resources (his time and the natural resources of the island) to survive and prosper. Consider one of the decisions Robinson must make: how much time to spend gathering food. Every minute spent gathering food produces food that Robinson can eat and so alleviate his hunger. However, every minute spent gathering food is time that is not spent on other important activities, including sunbathing; building shelter; or maintaining a signal fire in the hope of rescue. The question is: how many minutes should Robinson devote to gathering food?

An economist approaches this problem by realizing that there is a benefit and a cost to every minute spent gathering food and that benefit and cost will depend on how many minutes have already been spent gathering food. Economists call the benefit derived from the last unit of something the **marginal benefit** and the cost of the last unit of something the **marginal cost**

The first minutes spent gathering food confer on Robinson a very large benefit. He starts by gathering the low-hanging fruit so gets lots of food for every minute spent, and the food he gathers provides him with enough sustenance to survive. However, after Robinson has spent some time gathering food there is a lower benefit associated with each extra minute. For starters, he gathered all the low-hanging fruit in his first few minutes; in order to gather food now, he must climb trees and so gets less food for every minute spent gathering food. Additionally the food he gathers is no longer necessary for survival, and it may simply lead to his putting on weight. So the **marginal benefit** – the benefit of the last minute spent gathering food – starts very high, but then falls as more minutes are spent gathering food. The relationship can be drawn on a graph with the dollar-value of the benefits on the vertical axis, and the number of minutes spent gathering food on the horizontal axis.

The first minutes spent gathering food are relatively costless for Robinson. He is initially only sacrificing time he would otherwise have spent lazing on the beach working on his tan (well, it would be embarrassing coming back from being stranded on a desert island without a tan!) However, the more time he spends gathering food, the more time he must take from other activities that may well be more important than sunbathing. For example, after a while he must spend time that would otherwise have been spent building a shelter or maintaining a signal fire. So the **marginal cost** – the cost of the last minute spent gathering food – increases

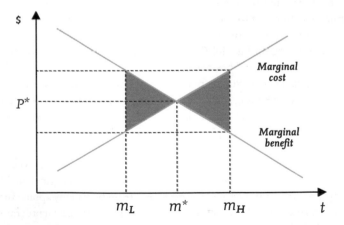

Figure 1.2: The marginal benefit and marginal cost of time spent gathering food when stranded on a desert island. The best quantity of time to spend is where the marginal benefit and marginal cost are equal.

as more minutes are spent gathering food. This could be drawn on a graph with a financial measure of cost on the vertical axis and the number of minutes spent gathering food on the horizontal axis. In fact both lines could be drawn on the same graph, as has been done in figure 1.2.

The question of the best number of minutes for Robinson to spend gathering food then becomes quite easy to answer. Robinson should spend m^* minutes gathering food so that the marginal benefit of the last minute he spent gathering food and the marginal cost of the last minute he spent gathering food are the same. Why is this so?

Suppose Robinson spent more time than this gathering food, for example, m_H in figure 1.2. Then the marginal cost of the last minute spent gathering food would have exceeded the marginal benefit of the last minute gathering food, so it would have been better not to have spent it gathering food, but to have spent it building shelter or stoking the signal fire. The same can be said for all of the minutes between m^* and m_H. Each of these minutes presents a net cost to Robinson in the amount by which the marginal cost of that minute exceeds the marginal benefit. So it is possible to represent the total amount by which Robinson's excessive foraging hurts him by the area between the marginal cost and marginal benefit curves between m^* and m_H. This area has been shaded in figure 1.2.

A similar argument can be used to show that spending any less time than m^* minutes gathering food cannot be the best thing for Robinson to do. If he were to spend less than m_L minutes gathering food, then the marginal benefit of another minute out gathering food would exceed the marginal cost: he'd be better off spending more time collecting coconuts instead of topping up his tan! Each of the minutes not spent gathering food between m_L and m^* has a foregone net benefit in the amount by which marginal benefit exceeds marginal cost. So the total foregone benefit as a result of spending too little time foraging for food is represented by the shaded area to the left of m^* in figure 1.2. Economists will treat benefits foregone as a result of a decision in exactly the same way as they treat a cost of a decision (see "Opportunity cost" below).

While our example of Robinson Crusoe may seem a little contrived, it serves an illustrative purpose. Economists would use this marginal analysis to optimize any number of other decisions, from how many apples and oranges a farmer should produce or consume to the tax rate a kleptocratic dictator should set. Unless the marginal benefit of the activity equals its marginal cost, they can always do better.

Opportunity cost

Economists think about the costs of activities in a slightly different way to the average person on the street and, importantly, in a way that is different from the accountant's concept of cost. Think of an owner-managed convenience store. To an accountant the costs of such a business operation would be measured in the amount the owner pays in wages to his employees; the amount he pays for the stock that he sells; the amount he pays in rent for the premises; and the amount he pays for the tills and CCTV cameras and other equipment used to run the store.

All of this would be included in the economist's concept of cost, but there is something the accountant has missed that the economist would include: the cost of the owner's time. If the owner of the convenience store were not running the store, he might be able to do something else with his time. The next best thing he could do might be lying on a beach somewhere, or it might involve a middle to senior management position in a large firm. Whatever the next best thing the owner could do with his time, not doing it is a cost of running the convenience store and should be included in the concept of cost.

This concept has actually been used above already! Recall that the cost of gathering food for Robinson Crusoe was that the time could have been spent on other activities. Sometimes these activities were not all that conducive to Robinson's welfare (sunbathing), but other times the alternative activities were extremely conducive to Robinson's welfare (stoking the signal fire). When the opportunity cost was low, all Robinson had to give up was sunbathing. But as Robinson spent more time gathering food, the only other activities from which the time could be taken were valuable activities, such as building shelter or stoking the signal fire. This is what made the marginal cost of gathering food increase: the opportunity cost was increasing.

Opportunity cost is a hugely important concept in economics and will be explained in more detail in **Chapter 3**. For now, simply remember the maxim that the opportunity cost of using time or an asset to do x is **the value of the next best alternative use of that time or asset which is foregone** when the time or asset is used to do x.

This book

This book is divided into seven parts. The remainder of this part explains the economist's model of the rational individual and psychological evidence that challenges this conception of the individual. **Part Two** sets out the ideas behind supply and demand and how they interact in markets, potentially leading to an ideal social outcome under certain circumstances. **Part Three** then considers how markets can fail in some way so that they do not convert individuals' self-regarding actions into the best outcome for society. **Part Four** looks at some of the more advanced topics in microeconomics involving strategic interactions between firms and difficulties in writing contracts. **Part Five** moves on to consider the basics of macroeconomics including how economic performance should be measured and what causes economic growth. It then looks at developments in macroeconomic thought from the classical economics through to Keynes and latterly the monetarists. **Part Six** brings together macro- and microeconomic ideas to consider some of the big economic debates including globalization and free trade, how poorer countries could develop, and the causes and consequences of the financial crisis of 2007–8.

Chapter 2

The economic mindset: *homo economicus* vs. behavioural economics

In most economic theories, the role of *homo sapiens* is played by an eccentric character known as *homo economicus*. According to popular wisdom, *homo economicus* is a clinical calculator of his own advantage, a ruthless pursuer of his own interest and, to top things off, an insufferable smartarse. What could be more "dismal" than a science based on such an account of human nature? This chapter presents an outline of how economists really do characterize human beings and examines the case for and against this approach, including the critique from **behavioural economics**. In so doing, it gives foundations for much of what follows as well as a more general critical perspective on the methodology of mainstream economics.

Meet *homo economicus*!
Stripping down *homo sapiens*

Chapter 1 argued that, just as scientists try to foretell the results of various physical processes, part of the job of an economist is to generate predictions about a range of economic phenomena. In contrast to the natural sciences, however, the observations of interest to economists – be it the number of jobs created in the last quarter or the effect on cigarette sales of a new tax – arise primarily as a result of **human decisions** rather than unmediated physical laws. The principal force at work in economics is therefore that of **free will**. And, as experience tells us, free will can produce all sorts of bizarre and self-destructive consequences, from drug use and religious fanaticism to falling in love with someone you shouldn't have.

Given this daunting diversity of human behaviour, why do economists insist on making assumptions about the way people make decisions? The simple reason is that if one were to make *no* substantive assumptions, one could not arrive at *any* interesting answers to the questions economists study. To see this, imagine you were a professional economist and your boss asked you whether an increase in the interest rate would lead to a rise or a fall in savings. If you were unwilling to make any generalization whatsoever about human behaviour, the best you could offer would be "savings could increase or decrease". This kind of thing would be unlikely to get you promoted. Assumptions about human behaviour are thus an essential starting point for any economic argument worth listening to, even if it is inevitable that these assumptions will fail from time to time.

There are all sorts of assumptions one could make about the way people make decisions, but economists focus overwhelmingly on **rationality conditions**. These require, roughly, that people pursue a set of interests in a consistent fashion. Why characterize human behaviour in this way when other disciplines (most notably psychology) tend not to? The most important reason is that economists are interested in a particular domain of human activity – one where people sign contracts, trade goods, and decide what to do with their money on a day-to-day basis – where this seems reasonably **accurate**, has a great deal of **predictive power**, and has a high degree of **generality**.

Economists focus overwhelmingly on rationality conditions.

For instance, consider a farmer deciding which crop to plant in a field. An economist would typically assume he chooses in order to maximize the profit of his farm (taking all things, including the cost of his own labour and the long-term fertility of his land, into account). This gives a very clear prediction as to what the farmer will do – the assumption that he maximizes profit has tremendous predictive power. What's more, since he can use whatever income he raises from the field to spend as he pleases, he has every incentive to behave as the economist assumes. **Profit maximization** therefore seems like it should be accurate in this case (see p. 23). And, finally, any firm can profit maximize, so the same assumption can be applied to a wide range of cases – it is a very general assumption.

Assuming people are rational may not seem very sensible or get us very far in some spheres of analysis – it is of little use in telling us why people fall in love or cry over Celine Dion – but for most purposes economists are concerned with it is an incisive and broadly accurate standpoint. This explains why most practitioners in the field use these assumptions (though see p.35 for some dissenting voices). In addition to this, however, there are a number of other less reputable reasons why rationality conditions are popular. They include the following:

Celine Dion: not on *homo economicus*'s playlist.

- ► As well as coming up with predictions (what is known as **positive economics**), economists are also interested in dispensing advice to investors, policymakers, and others over what they *should* do. This is the sub-discipline of **normative economics**. Since no cogent advice would ever suggest irrational behaviour, using rationality conditions in positive economics means that positive and normative economics share many of the same tools. Though this is convenient for economists who do both positive and normative economics, this convenience is not a good reason to orient positive economics in a particular way.
- ► Assuming that humans are rational, autonomous beings with diverse tastes and interests fits an eighteenth-century liberal ideological perspective. Subscribers to this credo – including one Adam Smith – have therefore found it an attractive foundation for economic analysis. (See p.23). But the question of how to think of people in a morally palatable way is clearly distinct from that of how to think of them in an economically useful way.
- ► Finally, certain political doctrines have found the *conclusions* generated by rationality conditions to be palatable, and thus have embraced the assumptions on that basis. The libertarian right has been particularly swayed by the welfare theorems described in **Part Two**, while the social democratic left has found solace in some of the "market failure" arguments presented in **Part Three**.

Milton Friedman on "unrealistic assumptions" in economics

Assumptions about decision-making are a fact of life in economics – it is impossible to deduce anything but the most vacuous conclusion without making them – and in some cases these assumptions are likely to prove unrealistic.

Indeed, as Milton Friedman (1912–2006) argued in his classic 1953 essay "The Methodology of Positive Economics", it is often the case that the *stronger* – i.e. more unrealistic – the assumptions, the sharper the conclusions will be. For example, the supposition that firms maximize their profits is a very strong assumption, but it also yields an impressive range of insights as to how companies behave *when* it is true (see **Chapter 4**). It is sometimes sensible for economists to sacrifice a degree of accuracy – and allow more instances when their assumptions fail – for additional predictive power.

So far so uncontroversial, but Friedman goes further. Some assumptions such as profit maximization may not *ever* be true precisely. But, as they are to do with rational behaviour, in general they must at least hold *approximately*. Firms that fail "by a long way" to maximize profits have a strong incentive to learn from their mistakes and change their ways, so one would expect them to tend towards profit maximization over time. Similar arguments can be made for any sort of rational behaviour.

There is surely a large measure of truth to Friedman's argument, but one shouldn't let it breed complacency about rationality conditions. Economists should be open to revising their assumptions if faced with sufficiently strong evidence that they fail to hold even approximately.

Three fundamental assumptions

So what are these rationality conditions and how convincing are they? The details vary from theory to theory, but there are three assumptions that are common to almost all economic analysis, and which form the essence of *homo economicus*. These are set out and scrutinised below.

Stating the assumptions will involve adopting a very abstract perspective on decision making. Though this will probably seem unnatural to begin with, conceiving of decisions in this way means economists can arrive at a theory that applies to a very wide variety of cases.

At the highest level of abstraction, then, making a decision involves selecting an alternative from a set of options. Economists call the set of all possible options the **choice set**, and assume that people have **preferences** over the alternatives in this set – that is, they may prefer some options over others. These preferences can be observed by looking at the decisions people make: if they choose one option when another one is available, then the former cannot be any worse, according to their preferences, than the latter. To use the jargon, the first option is **revealed preferred** to the second. Rationality conditions take the form of restrictions on the kinds of preferences people are allowed to have – that is, they restrict the kinds of decisions people can make. In economics there are three conditions that preferences have to satisfy to conform to the model of *homo economicus*: transitivity, continuity, and completeness.

Transitivity

The first condition is called **transitivity** and rules out "cyclical" preferences – for example, preferring beer to wine, wine to whisky, but whisky to beer.

Having preferences like this seems obviously contrarian. Imagine Sophie has these cyclical preferences over beer, wine, and whisky and currently has a beer. The fact that she prefers whisky to beer means she'd pay a small sum to exchange her beer for a whisky. Likewise, her preference for wine over whisky means she'd pay a small sum to trade her whisky for wine, but then since she prefers beer to wine she'd also pay to swap her wine for a beer. She'd therefore make a series of transactions that would all cost her money but, overall, would leave her exactly where she started. And this without even touching a drop! Sophie would have fallen victim to what economists call a **money pump** and this looks like irrationality *par excellence*.

In real life, people are very seldom as irrational as Sophie – if they were, opportunities for money pumping would abound. The fact that they don't should inspire some confidence that transitivity is a reasonably accurate assumption to make about the way people behave.

Continuity

Continuity's formal statement is mathematically complicated, but it's possible to get an accurate impression of what it requires by thinking of a choice set made up of "bundles" of different goods. For example, one might imagine someone with a shopping basket containing eggs and bacon. At an abstract level, the axiom says: *if X and Y are two different goods in a bundle, there is always another bundle, containing one unit fewer of X, some more of Y, and the same amount of everything else, that is preferred to the original bundle.* Where X is bacon and Y is eggs, this means there must be *some* number of eggs that you'd willingly accept in return for giving up a single rasher of bacon.

Is continuity really a rationality condition and do people typically behave in accordance with it? In answer to the first question, it is not a rationality condition in the same way that transitivity is – people who do not follow it are not exposed to money pumps or such like. However, "discontinuous" preferences are generally somewhat odd (see the box below for an example).

In response to the second question – whether continuity is an accurate assumption about real-life decision-making – many people's instinctive response is negative. For example, suppose one of the "goods" in the bundle was "health" or "safety": surely, or so the argument goes, plenty of reasonable people would be unwilling to sacrifice *any* amount of health for something as quotidian as a rasher of bacon. Sensible though this may seem, in fact this isn't what is observed. To see why, imagine that someone placed a rasher (on a suitably clean surface) across a road or up a flight of stairs and then offered you the chance to go and get it. Provided you liked bacon, the chances are you'd cross the road or climb the stairs – thereby jeopardizing your health to some minimal degree – in order to claim it. Your preferences would then be consistent with continuity.

The assumption of continuity should not, therefore, be a major source of worry, at least when applied to the domain of activity economists usually study. Indeed, the idea that people are willing to "**trade off**" different goods for each other at *some* rate of exchange is quite fundamental to the

Fools' gold

An example of "preferences" that disobey continuity is the Olympic Games medals table. One can think of a country's medal haul as a "bundle" where the "goods" are gold, silver, and bronze medals, and say that one country is "preferred" to another whenever it is ranked ahead in the medals table. This ranking is based, first, on how many gold medals each country has won then, in case of a tie, on the number of silver medals they have; and finally on the number of bronzes. The technical name for this kind of ranking is a **lexicographic order**, since the way it works is analogous to the way words are ordered in the dictionary.

The medals table is inconsistent with continuity because there is *no* number of silver medals that a country could win that would be as good – according to the table – as a single gold medal. As a result of this, the table often gives a distinctly perverse account of how well different countries have performed at the Games. For example, at London 2012, Spain (three gold medals, ten silvers, and four bronzes) was ranked below North Korea (four golds, no silver, two bronzes), despite winning almost three times as many medals.

"On matters of taste there can be no argument"

Imagine you were offered the choice between a round-the-world tour and a bus ticket to the local supermarket and you chose the bus ticket. Would that make you irrational? Arguably, but it certainly wouldn't cause you to violate any of the three rationality conditions set out here. By and large, economists make few claims about *what* people should prefer: they just assume people's preferences to have a certain structure (to be transitive, continuous, and complete). In particular, economists can allow people's preferences to be altruistic – it is a common misconception that *homo economicus* is by nature purely self-interested.

The principal advantage of this is that it means that economic theories can accommodate a very diverse range of tastes. It also means that the discipline is founded in a way that is consistent with the liberal maxim *"de gustibus non est disputandum"* – "on matters of taste there can be no argument".

way economists think of human decision-making. **Part Two** gives some far-reaching consequences of this and other assumptions.

Completeness

Finally, economists assume that people's preferences are **complete** in the sense that, when offered the choice between two alternatives, they either prefer one to the other or are indifferent. Put another way, the only thing that completeness doesn't allow is that people respond to the problem of decision-making with "I don't know". However, as anyone who has taken elderly relatives to a Thai restaurant will attest, "I don't know" is a common response, especially in unfamiliar settings. Furthermore, knowing what you want doesn't seem to be an obvious prerequisite for rational decision-making.

Formally stated, completeness therefore says: *for any pair of options, A and B, either A is preferred to B, B is preferred to A, or the two are regarded as equally good.* It is the least convincing of the three basic rationality conditions used by economists, and constructing economic theories that don't require it remains an active area of research. However, it's worth remembering that the loss of a little realism can be a price worth paying for predictive power. And what economists gain by making these assumptions is the topic of the next section.

Utility maximization

One highly mechanical way of making decisions is as follows. First, the decision-maker assigns a "score" to every alternative in the choice set representing its "rank" in her preferences, with a higher score indicating a higher ranking. The score can be on whatever scale the decision-maker likes – from nought to a hundred, one to ten, or the set of all numbers from zero to infinity – all that matters is that the scores accurately reflect the order in which things stand in her preferences.

Then, whenever she has to make a choice, the decision-maker always opts for the alternative with the highest score available. For reasons that will become apparent, economists are profoundly interested in this type of decision-making. They call the score given to each alternative its **utility**, and describe anyone who chooses in this way as a **utility maximizer**.

If people are utility maximizers, then there is a clear mathematical structure to the way they make decisions – their choices are determined by the numerical values of the utilities they give to things. As will be shown in later chapters, it is possible to exploit this structure to arrive at detailed propositions about the way people will behave in a wide range of economically important settings. Utility maximization thus buys enormous **predictive power**. For this reason, economists across the discipline tend to treat human beings as utility maximizers as a matter of course: it would be no exaggeration to say that this is a cornerstone of almost all modern economic analysis. In this book, the use of utility maximization is most evident in **Chapter 3**, which shows how it gives rise to a theory of consumer demand, and **Chapter 8**, which uses it to analyse "strategic" decision-making, where one person's decision has a bearing on the wellbeing of many others.

> Economists are only interested in making predictions about what people decide, not how they decide.

However impressive all this analysis may be, there remains a striking – and at first sight rather troubling – catch. *Nobody actually thinks like a utility maximizer.* Even the most cold-blooded, Gordon Gekko-esque people don't work out what provides them with the greatest utility before making any decision – and anyone who did would probably find they could gain more utility by living their life in a less obsessive fashion. But this in itself is not a problem at all for economists, since they are only interested in making predictions about *what* people decide, not *how* they decide.

Provided utility maximization is acceptably accurate in this regard, it is fine to base economic theories on it – particularly if the theories founded on it give sharper conclusions than their rivals.

So how is it possible to test whether utility maximization delivers accurate predictions? This is where the three assumptions set out in the previous section come into use, via the following observation:

> Anyone whose preferences are consistent with **transitivity**, **continuity**, and **completeness** behaves as if they were a utility maximizer.

In other words, provided people behave consistently with the three rationality conditions, it is fine for economists to treat them *as if* they were utility maximizers. People may not think like utility maximizers, but that doesn't mean they don't act like them.

Cardinal sins?

The "utility" discussed previously is an example of an **ordinal scale**: the numerical value of something's utility reflects nothing more than its position in a person's order of preference. This implies, for instance, that the fact that someone assigns an apple double the utility of a pear does not make it "twice as good" for that person; all it means is that the person would prefer an apple to a pear.

Economists haven't always thought of utility in this way. Influenced by the utilitarian philosopher Jeremy Bentham (1748–1832), nineteenth-century economists tended to imagine "utility" as a measurable quantity reflecting "how happy" decision makers were. This kind of utility is known as **cardinal utility**. Francis Edgeworth (1845–1926) went as far as postulating a "hedonimeter" that could be rigged up to a person's brain, "continually registering the height of pleasure experienced by an individual" as determined by "a sort of hedonico-magnetic field".

Many economists find this kind of thing hilarious. There are, however, still those who maintain that happiness can be usefully measured (see the discussion of "Happiness economics" in **Part Five**), while the use of neuroscientific methods to examine economic questions is a burgeoning area of research (see the box on p.41). Furthermore, the theories of expected and discounted utility maximization use a type of utility that is cardinal in the sense that it can be measured from people's choices (though it most certainly does not stand for "how happy" they are).

Ben Bernanke, chairman of the Federal Reserve from February 2006 to January 2014. His interest rate decisions were always conducted under uncertainty conditions.

Uncertainty and expected utility maximization

Treating humans as utility maximizers is a hugely powerful step, but on its own it isn't enough to make headway with many of the most important questions economists study. One area where more assumptions are helpful is **decision-making under uncertainty** – choosing when the outcome of one's choice is not known in advance. Uncertainty is ubiquitous in everyday life, from the weather forecast before you leave for work, to the traffic in town as you drive in, to the mood of your boss when you arrive. Economically important examples of decision-making under uncertainty include the following:

▶ Investors in the stock market choose which shares, and how many, to include in their portfolios. Since they don't know whether the value of their chosen shares will go up or down, or how large a dividend they will pay out, they cannot be sure how their portfolios will perform.

▶ The chairman of the Federal Reserve ("the Fed") sets interest rates in the US, and the effects of his decision on the domestic economy are not felt fully until several months after it has been taken. Because the economy's performance over this period is uncertain, he never knows whether his decision will turn out to be the right one.

▶ Managers hire new workers from a field of applicants on the basis of their CVs, references, interviews, and other indicators. But – even in rare cases where everyone tells the truth – these give only partial accounts of how effective the various candidates would be as employees. As a result, managers don't know for sure how productive their chosen recruits will turn out to be.

The impact of uncertainty on investors' portfolios, the chairman of the Fed's choice of interest rate, and managers' decisions over who to employ (and on what terms) are all of keen interest to economists. How, for example, might the investor choose between investing in "risky" firms (e.g. nascent technology firms with uncertain prospects) and "safe" ones, such as long established manufacturers? To get a handle on these issues, some sort of account of the way people make decisions under uncertainty is needed. One highly structured, artificial story goes as follows:

❶ As a first step, you think through all of the possible consequences that could result from any action you might take and translate each consequence into its financial value to you. So if you consider getting punched in the face to be as bad as losing £100, you think of, "a punch in the face" as being the same thing as -£100; if you reckon "a smile from a stranger" is as good as a £10 windfall, you think of this as just being +£10.

❷ Then you work out your **utility of income** using the following procedure. You start out by giving £0 a utility of 0 and £100 a utility of 100. Then, to work out the utility of any other amount, you reason as follows:

▶ If the amount is between £0 and £100, say £10, you ask yourself: "If I were offered the choice between £10 for sure and £100 with a probability of x, what would x have to be for me to be indifferent between the two options?" If x is 25%, then you give £10 a utility of 25.

▶ If the amount is less than £0 – say a loss of £100 – you ask yourself: "If I was offered a gamble that lost me £100 with probability y or else gained me £100, what would y have to be in order for me to be indifferent between the gamble and £0?" You then calculate the utility of losing £100 with the formula:

$$- \frac{100\,(1-y)}{y}$$

So if y is 40%, then the utility of losing £100 is equal to minus 100 x (0.6/0.4) =-150.

▶ If the amount is more than £100 – a gain of £200, suppose – you ask: "If I was offered the choice between £100 for sure and a gamble that paid £200 with probability z, what would z have to be for me to be indifferent?" £200 then gets a utility of 100/z.

❸ Now, for any course of action you can take, you list the **probabilities** that it ends up giving you any of the consequences. So, for example, you may reason that flashing a flirtatious smile at someone across a bar could get you a smile in return with a probability of 80% and a punch in the face the remaining 20% of the time.

❹ Fourth, you work out the average utility – known to economists as the **expected utility** – of any action by multiplying each utility level by the probability that the action gives you that utility, then summing up. To illustrate, if a punch in the face is as good as a £100 loss and that has

According to Bayesianism, the bets you make at the dog track reflect the probabilities you give to each dog winning.

Going Dutch

At the heart of expected utility maximization is the idea that people behave as if they weigh uncertainty using probabilities. For people who have studied statistics at school, this might seem like an obvious – trivial, even – step to make, but it isn't. For some events, such as rolling a six on a (normal, unbiased) die or writing off your car during your first year of driving, there is sufficient data available to estimate probabilities very accurately. But for others, such as the Republicans winning the next US presidential election or Manchester United winning the Premier League next season, there is no clear probability "out there" that people can easily access. And for events such as the Republicans winning the 2024 presidential election or Manchester United winning the 2023–24 Premier League, the probabilities seem utterly obscure. Is it really plausible to assume that people behave as though they can conjure up the probabilities of events as distant as these where so many diverse factors seem to be at play?

According to a school of thought known as **Bayesianism** – named after the English mathematician Thomas Bayes (1701–61) – it must be so, since any behaviour that is *not* consistent with the use of probabilities is irrational. To get an impression of the argument, imagine you went to watch a greyhound race between two dogs, Mighty Monty and Furious Freddie, and were given the chance to buy or sell betting slips that paid out £1 in case either of the dogs were to win. Suppose you valued a bet on Mighty Monty at 60 pence. This would mean you thought a fair price to buy or sell the betting slips would be 60 pence – you'd definitely want to sell for any higher price and buy for anything lower.

How, then, might you value a betting slip on Furious Freddie? Assuming that the race will definitely have only one winner, a Bayesian would say the price must be 40p. Any more – say 45p – and you'd be willing to pay 60p + 45p = £1.05 for a pair of betting slips that between them will guarantee you £1: i.e. you'd be willing to fritter 5p away for nothing. Any less – say 35p – and you'd be willing to *sell* a pair of betting slips that committed you to giving out £1 in return for 60p + 35p = 95p: another pointless sacrifice of 5 hard-earned pennies.

This argument shows that, if you were rational, your valuations of the betting slips should add up to £1 – if they didn't, there'd be some combination of transactions, known for obscure reasons as a **Dutch book**, that you'd be willing to perform that would be guaranteed to lose you money. And accepting a Dutch book is obviously not a rational thing to do. The twist is that in adding up to £1, your valuations are *just like* probabilities – thus, you can be treated as if you believed the probability of Mighty Monty winning was 60% and that of Furious Freddie was 40%.

a utility of -150, and a smile is as good as £10, which has a utility of 25, then the expected utility of flashing a flirtatious smile is 80% x 25 plus 20% x -150 = -10.

⑤ Finally, having computed the expected utilities of all of the possible courses of action, choose the one with the highest available expected utility – in this case probably playing it cool.

This procedure is known as **expected utility maximization** and is used by economists to model behaviour in all the situations listed above and very many more. As with utility maximization, economists don't claim that it gives an accurate impression of what goes on in people's heads when they make decisions under uncertainty. Instead they argue that, provided people follow a set of rationality conditions, they act *as if* they were expected utility maximizers. So long as these rationality conditions prove accurate, the predictions generated by expected utility maximization will be borne out.

Describing all the rationality conditions required for expected utility maximization demands a level of mathematical sophistication that isn't worth the trouble here, but the box "Going Dutch" gives an argument for why behaviour consistent with step 3 above might follow from rationality. The section on behavioural economics on pp.35–44 looks at some evidence on whether expected utility maximization is an accurate characterization of people's behaviour.

As a final note, it's important to be clear that while the "utility" in expected utility maximization most certainly doesn't refer to anything going on in people's brains as nineteenth century economists imagined, the *scale* does have a significance that the "ordinal" utility in straightforward utility maximization does not (see the box on p.25). Setting the utility of £100 at 100 and £0 at 0 in step 2 above was arbitrary – a bit like the decision whether to measure temperature in fahrenheit or centigrade – but once this decision had been made, the particular utility given to any amount had a meaning in terms of the gambles you were willing to take. This feature of the model is put to use in the next section.

Risk aversion

In everyday parlance, being described as "risk averse" has a variety of connotations. On the one hand, it is almost a badge of honour for chastened post-crisis financial institutions. On the other, it has been an epithet for an array of maddening health and safety directives: the sort of rule that prevents children in the UK playing "conkers" or forces passengers on some US flights to sit – many of them with legs crossed á la Gérard Depardieu – for the last hour before their plane lands.

As one would expect, economists use the term in a more sober and precise fashion. They describe someone as risk averse whenever, given the choice between two options that lead to the same average outcome, they always opt for the less uncertain of the two. Used in this sense, risk aversion can explain why investors in the stock market will accept a lower return from shares in "safe" companies than "risky" ones (see **Chapter 10**), and why workers on performance-related pay need to be paid more, on average, than people on fixed-wage contracts (**Chapter 9**). One of the great advantages of the model of expected utility maximization is that it gives a very neat way of expressing the concept of risk aversion.

To see how this works, imagine you had to choose between a €5 note and a bet on a coin toss that would pay you €10 in case it landed showing heads and nothing if it showed tails. Both of these options pay you the same amount on average – €5 – but the amount you gain from the bet on the coin toss is clearly more uncertain than what you get from the €5 note, which isn't uncertain at all. This means that if you were risk averse then you'd opt for the €5 note.

What does this imply if you act like an expected utility maximizer? Since you prefer a 100% chance of €5 to a 50% chance of €10 and a 50% chance of €0, then it must be that the utility of €5 is greater than 50% times the utility of €10 plus 50% times the utility of €0. This is illustrated in figure 2.1 below.

One striking feature of figure 2.1 is the slope of the line describing the utilities of different amounts of money – as you move to the right, it gets less and less steep. This means that the utility increase from an extra euro beginning from a low sum of money – say, the increase in utility as you

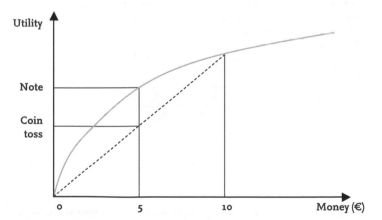

Figure 2.1: Utilities for a risk averse person. The yellow line gives the utilities the person assigns to different amounts of money, so the expected utility of a €5 note is just the level marked note. To work out the expected utility of the coin toss, simply draw a straight line between the utilities of €0 and €10 and read off halfway along – this means the expected utility is at the level marked coin toss.

The St Petersburg paradox

The idea of using diminishing marginal utility of income to explain risk aversion traces its roots to the gambling salons of eighteenth-century Europe.

A problem first posed by the Swiss mathematician Nicolaus Bernoulli (1687–1759) imagines the following bet, consisting of an indefinite sequence of coin tosses. To begin with you are given a pot of one dollar, and then a coin is tossed: if it lands on tails the gamble ends and you walk away with the pot; if it lands heads then the pot doubles in size to two dollars and you toss again. The process then carries on in the same fashion – for each coin toss, a tails ends the gamble and you walk away with the pot, and a heads doubles the pot and prompts a further toss.

Bernoulli's question is: how much is this gamble worth? In other words, how much should someone be willing to pay in order to take part in it? One natural way of valuing it would be to work out the average or expected winnings it yields by summing up all the potential winnings multiplied by the probability of ending up with them. Working from the table below, this gives (1 x ½) + (2 x ¼) + (4 x 1/8) + (8 x 1/16) + ..., which is the same as ½ + ½ + ½ + ½ + ... But this equals infinity! And no sane person would part with everything they had in order to play this extremely risky gamble, which pays out less than $10 almost 95% of the time. The fact that people are unwilling to pay a significant sum for a gamble whose average winnings are infinite has been dubbed the St Petersburg paradox.

The solution Bernoulli proposes is that, as the sums of money increase, the value of an additional dollar to the gambler – what economists would call marginal utility of income – goes down. For example, if utility is as in the table, the one-dollar move from $1 to $2 gives one additional unit of utility, the same amount as the two-dollar move from $2 to $4, the four-dollar increment from $4–$8, and each subsequent jump in the possible winnings ad infinitum. This is a case of diminishing marginal utility of income – the same as **risk aversion** in expected utility theory. It implies the expected utility of the gamble equals 3, which, reading from the table, makes the gamble worth a much more realistic $2.

Coin tosses	T	HT	HHT	HHHT	...
Winnings	$1	$2	$4	$8	...
Probability	½	¼	1/8	1/16	...
Utility	2	3	4	5	...

move from €0 to €1 – is more than the increase if you start out at any higher amount – for example, the gain if you move from €10 to €11. Economists call the extra utility from an additional unit of money the **marginal utility of income** and, whenever this decreases as the amount of money increases, say that the person in question has **diminishing marginal utility of income**.

A startling – not to mention extremely analytically powerful – feature of expected utility maximization is this:

> Having diminishing marginal utility of income is the same thing as being risk averse.

For a rough idea of why this is so, have another look at figure 2.1. For anyone who is risk averse, the expected utility of the coin toss must lie below that of the €5 note, which means that the purple dotted line must lie below the yellow line €5 along the money axis. This can only happen if the utility increase as you move from €0 to €5 is bigger than the gain as you move from €5 to €10. And *this* is always true when the person in question has diminishing marginal utility of income. The box "The St Petersburg paradox" gives some more illustration of this.

Time and discounted utility maximization

Time

One of the few overlaps between economics and stand-up comedy is that, more often than not, it's all about timing. Time can matter in economic settings when the costs and benefits of a decision aren't all collected at the same moment the decision is taken. For example, an entrepreneur setting up a business usually has to stump up some initial outlay in order to make her business operational, then hopes to recoup the money through the profits the business earns over the following years. Similarly, policymakers working on mitigating the impact of climate change on the economy consider measures that are costly to begin with – installing energy efficient equipment, investing in low-carbon electricity generation, and so forth – but which yield benefits over the longer term by protecting people from the effects of climate change (see the box on p.34).

Decisions such as these that involve "streams" of costs and benefits over time are examples of what economists call **intertemporal choice**.

Just as it's helpful to analyse choice under uncertainty through the lens of expected utility maximization, one can gain useful insights into intertemporal choice by using the model of **discounted utility maximization**.

A heated debate

Small differences in people's discount rates can have dramatic effects on how they value costs and benefits in the distant future. For instance, if someone discounts cash amounts at 1% per annum, then $1 million in one hundred years' time is worth $370,000 to them today, while if they discount them at 5% per annum, the same sum at the same time is worth only $7,600 to them now. The question of what to do about climate change, where the projected costs of carbon emissions extend far into the future, brings this into sharp relief.

In 2006, a team led by Sir Nicholas (now Lord) Stern of the London School of Economics published a report for the British government surveying the evidence on the economic impacts of climate change and presenting an array of policy recommendations. The report was hugely influential and made front-page news across the globe – an achievement few economic researchers can ever hope to match. Part of the reason for all this publicity was the clear and accessible way in which the review was written and presented, but another was the striking conclusions it arrived at: it estimated that, without policy intervention, the future costs of climate change would be equivalent to a 5–20% fall in GDP "now and forever", much more than most previous studies had reckoned. As a number of critics, including William Nordhaus of Yale University, were quick to point out, the divergence between Stern's cost estimates and those of other authors largely derives from differences in the choice of discount rate. Stern uses a much lower discount rate than his peers – approximately 1.5% as opposed to around 5.5% – and consequently places a far greater weighting on the costs of climate change, most of which will be incurred in future centuries.

Why does Stern go it alone on discounting? In the report, he argues that the high discount rates used by other researchers reflect the observed behaviour of "impatient" human beings in settings such as financial markets. But policymakers shouldn't be impatient in the same way people are – this would give a precedence to people alive today over future generations that is hard to justify ethically (his 1.5% rate reflects the fact that future generations are projected to be richer than us, rather than any impatience per se).

Stern's assertion that policymakers should make decisions on the basis of ethical principles rather than everyday behaviour is surely correct, but so is Nordhaus's counter that the moral arguments in favour of Stern's particular methodology are hardly cut and dry. The controversy has spawned a large literature that shows little sign of reaching a consensus at the moment.

Discounting

Generally speaking, time matters because people have preferences for earlier or later reward. If, for example, Lucy prefers gratification as early as possible, she would choose a fancy meal out tonight ahead of one in a year's time, and prefer a fancy meal out in a year's time to one in ten years'

As the planet heats up, Lord Stern's calculations on the economic costs of climate change generated their own heated debate about discounting.

time. Thinking in terms of utility maximization, one could regard her as giving less weight to the utility of anything she consumes the further into the future this consumption takes place. She **discounts** utility more and more the later she "experiences" it.

The model of discounted utility maximization expresses this very simply via the **discount rate**, usually given as a percentage. As the name suggests, the discount rate is just the rate at which a person discounts future utility per year. Positive discount rates imply impatience – that a meal in a year's time is worth less than the same meal today – while negative discount rates imply the opposite. The higher someone's discount rate, the more impatient that person is.

The role of the discount rate is to translate future utility values so they are comparable with present ones. So, for example, if Lucy prefers Indian to Chinese food, she may give an Indian meal a utility of 120 and a Chinese one a utility of 100. If she is also impatient, however, she may consider a Chinese takeaway tonight to be just as good as an Indian takeaway in a year's time. This means that the **present value** to her – in utility terms – of 120 in a year's time is only 100. A discount rate of 20% would capture this.

Discounting thus conveys the fact that different degrees of patience means people are willing to sacrifice more or less in the present in order to gain some future reward. A person's discount rate neatly sums up her patience or lack thereof in a single number.

Daniel Kahneman and Amos Tversky

Daniel Kahneman (1934–) and Amos Tversky (1937–1996) were amongst the first to use experiments to test the rationality assumptions underpinning models of *homo economicus*. Working together at the Hebrew University of Jerusalem in the 1970s, they published a series of seminal works that challenged the way economists represent human behaviour, especially in choice under uncertainty. Their paper "Prospect Theory: An Analysis of Decision Under Risk", which appeared in *Econometrica* in 1979, was particularly influential in showing various ways in which people seemed systematically to contradict the model of expected utility maximization. After Tversky's early death, Kahneman was awarded the 2002 Nobel Prize in Economics for the pair's work.

Behavioural economics – a different beast

Introduction

So far this chapter has examined the three most important species of *homo economicus* – the utility maximizer, the expected utility maximizer, and the discounted utility maximizer. Nobody believes that these models accurately describe the way people come to decisions: it's clear that, in fact, people are nothing like as calculating as they suggest. But economists are primarily interested in what people do, rather than how they think. And provided they make choices that are consistent with the relevant rationality conditions, the models will give an accurate account of what people do.

How tenable, then, is it to assume that people follow these conditions? In the sort of data economists deal with – daily fish sales at New York's Fulton Market, subsistence farmers' choices of crops, and so on – it's usually impossible to identify whether any particular assumption has failed : there are simply too many factors at play. This general identification problem is why a branch of economics, known as **experimental economics**, has emerged that tries to test assumptions "in the lab".

A discipline that strongly overlaps experimental economics, known as **behavioural economics**, focuses on the rationality conditions that underpin *homo economicus* in its various guises. It attempts, through experiments and insights garnered from psychology and neuroscience, to uncover where these conditions are likely to fail and thus to set out more realistic accounts of how people make decisions. They then draw out the implications this has for people's behaviour in economic settings. Two of the pioneers of the field were Daniel Kahneman and Amos Tversky.

The next three sections present a few findings from behavioural economics that challenge, in turn, each of the models of decision-making described earlier on in the chapter. Many orthodox economists remain deeply sceptical of the contributions made by their behavioural colleagues, and the final section of the chapter presents some of the criticisms of behavioural economics.

Framing and loss aversion

In their 1981 paper "The Framing of Decisions and the Psychology of Choice", Kahneman and Tversky invited subjects to carry out the following thought-experiment:

> Imagine that the US is preparing for the outbreak of an unusual Asian disease, which is expected to kill 600 people. Two alternative programmes to combat the disease have been proposed. Assume that the exact scientific estimates of the consequences of the programmes are as follows:
>
> If programme A is adopted, 200 people will be saved.
>
> If programme B is adopted, there is 1/3 probability that 600 people will be saved, and 2/3 probability that no people will be saved.
>
> Which of the two programmes would you favour?

(At this point, you should note what you would do.) Next they asked subjects to imagine the same scenario, but where the available programmes were given as follows:

> If programme C is adopted, 400 people will die.
>
> If programme D is adopted, there is a 1/3 probability that nobody will die, and 2/3 probability that 600 people will die."

What would you have chosen? If you opted for programme A in the first problem, then D in the second, then your instincts towards civil protection match those of the majority of Kahneman and Tversky's subjects. Hopefully this strength in numbers is of some comfort as your choices are also clearly irrational. If you look at the problem carefully, you should be able to see that

C and D are respectively rewordings of A and B – this means that if you prefer A to B you should also prefer C to D. Preferring A to B and D to C contradicts utility maximization because, in that model, either A has a greater utility than B *and* C has a greater utility than D or vice versa: you can't have one without the other because the pairs A and C, and B and D are identical.

Kahneman and Tversky claim their experiment highlights two fundamental features of decision-making, both of which have been corroborated by other studies. One is **framing** – that people's decisions depend on how they conceive of the alternatives they are presented with, and that this can depend on the way in which their decision is portrayed or framed. The use of framing to manipulate other people's perceptions is ubiquitous in everyday life: from advertisers using celebrity endorsements to glamourize hair conditioner (active ingredient – quaternary ammonium), to politicians propounding public service "reform" (read – cuts).

The second phenomenon at play in the experiment is **loss aversion**. This refers to a tendency to be risk averse when evaluating gains but risk-seeking when presented with possible losses, the idea being that people dislike incurring losses and so are willing to take risks in order to avoid them. Kahneman and Tversky's experiment works by framing the choice between A and B as one between lives *gained* – and inducing subjects to choose the safer alternative A – and the choice between C and D as one between lives *lost*, which leads them to opt for the riskier programme D.

Certainty effects and regret

Another thought-experiment proposed by Kahneman and Tversky, based on an earlier suggestion by the Nobel laureate Maurice Allais (1911–2010), runs like this.

First, you have to choose between the following two gambles:

A Receive $4000 with a probability of 80%, and $0 the remaining 20% of the time.
B Receive $3000 with certainty – i.e. 100% of the time.

Having decided between A and B, now select one of C and D below:

C Receive $4000 with a probability of 20%, and $0 the remaining 80% of the time.
D Receive $3000 with a probability of 25%, and $0 the remaining 75% of the time.

Certainty effects and expected utility maximization

To see why choosing B ahead of A and C ahead of D is inconsistent with expected utility maximization, use x, y, and z as shorthand for the following amounts:

x is the utility of $3000

y is 80% times the utility of $4000 plus 20% times the utility of $0

z is the utility of $0

If you are an expected utility maximizer who prefers B to A, then x (the expected utility of B) must be a larger number than y (the expected utility of A). This implies that 25% times x is a bigger number than 25% times y, and therefore that 25% times x plus 75% times z must be *more* than 25% times y plus 75% times z.

But the expected utility of C equals 25% times y plus 75% times z, while the expected utility of D is 25% times x plus 75% times z. So if you are an expected utility maximizer who prefers C to D, then 25% times x plus 75% times z must be *less* than 25% times y plus 75% times z – contrary to what was implied by preferring B to A. The two choices are therefore contradictory under expected utility maximization.

If you chose B over A and C over D, then your stated preferences match those reported by most subjects in Kahneman and Tversky's study. However, once again the majority verdict contradicts that of *homo economicus*, as explained in the box above.

What lies behind these choices? One suggestion is the lament "if only". Imagine choosing A over B, then ending up in the unlucky twenty percent who receive $0 rather than $4000. The chances are you'd feel a pang of regret or even foolishness for not having chosen B, which would have guaranteed you $3000. Anticipating this might spur you to choose the smaller, but certain prize offered by B.

By contrast, even though D offers a higher chance of winning $3000 than C does of getting you $4000 – indeed, the chance of winning is higher by the same proportional amount as it is for B over A – it may be that in this case you'd experience little regret were you to end up with $0 having chosen C. You could console yourself that there was still a decent chance of coming away empty-handed after choosing D – your choice of C was a reasonable gamble that just failed to come off.

In short, the **certainty** offered by B might cause regret-fearing decision- makers to play it safe when deciding between A and B in a way they don't when deciding between C and D, where regret is less of a concern. This kind of decision-making cannot be squared with expected utility maximization.

Present bias and time consistency

In the model of discounted utility maximization, a person's degree of impatience is given by a single number – the discount rate – that gives the rate at which that person discounts utility per year. An implication of this is that people's willingness to "trade" utility between points in time depends only on the *number of years* between the two different points – not on how close they are to the present. For example, if, thinking about it today, Greg reckons that the "pain" of a visit to his excruciating-but-wealthy grandmother next year will be worth the "gain" of a better Christmas present the following year, it must be that, when the time comes for the visit, he is still willing to make the same "trade". In other words, he doesn't use one discount rate when weighing utilities one and two years into the future, and another one for weighing present utility and utility in a year's time.

Unfortunately, this aspect of the theory has been very widely refuted in experiments, where people tend to be far more willing to defer future benefits than they are present gratification – a phenomenon known as **present bias**. For instance, Greg might cheerfully pencil in a visit to his insufferable granny for one year's time – reasoning that it's worth the superior Christmas present that will follow the year after – but then call in sick when the appointed date arrives, since the "trade" seems far less favourable when his present wellbeing is at stake. Another example that gets to the core of the issue comes from Richard Thaler of the University of Chicago: many people would prefer an apple today to two apples tomorrow, but prefer two apples in fifty-one days to one apple in fifty days.

By and large, people do not therefore seem to behave in a way that can be reconciled with discounted utility, where there is a single discount rate. Instead they seem to make decisions that are more easily explained by a model of **hyperbolic discounting**, where people have a high discount rate – they are very impatient – when choosing between present benefits and gains a short time into the future, which gets progressively smaller – showing greater patience – the further out into the future the gains are shifted.

> We don't see very far in the future, we are very focused on one idea at a time, one problem at a time, and all these are incompatible with rationality as economic theory assumes it.
>
> Daniel Kahneman, *Thinking Fast and Slow*, 2011

An intriguing implication of this is that people make decisions that are not **time-con-sistent** in the sense that, once they have made

Neuroeconomics

An offshoot of behavioural economics, known as *neuroeconomics*, has followed psychologists in using brain-imaging technologies such as MRI-scanners to examine the neurological processes that underlie economic decision-making.

Some claim that the findings of neuroeconomics lend credence to various behavioural or rational theories of choice. For example, a 2004 study by Samuel McClure and colleagues published in *Science* found that when people made any sort of intertemporal decisions, their pre-frontal cortex – an area associated with rational decision-making – showed heightened activity. However, when these decisions involved present rewards, this was accompanied by increased activity in the midbrain, which is more connected with impulsive actions. This seems to fit the model of present-biased decision-makers, who are relatively patient when balancing long-term costs and benefits but strongly impatient when it comes to immediate rewards.

For many economists, however, the area of neuroeconomics remains less MRI, more WTF. As has been repeated endlessly in this chapter, economists are concerned with what people do, rather than what they think. Unless there is a clear mapping from brain-images to the choices they make, it's not clear what the value of neuroeconomic results can be for the field. And, as yet, this is a very distant prospect.

them, they stick to them. For example, consider a present-biased smoker deciding whether to give up this week, next week, or the week after that. She might reason that the long-term health benefits of quitting justify giving up smoking next week and enduring seven days of cravings then, but that, owing to her present bias, she is unwilling to suffer the cravings at present. She therefore decides to give up next week. But then when next week arrives, she's in the same position as she was to begin with, so she decides to postpone quitting for another week; and then when the following week comes, she does the same again. The result is that, even though at every point in time she realizes it would be a good idea to give up smoking *in the future*, her present bias means she never gets round to doing it.

This type of behaviour has all sorts of interesting economic consequences, including addiction, **procrastination** (something academic economists are particularly expert on), and failure to save enough money for retirement. Sophisticated people who realize that present bias might lead to these problems often use **commitment devices** to lock in their current decisions, making it impossible for them to reverse them in the future. For example, people might pour their savings into illiquid assets – stores of wealth such as artwork or housing that are relatively difficult or expensive to sell quickly – as a way of guarding against any raid by their future present-biased selves. Similarly, workers who know they are prone to procrastination may set themselves binding deadlines to finish work, for instance by making promises that are not easily reneged upon, thereby preventing their future selves from faffing around on Facebook instead of being productive.

Problems with behavioural economics

Do the findings of behavioural economics mean it's time to consign the workhorse of economic analysis, *homo economicus*, to the knacker's yard? Most economists probably wouldn't say so, for reasons including the following.

A general criticism of experimental economics is that people's behaviour in the lab may not reflect what they do in the field – in the jargon, some experiments may lack **external validity**. This seems particularly pertinent to some of the work in behavioural economics, where the choices people are asked to make are often distinctly contrived and artificial – not, in other words, representative of the sort of choices they make as they go about their daily business. (Ask yourself when the last time was that you made a decision that bore any resemblance to those described under "Framing..." and "Certainty effects..."). Perhaps, then, all these experiments do is exploit the fact that people are liable to make mistakes in unfamiliar environments – errors they generally correct as they get to grips with their surroundings.

There is surely something to this. It would be bizarre, for example, if people who slipped up in the "Framing..." experiment persisted in their irrationality once they had realized that C and D were simple rewordings of A and B. And the fact that present-biased people turn to commitment devices suggests that they wish to make time-consistent intertemporal choices where they can. Indeed, there is some experimental evidence that people do learn from the "mistakes" these experiments highlight. The idea that people tend towards rational decision-making echoes Milton Friedman's contention that rationality conditions tend to hold "approximately" (see the box, p.20).

A second, related, complaint concerning experiments in behavioural economics is that they usually offer **hypothetical choices** (such as those in "Framing..." and "Certainty effects...", where the "winnings" aren't really paid out) or real gambles with **low payoffs**. The charge is that, because people aren't playing for large enough stakes, the incentive to report "correct" answers is swamped by other considerations that are peculiar to the

The best laboratory behavioural economics can find? Howie Mandel cranks up the tension in the US version of the TV quiz game, *Deal or No Deal*.

lab – the pressure of being observed, the unfamiliarity of the situation, the desire to look good in front of the experimenters, and so forth.

The grim reality of research funding means it isn't typically possible to carry out high-stakes experiments, so it's not yet clear whether this criticism carries weight. An imaginative approach to investigating it has been to analyse the behaviour of decision-makers in game shows such as *Deal or No Deal*, where the stakes are very high and decisions have similar structures to those in experiments (a 2008 *American Economic Review* paper by Thierry Post and colleagues does just this). But then these studies seem vulnerable to the criticism that people are in unfamiliar environments. (Sad is the lot of those for whom the goading features of Noel Edmonds/ Howie Mandel/ Andrew O'Keefe are an everyday sight.)

A third rebuttal to the behavioural critique is that accuracy isn't the sole object of an economic theory. As explained in the section "Stripping down *homo economicus*", other worthy features are predictive power and generality. And it's easy to imagine how incorporating all the psychological foibles revealed by behavioural economics might reduce the incisiveness or applicability of the conclusions drawn by economists, replacing utility with futility. Nonetheless, there are certain

> **Arriving at recommendations of what decision-makers should do is surely best done with reference to what a rational person would do.**

areas where adding behavioural considerations can sharpen mainstream economic theory – for example, the idea that people have an overriding concern for fairness suggests people will tend to "split the difference" in negotiations, whereas standard economic analysis says many other outcomes are possible.

Finally, even if you are convinced that *homo economicus* is a hopeless starting point for positive analysis – i.e. coming up with predictions about economic phenomena – it surely makes sense to stick to models of rational choice for normative work. That is, arriving at recommendations of what decision-makers *should* do is surely best done with reference to what a rational person would do.

Conclusion – time to evolve?

In conclusion, it's worth bearing in mind that these criticisms apply with different force to different experiments. For instance, if people were exposed to "Framing..." type problems often enough, and with sufficiently high stakes, one would expect them to right their ways, since the behaviour revealed in Kahneman and Tversky's experiment is obviously irrational. For other phenomena, such as present bias, the issue of rationality is less straightforward.

Another point to emphasize is that we don't necessarily face an either-or choice between *homo economicus* and his behavioural cousin. It's perfectly acceptable, for example, to regard expected utility maximization as a suitable foundation for a theory of stock market investment, but framing and loss aversion as a better starting point for the analysis of betting behaviour at the Melbourne Gold Cup.

In the remaining chapters of this book – especially those covering topics in microeconomics – the power of the *homo economicus* model will become apparent through the elegant and flexible way it can be used to answer an array of important economic questions. Though it's possible that comparable or even better theories could be built up using behavioural economics or other methods, nobody's managed it yet.

PART TWO:

Markets and competition: the invisible hand

In the classical portrayal of the free market, the self-interested actions of producers and consumers play out in a sublime harmony, collectively furthering the general good as though guided by an "invisible hand". The formal demonstration of this – collected in the **fundamental theorems of welfare economics** – has been essential to liberal economic thinking over the last two centuries and was instrumental in promoting the Thatcher–Reagan doctrine of deregulation and privatization in the 1980s. The ideas of **competition** and the **price mechanism**, which are central to the theorems, remain of keen interest to economists today – they help explain how (and if) online retailers benefit consumers, and how to solve problems such as pollution and climate change.

This part of the book sets out the models of **demand**, **supply**, and **market equilibrium** that underpin the theorems, taking in some of the most important concepts of microeconomics along the way. **Chapter 3** shows how **prices** and **income** levels shape the overall demand for a good, calling *homo economicus* into service, before **Chapter 4** explains how prices determine the supply decisions of **profit-maximizing firms** in **competitive industries**. This culminates in the welfare theorems presented in **Chapter 5,** which show how the price mechanism ensures that production and consumption are **efficient** in the sense efficient in the sense that it is impossible to reorganize things so some people benefit and nobody loses out. It concludes with a critical discussion of the theorems, considering their relevance to a world that is less perfect than they postulate, and asking whether the notion of efficiency has any room for fairness or equality.

Beyond paving the way for the welfare theorems, the models of supply and demand are essential parts of any economist's toolkit. They'll be used later on in this book to get a handle on financial markets (**Chapter 10**) and trade (**Chapter 17**), and also to see how things play out when the economy fails to work as the welfare theorems envisage (**Part Three**).

Chapter 3

Demand

Demand is one of the most important concepts in all of economics. It reports the relationship between prices, incomes, and other variables of interest and the amount of any particular good – be it cigars, sunbeds, or stilettos – that buyers will choose to purchase.

A useful way of thinking about "the demand" for a consumer good is as the summation of the **individual demands** of all potential buyers in the market, so this chapter begins at the level of individual decision-making. It starts by describing the set of things a consumer *can* buy – her **budget set** – before considering what she *wants* to buy, as given by her preferences represented by her **indifference map**. The consumer's individual demand is then simply the bundle of goods that she can afford that she likes the most out of all the bundles she can afford.

Setting things up in this way makes it possible to identify the effects of changes in prices and income on individual demands, and thus to distinguish various types of good: normal and inferior, ordinary and Giffen, and substitutes and complements.

Finally, the focus broadens to the overall demand for particular goods, with related concepts such as the **price elasticity of demand** investigated and explained.

Consumer choice

Imagine a very simple case of consumer choice where there are only two goods – say apples and bananas – and an individual – let's call her Cherie – deciding how to divide her expenditure between them.

To begin with, suppose apples cost $1 and bananas $2, that Cherie's **income** is $20, and that she isn't allowed to spend more than this amount

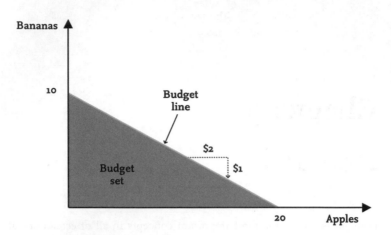

Figure 3.1 The budget set shows the combinations of goods the consumer can consume given their income.

(think of her "income" as including all of her savings plus her credit-card limit). This means that only certain **bundles** of apples and bananas are affordable to her, and the set of those that are affordable is called her **budget set**. The consumer's budget set is represented in figure 3.1 above.

As shown in the figure, the right-hand boundary of the budget set – those bundles where Cherie cannot afford to increase her consumption of *both* apples and bananas any further – is a straight line down from the apple axis to the banana axis. This boundary is known as the **budget line** and is made up of all of the bundles where the consumer is spending all of her income. For current purposes, there are two important things to note about it.

First, the budget line's *slope* is given by the ratio of the banana price to the apple price. To get some idea why, imagine Cherie starts off with some bundle on the budget line, meaning that the only way she can increase her consumption of apples is by taking some of the bananas in her bundle back to the shop and vice versa. Suppose also that she wants to move down along the budget line by trading in bananas for a certain number of apples. The more expensive bananas are, the fewer she'll need to give up to pay for her apples, and so the shallower the budget line will be; likewise, the higher the apple price is, the more bananas she'll need to part with to fund her apple purchase, so the steeper the budget line will be. The slope is therefore determined by the relative prices of the two fruits, with dearer bananas equating to a shallower budget line and more expensive apples making it steeper. The ratio of the two, which is the numerical value of the slope, is called the **market rate of exchange** between the goods.

The second thing to notice about figure 3.1 is that the budget line intersects the apple axis at the point 20 and the banana axis at 10. The explanation here is simple: if Cherie's bundle is at the point where the budget line intersects one of the axes then she's spending everything she has on one of the goods; and if she's doing this then the quantity of the good she must be buying is just her income divided by the price of of that good.

Indifference maps

With her budget set in place, how will Cherie choose from it? The first step in answering this question is to assume that her behaviour is consistent with **utility maximization**, meaning she acts as if she attaches a utility to every possible bundle and then chooses the one with the highest utility available. This means one can draw a "contour map" over all the bundles to represent her preferences, where the "height" of any bundle is the utility she assigns to that bundle. Figure 3.2 (overleaf), where yellow lines are contours, gives an example of this.

Economists call the "contours" on pictures such as figure 3.2 **indifference curves** because if any two bundles lie on the same contour they must be assigned the same utility, and this just means the utility-maximizing consumer is indifferent between them.

There are two important things to note about figure 3.2.

▶ **The slope of the consumer's indifference curves indicates the *rate* at which she's willing to exchange bananas for apples**. To see this, imagine a trader offered Cherie the opportunity to swap some apples for a banana. If her indifference curve was shallow, then she could hand over a large number of apples in exchange for a single banana and end up with a bundle on the same indifference curve – meaning the trade would leave her just as well off as she had been before. On the other hand, if Cherie's indifference curve was steep and the trader asked for many apples, she'd tell him where to stick his banana – she could only remain on the same indifference curve by giving up a small number of apples in exchange for a single banana. Trades (1) and (2) on the figure illustrate these respective cases. The slope of the consumer's indifference curve therefore gives her **personal rate of exchange** between the two goods (technically known as her **marginal rate of substitution**).

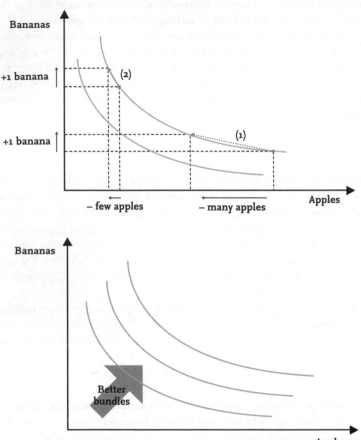

Figure 3.2: Smooth, well-behaved preferences lead to indifference curves gradually less steep to the right and a direction of preference away from the origin.

▶ **The way the indifference curves are drawn involves assumptions about Cherie's preferences.** The direction of preference (given by the big arrow) points away from the origin, indicating that she prefers to have more bananas or apples to less, and, moving from left to right, the indifference curves get gradually less steep, implying that, the more bananas she has, the fewer apples she's willing to give up in order to get one more of them. Anyone whose indifference curves have these two properties is said to have **well-behaved preferences**.

Though there's nothing irrational about having "badly behaved" preferences, it's easy to see by introspection that in most conceivable cases preferences are indeed well behaved. The indifference curves are also drawn so that they have a "smooth" slope with no kinks. In this case, the assumption that the consumer's preferences aren't "kinky" is no sign of prudishness on Cherie's part – all it means is there are no sudden jumps in her personal rate of exchange.

Choice

By putting figures 3.1 and 3.2 together, it's possible to deduce Cherie's demand for apples and bananas when her income is $20 and the prices of the two goods are $1 and $2. This is shown in figure 3.3.

As Cherie behaves as if she's maximizing a utility function, she'll always choose the bundle in the budget set that lies on the "highest" indifference curve. In figure 3.3, this is at the bundle made up of eight apples and six bananas, where the slope of her indifference curve is equal to the slope of the budget line. This is an instance of the more general fact that, provided she has smooth well-behaved preferences and chooses a positive amount of both goods, **a rational consumer will demand a bundle where her personal rate of exchange between the goods equals the market rate of exchange**.

This feature of Cherie's demand is much more important than it may initially seem and, when you think about it, actually very intuitive. Imagine what would happen if her personal rate of exchange differed

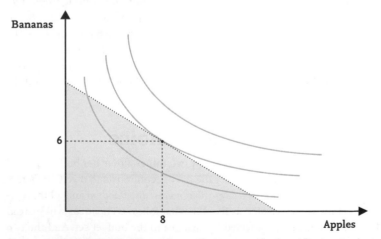

Figure 3.3: Cherie's demand for apples and bananas can be found by showing her indifference map on the same graph as her budget set.

from the market rate – if her personal rate of exchange was, say, one apple for one banana but the market offered something else:

▶ If the market rate was *more* than one apple for one banana, then the consumer could exchange one banana on the market and be made better off – after all she only thinks that one banana is as good as one apple and the trade gives her more than one apple, so she makes a "profit".

▶ Likewise, if the market rate was *less* than one apple for one banana, then she could obtain one extra banana by giving up less than a single apple. Once again, this nets her a "profit" as she would have been willing to give up an entire apple for a banana.

This argument shows that the consumer can *only* be choosing her best affordable bundle if her personal rate of exchange equals the market rate of exchange.

The conclusion belongs to an illustrious family of propositions in economics that use **marginal analysis**. The claim is that a rational consumer chooses a bundle where her personal rate of exchange is the same as the market rate. And the argument says that if the consumer was given any bundle where this wasn't true, then starting from that bundle – i.e. *at the margin* – there would be a trade that would make her better off. Since a rational consumer would always make that trade, the bundle could not be her final choice.

To be clear, the argument *does not* say that any two consumers with the same budget set will always choose the same bundle – Cherie might like bananas more than Sharon and end up choosing more of them. But it *does* say that, at the margin, their personal rate of exchange must be the same whenever they face the same prices, and thus that they can't *both* benefit from trading *with each other*. This is a crucial part of the argument for the efficiency of competitive markets, explored in greater depth in **Chapter 5**.

Prices, income, and choice

Cherie's choice is determined here by two things alone: her budget set and her preferences. As it's not really the job of economists to dwell on factors that influence preferences – *de gustibus non est disputandum* and all that (see p.23) – these will be treated as fixed in what follows. The focus will instead be on how choices are affected by changes in the budget set. And the two things that influence this are prices and income.

Income and demand: normal and inferior goods

Start with income and consider Mark, who is in the fortunate position of choosing between bundles of champagne and lager. If his income were to increase, then clearly he'd be able to afford bundles of the two drinks that had previously been out of his reach. Thus, increasing his income causes his budget line to shift away from the origin and his budget set to expand. Provided the prices remain constant, the market rate of exchange between the two goods would be unchanged and the *slope* of his budget line would therefore stay the same. This means that an increase in income leads to a parallel, rightward shift in the budget line as illustrated in figure 3.4 below.

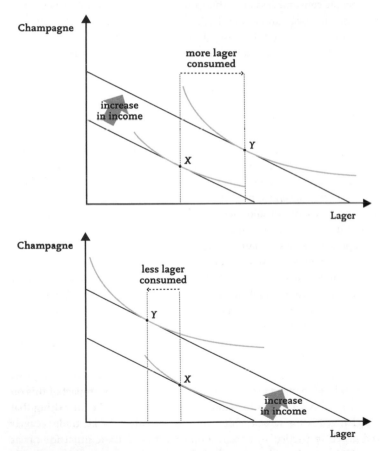

Figure 3.4: An increase in income normally leads to an increase in consumption unless a good is inferior.

How this affects Mark's choice depends on his preferences. In panel (a) of figure 3.4, increasing income leads him to choose more of both goods, while in panel (b) he buys more champagne but less lager. Two types of good may thus be distinguished here: **normal goods**, which the consumer chooses more of as his income increases, and **inferior goods**, for which his demand falls as his income rises. Champagne is (in this sense) a normal good in both panels of the figure, while lager is normal in panel (a) but inferior in panel (b).

The nomenclature is significant here. As people's incomes rise they spend more and so buy more "stuff": it's therefore "normal" for them to buy more of a given good as they get richer. There are, however, some goods that people consume less of as their finances improve – think tatty clothes, processed food, or caravanning holidays. People tend to reduce their consumption of these goods because, given their improved circumstances, they can now afford more agreeable alternatives, hence the goods are "inferior".

Prices and demand: ordinary and Giffen goods

Now turn to prices and imagine Karen, choosing between bundles of caviar and gruel. Suppose there's a change in the price of one of the goods – say, a fall in the price of gruel. This has two effects on the budget set. First, the market rate of exchange between the two goods – and therefore the slope of the budget line – changes. This reflects the fact that gruel is now cheaper, so Karen can exchange a portion of caviar for more gruel than previously. Second, the maximum amount of gruel she can afford – the point where the budget line intersects the "gruel" axis – goes up. In other words, the fall in gruel price increases the **purchasing power** of her income.

As the two effects have different economic meanings – one is a change in the market rate of exchange, the other is a change in purchasing power – it is enlightening to look at their impact on Karen's demand separately. Doing this will involve carrying out a thought-experiment where, instead of being confronted by both changes at once (as happens in real life), Karen responds *first* to the movement in the market rate of exchange and *then* to the change in her purchasing power.

So, imagine Karen's purchasing power remains constant, but that gruel can now be exchanged for less caviar on the market. The impact of this on her demand is known as the **substitution effect**, since the only thing that has changed is the rate at which she can "substitute" – i.e. trade – caviar and gruel. In particular, Karen's opportunities to trade gruel for caviar are now *worse* than they were before, while the opportunities to trade

Caviar, an ordinary good in the example of Karen, contrasted with gruel an inferior, possibly even a Giffen good.

caviar for gruel are *better*. This means that – *at the margin* – she will find it attractive to swap some caviar for gruel. So the substitution effect would lead her to demand more gruel and less caviar.

The remaining impact of a fall in gruel price is an increase in her purchasing power, keeping the market rate of exchange fixed. This is *just like* increasing her income, and it's already been shown that the effect this has on Karen's demand for gruel and caviar depends on whether they are normal or inferior goods. For obvious reasons, this effect of the price change on her demand is known as the **income effect.**

This two-stage analysis of the effect of a gruel price change on the consumer's demand for gruel is summarized in the equation below.

The equation raises an intriguing prospect. If gruel is not only inferior, but *so* inferior that the income effect outweighs the substitution effect,

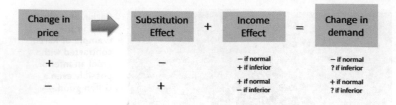

Change in price		Substitution Effect	+	Income Effect	=	Change in demand
+		−		− if normal + if inferior		− if normal ? if inferior
−		+		+ if normal − if inferior		+ if normal ? if inferior

then a reduction in the gruel price will lead to a *fall* in the consumer's demand for gruel. This kind of good – for which the change in demand has the *same* sign as the change in price – is called a **Giffen good**. As relatively few goods are inferior and only a proportion of these will be Giffen goods, any commodity that is not a Giffen good is termed an **ordinary good**.

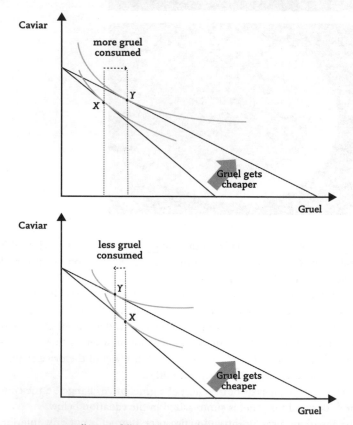

Figure 3.5: As gruel's price falls, more is consumed – unless it is considered so inferior that the income effect outweighs the substitution effect: then consumption might fall with the price.

Bending over backwards: more pay means more play

One ingenious way economists have put the indifference curves/budget sets framework to use is in modelling a worker's decision over how many hours to work. The worker is portrayed as choosing bundles composed of two "goods": leisure, meaning hours spent not working; and consumption of goods purchased using the proceeds of her employment. She trades off leisure and consumption by altering the number of hours she works, and the rate at which she can do this is determined by the ratio of her wage to the price of consumption.

Imagine the worker's wage increases. The analysis is slightly different to that of a price change studied earlier, because the labourer here is a "seller" of her own leisure. But once again the overall impact on the hours she works is determined by a substitution effect – each hour of leisure she sells buys her more consumption – and an income effect – she can afford more consumption no matter how much she works.

As one would expect, the substitution effect must induce the labourer to work more hours (i.e. "demand" less leisure). However, if leisure is a normal good, the income effect will tend to make her work less, meaning her overall response to a pay rise might be to work less. Workers like this are said to have "backwards-bending labour supply curves" because, beyond some threshold, as wages go up, the number of hours worked goes "backwards".

With a number of dishonourable exceptions in the financial services industry, backwards-bending labour supply curves are the norm rather than the exception. Offer most people thousands of dollars an hour and they'll soon stop putting in nine-to-five shifts.

The two cases of ordinary and Giffen goods are illustrated in figure 3.5 opposite.

Examples of Giffen goods studied by economists have tended to be staple foods in agrarian settings, such as rice in rural China and potatoes in 19th century Ireland. If the price of these goes down, there is little tendency to respond to the change in market exchange rate (they are essential staples, so the substitution effect is weak), but the increase in purchasing power leads the consumer to replace them with more gastronomic foodstuffs – truffles or saffron, anyone? – so they are inferior goods.

Substitutes and complements

So far little attention has been paid to the effect of a change in price of one good on a consumer's demand for *different goods*, but this can be analysed using exactly the same approach set out above. Consider Derek, who is choosing between bundles of ham and eggs, and imagine the egg price goes up. What will happen to his demand for ham? First, there is a substitution effect – which will have the *same* sign as the egg price change – and, second, an income effect, whose sign depends on whether ham is a normal or inferior good. The decomposition is summarized by this equation:

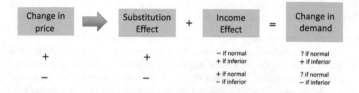

Change in price		Substitution Effect	+	Income Effect	=	Change in demand
+		+		− if normal + if inferior		? If normal + if inferior
−		−		+ if normal − if inferior		? if normal − if inferior

Taking it for granted that ham is a normal good, the sign of the change in ham demand depends on which is stronger out of the income and substitution effects.

If Derek regards ham and eggs as interchangeable – perhaps he's only interested in them as a source of calories – then a change in the market exchange rate will have a big effect on his chosen bundle. This means the substitution effect is likely to dominate, so the sign of the change in egg price will be the same as that of the change in ham demand. If this is the case ham and eggs are said to be **substitutes** – so-called because the calorie-focused consumer is happy to "substitute" ham for eggs. Any pair of goods that perform similar functions – trains and buses, whisky and gin, domestic and international holidays – are likely to be substitutes for each other.

Another possibility is that Derek finds his enjoyment of eggs to be greatly enhanced by the addition of ham – maybe he wants to make an omelette – and so is unwilling to alter the relative amounts of ham and eggs by much just because the market exchange rate changes. If this is so, it's probable that the income effect will outweigh the substitution effect, so the change in demand for ham will go in the same direction as the change in the egg price. In this case ham and eggs are called **complements**, because the ham "complements" the eggs Derek eats. Cars and petrol, gin and tonic, and mistletoe and wine are all examples of complementary products.

Demand curves

Rational individuals treat most goods as ordinary goods – when the price goes up, the amount they demand goes down and vice versa. This means that in an overwhelming majority of cases, the *sum* of everyone's demand for a good will be higher when its price is lower, and lower when the price is higher. Thus, if you plot the relationship between a good's price and the total amount demanded by all consumers, you end up with a downwards-sloping line called the good's **demand curve** or simply the good's **demand**. Two demand curves are illustrated in figure 3.6 below.

Demand curves crop up all over economics – in this book alone they'll be used to discuss topics ranging from pollution to protectionism. So it's worth spending a few moments dwelling on their properties.

A first thing to note is that the slope of a good's demand curve indicates how quickly the amount of it people buy changes in response to changes in the good's price. This information is of interest, for example, to firms such as Toyota and Guinness who may wonder how much more of their products they'll be able to shift if they cut their prices. However, a problem with using the "raw" slope of the demand curve to measure this is that its numerical value depends on the units in which prices and quantities are denominated – euros or yen, pints or litres, and such like. This is why economists tend to use the **price elasticity of demand** to measure the sensitivity of the amount demanded to a change in price. It is calculated using this formula:

$$Price\ Elasticity\ of\ Demand = \frac{\%\ Change\ in\ Demand}{\%\ Change\ in\ Price}$$

One way of thinking about the price elasticity of demand is as the proportional fall in the amount purchased in response to a one percent increase in

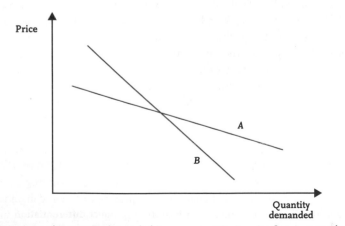

Figure 3.6: The quantity demanded is more sensitive to price for some goods than for others.

Irrational demands?

The demand curves set out here are built up from the choices of utility-maximizing consumers. But what if, having read **Chapter 2**, you don't believe utility maximization is a good model of behaviour? Does that mean you should reject the whole theory of demand?

Not really. Many even rougher guides to economics would just present you with a downward-sloping line and claim that it models demand – with no rigorously stated basis in consumer choice. Provided you still believe that when prices go up, the amount people will buy goes down, there is no problem in this. You can use the tools here without signing up to any particular paradigm of human decision-making.

So why bother with all the foundational stuff? One reason is that it allows economists to delve deeper into the determinants of demand – so they can talk about income and substitution effects and so forth. Another is that economists are interested in the effects of things like price changes on people's **welfare**, and one can only talk about this with reference to some underlying account of their preferences. This will be the focus of **Chapter 5**.

price. Though it is not the same thing as the slope of a demand curve, the flatter the curve is, the greater its price elasticity is (in the jargon, "the more elastic its demand is"). One would therefore say demand curve A in figure 3.6 is **more elastic** than demand curve B, meaning that the quantity demanded according to A is more sensitive to changes in price than it is according to B.

Generally speaking, the elasticity of a good's demand depends on the availability of alternatives that might fulfil the same purpose or, in other words, the availability of substitutes. For example, there are plenty of close substitutes around for steak and ale pies – you don't have to go far (in London, at least) to find a chicken and mushroom pie or Cornish pastie, which scratch essentially the same gustatory itch. This means that if the price of steak and ale pies goes up, consumers will respond by diverting their spending to these alternatives, leading to a big fall in sales of steak and ale pies. For similar reasons, if the steak and ale pies were to become cheaper, a steep increase in their sales would be expected. The existence of substitutes makes the demand for steak and ale pies elastic.

The opposite is true for goods such as petroleum, basic foodstuffs, alcohol, and tobacco, for which there are few, if any, other goods that serve the same purpose. For these goods the absence of substitutes means that sales are relatively unresponsive to changes in their prices – that their demands are inelastic. Firms often engage in branding (**product differentiation** in the economist's argot) to reduce the seeming availability of substitutes –

Staring down the barrel: demand elasticity and the Oil Crisis

In the wake of the 1973 Yom Kippur War, Arab members of the Organization of Petroleum Exporting Countries (OPEC) declared a reduction in oil production of 5% per month until various political demands were met. Over the course of the next six months, global oil production fell by around 7.5% and the price of oil quadrupled, wreaking social and economic upheaval across Europe and North America.

It's easy to see why a fall in production had such a dramatic effect on prices – at that point, Western economies were dependent on oil to fuel their energy, transport, and industrial sectors. There was simply nothing else out there that could do the same job. This meant that demand for oil was extremely inelastic: a small drop in volume equated to an enormous spike in its price.

Over time, however, persistently high prices gave oil consumers a strong incentive to explore substitutes, including alternative energy sources such as natural gas and new fuel-efficient technologies. By 2007, leading economies used less than half as much oil to produce a dollar's worth of GDP as they had in 1970. From a longer-term perspective, the demand for oil therefore appears much more elastic than it did in 1973.

The same story will be true of any good. The longer the period over which demand for a good is measured, the more flexible consumers' behaviour becomes, and the greater their readiness to substitute away from any good is. Thus, a good's demand is always more elastic over longer timescales.

Price inelasticity in action in this queue of motorists during the 1973 oil crisis. A drop in output pushes prices sharply up (in the short term) for a good with no obvious substitute.

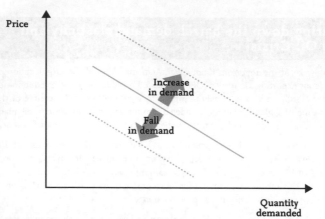

Figure 3.7

how much would it take to make you swap your Starbucks coffee for one from McDonald's? – allowing them to raise prices without suffering big losses in sales.

Finally, one of the conclusions from the discussion of individual demand was that demand for a good also depends on consumers' incomes and the prices of other goods. As these change, the amount of a good consumers will purchase changes for all prices, meaning the demand curve will move about as in figure 3.7. Rightward shifts in the demand curve – more goods sold at all prices – are called **increases in demand** while leftward movements correspond to **falls in demand**.

Just as economists measure the effect of a change in price on demand using the price elasticity of demand, the effect of changes in the overall income and the prices of other goods are given by the **income** and **cross-price elasticity of demand**. The formulae for these are:

$$Income\ Elasticity\ of\ Demand = \frac{\%\ Change\ in\ Demand}{\%\ Change\ in\ Income}$$

$$Cross\text{-}price\ Elasticity\ between\ A\ and\ B = \frac{\%\ Change\ in\ Demand\ of\ A}{\%\ Change\ in\ Price\ of\ B}$$

As was shown earlier, a positive income elasticity implies the good is normal, while a negative value means it is inferior. Positive cross-price elasticities of demand correspond to goods that are substitutes and negative cross-price elasticities denote complements.

Chapter 4
Production and supply

Along with demand, **supply** is the other great force of nature in microeconomics. Supply gives the relationship between factors such as prices, costs, and productivity on the one hand, and the amount of any good that will be offered for sale on the other.

The terms of this relationship rest on **production** decisions made by firms in the relevant industry, so the chapter begins at this level. Characterizing firms as **profit maximizers**, it shows how firms organize their production – and hence determine their supply – first in the **short run** and then in the **long run**. It then moves on to outline general properties of the overall supply of a good.

This chapter focuses entirely on the behaviour of **competitive** firms – those with very little **market power**. **Chapters 7** and **8** examine what happens when firms don't fit into this model.

Profit and the profit motive

Just as the analysis of demand in **Chapter 3** was predicated on rational consumer behaviour, it will be assumed here that companies are focused solely on the bottom line. In particular, it will be supposed that firms **maximize profit**. Unlike utility maximization – which, remember, means only that behaviour is consistent with certain rationality conditions – profit maximization involves attaining the maximum possible amount of some tangible quantity. In this sense, it is a *stronger* assumption to make than utility maximization. But is it a reasonable one?

The definition of profit used by economists is rather different to that tallied up by accountants and reported in the media. Everyone agrees that a firm's profit is equal to the revenues it generates minus the costs it incurs.

But whereas accountants and others count only those costs that arise as a *direct* result of doing business, economists also include **opportunity costs**. These reflect the fact that, in pursuing a certain line of business, a firm's owners incur the cost of *not* pursuing the next best alternative available to them.

As the box opposite highlights, the economist's way of measuring profit – **economic profit** – is much more sensible from a practical point of view. Whereas "accounting profits" are not a reliable guide to how lucrative a business prospect is, it is always true that more remunerative business opportunities generate a higher economic profit. From this point onwards, you should take it as read that all references to "profit" mean economic profit.

Given that profit accurately reflects the financial performance of any enterprise, it would seem that company owners have every incentive to maximize it – giving them more money to utilize for their own consumption. What's more, the Darwinian nature of competition between firms in certain industries can mean that any failure to maximize profits leads to bankruptcy and so *only* profit-maximizing firms survive (this point is revisited later on in the chapter). For these reasons, profit maximization generally gives a good approximation of firm behaviour in most real-world cases.

What, then, might cause a firm to fail to maximize profits? If firm owners are rational, then the only possible reason is that the profitability of an enterprise is not the only thing its owner cares about. In these cases, the neat separation between maximizing profit on the one hand, then using it to further their own ends on the other breaks down.

One scenario where this is likely to happen is when the firm's owner and the firm's manager are one and the same person, as is the case with self-employed businessperson and tenant farmers. Where this is so, maximizing profits might involve the firm's owner working so hard that she would prefer to consume less and enjoy a bit more leisure time (remember the "backwards-bending labour supply" on p.57).

Another oft-cited reason why firm owners might not be solely interested in profit is that they also have ethical or humanitarian concerns. Thus, for example, most Western clothing brands now avoid the use of low-cost child labour. However, though it would be naïve to claim that businesses never encounter trade-offs between profitability and righteousness, it's also very easy to overstate the argument that ethical behaviour and profit maximization are mutually inconsistent. In most examples – including, almost certainly, that of Western clothing brands and child labour – a firm's moral conduct serves to *enhance* its profitability by improving its reputation among consumers and motivating its employees.

Opportunity knocks: accountants vs economists

Imagine you are a wealthy entrepreneur with £1 million in the bank, and you have the chance to pursue one of two business ventures. One is to spend £1 million on a sushi bar, which will earn revenues of £600k per year but cost £500k per year to run. The other is to spend £500k on a jewellery boutique, which will make annual revenues of £280k from costs of £200k. The interest rate is 5%. Which venture makes the most profit?

Ask an accountant and the answer is straightforward. The sushi bar makes £100k per year while the jewellery boutique only makes £80k – the sushi bar therefore has the highest accounting profit. However, there is something more than a little fishy about the idea that you should open the sushi bar on this basis. If you were to open the jewellery boutique and then leave the remaining £500k in the bank, you would earn £80k per year in accounting profits plus £25k in annual interest, leaving you with a total of £105k in income. You'd therefore be better off to the tune of £5k per year if you opened the boutique.

The economist's notion of profit reflects this. By spending £1 million on the sushi bar, you forgo the alternative of spending £500k on a jeweller's and leaving £500k in the bank. This means that, on top of the £500k in annual running costs, you incur a £105k annual opportunity cost, and therefore make an economic loss of £5k. By contrast, opening the jeweller's nets you an economic profit of £5k.

The profit-maximizing firm

What, then, does the assumption of profit maximization imply about the way firms organize their production and how much they decide to supply?

From an abstract point of view, a firm can be thought of as an entity that makes various goods to sell – its **outputs** – using combinations of various ingredients known as **inputs** or **factors of production**. The relationship between a firm's inputs and outputs is given by its **production technology**, which says, for each combination of inputs, what combinations of outputs the firm can make.

Now a firm's profit is equal to the value of the output it sells – its **revenues** – minus the **costs** it incurs in employing inputs (including, of course, opportunity costs of not using them for something else). To maximize its profits, it therefore needs to find the level of output where the surplus of revenues over costs is greatest. The best way to work out this level of output is by using marginal analysis.

> The idea that firms organize their production so that their marginal cost equals their marginal revenue is a vital cornerstone of economic analysis of firm behaviour.

Ever finer margins

A firm's **marginal cost** is the additional cost it incurs when it increases its output by one unit and its **marginal revenue** is the extra revenue generated by selling another unit. So if, for example, a dairy could sell 1000 pints of milk for £700 at a cost of £500 and 1001 pints for £701 at a cost of £505, then its marginal revenue (starting from 1,000 pints) is £701–£700=£1 and its marginal cost is £505–£500=£5.

Most of the time, economists make the simplifying (and mostly harmless) assumption that goods can be divided endlessly into smaller and smaller chunks – so, for example, the dairy could sell *any* volume of milk, down to the last molecule (or smaller). This has the effect of making the difference between the extra cost or revenue of the *next* unit produced and that of the *last* one disappear, so the terms marginal cost or revenue can be used to refer to either interchangeably.

With this in mind, the following shows what a firm must do in order to maximize its profits:

▶ Imagine the firm set its output at a level where marginal revenue was greater than marginal cost (see the box above for definitions). This means that by producing one more unit, it would generate more revenue than it would cost – so its profits would increase. The fact that it could do this would imply that whatever output it had chosen to begin with couldn't have been a profit-maximizing one.

▶ Alternatively, if it set output where marginal revenue was *less* than marginal cost, then the cost of the last unit it made would be higher than the revenue it brought in, so it would have been better off not making it. Once again, this would mean its initial choice of output couldn't have been the profit maximizing one.

▶ Consequently, the only remaining possibility is for the firm to set output at the point where marginal cost and marginal revenue are at the *same* level. Here, the firm can't squeeze any more profit out of its operations by marginally increasing or decreasing its production as the costs and revenues of any such move would cancel each other out. This leads to the conclusion that a profit-maximizing firm always produces output where its **marginal cost equals its marginal revenue.**

The idea that firms organize their production so that their marginal cost equals their marginal revenue is a vital cornerstone of economic analysis of firm behaviour. Most of the rest of this chapter (and large parts of **Chapters 7** and **8**) trace out its implications.

The short and the long run

A useful distinction that crops up in many areas of economics is between the **short** and **long run**. Its precise meaning varies according to the context: in particular, the usage in **Part Five** will be somewhat different to that here. But the general idea is that, when faced with a sudden change, there are some things people can alter very quickly in response – that is, they can change these things in the short run – while there are others that they can only alter over a more protracted period – in the long run. For instance, if Harry suddenly lost his job, he could adjust his weekly grocery shop immediately to reflect his changed circumstances, but he would have to wait until his current tenancy agreement expired before he could move to a cheaper house. One might then say that his grocery shopping was flexible in the short run but his living arrangement could only be changed in the long run.

For most firms, there is a similar distinction. In responding to a change, there are some aspects of their production they can adjust in the short run, but others that are fixed until the long run. To capture this it will be assumed that firms produce a single type of good as an output, using two different inputs, one of which the firm can vary in the short run while the other is fixed until the long run. It would be possible to have many more inputs and outputs and all the same conclusions would follow – so this really is just a way of keeping things simple.

A capital argument or a laboured point?

Unlike bankers and financial journalists, who use the term interchangeably with "money", economists use "capital" to refer to any inanimate assets a firm might use in production such as factories and machinery.

The assumption that capital is fixed and labour is variable is therefore natural in traditional manufacturing industries where production lines take a long time to construct or dismantle, but where labour can be hired and fired relatively easily. Indeed, the theory of short- and long-run production set out here was developed in an era when these industries were predominant in leading economies.

This seems a much less accurate sketch of life in modern services-oriented economies, where buying (or dumping) a couple of extra computers is normally far more straightforward than recruiting (or sacking) a specialist employee. However, this doesn't really undermine the theory, as all the same analysis set out below could be carried out with the roles of the inputs reversed.

The two inputs will be assumed to be **labour** and **capital**, where, as the box below explains, capital is yet another word that economists use in a somewhat idiosyncratic fashion. In the short run, firms will be allowed to vary the number of workers they employ as they please, but the amount of capital at their disposal will be assumed to be fixed. Capital is therefore treated as a **fixed input** while labour is **variable**.

Short-run production and costs

Starting out in the short run, imagine that a firm decides it wants to raise its output by a certain amount. If it was profit-maximizing to begin with, all of its employees will already be working as hard as they possibly can (or can be made to), so there's no use piping motivational mood music down the company PA in the hope of pepping up their productivity. And as it's the short run, the amount of capital the firm can use is fixed, so there's no prospect of raising output by installing new machines. This means the *only* way it can increase its production is by employing more workers. And the number of workers it will need to hire depends on the incremental output each one of them produces. This amount – the extra output added by recruiting one more worker – goes by the technical name of the **marginal product of labour**. Figure 4.1 below graphs the marginal product of labour versus the overall number of workers for a typical firm.

Why might a graph of the marginal product of labour look like it does in the figure? The easiest way to see this is to imagine a firm with a load

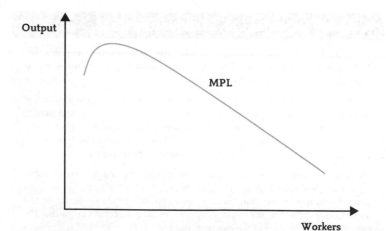

Figure 4.1: The marginal product of labour (MPL).

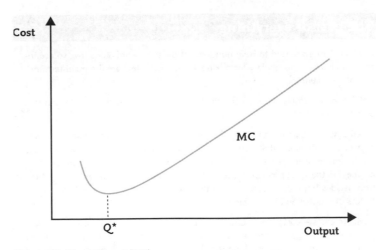

Figure 4.2: Marginal cost (MC).

of machines (i.e. a stock of capital) but no workers to operate them, which then progressively adds more workers to its payroll. The first few workers the firm employs will dramatically raise its output – the marginal product of labour is high when the workforce is small – and it may well be that, because they can start working as a team, early additional workers increase output by more than their predecessors: the marginal product of labour sometimes rises while the number of people employed remains low. Eventually, however, the shop floor gets crowded and there's less for new recruits to do, so the marginal product of labour begins to dip. This last effect, known as **diminishing marginal product of labour** or **diminishing returns to labour**, is likely to set in at some point for any firm with a fixed amount of capital.

Now turn to the question of how this affects the firm's **costs of production** – the amount it costs them to produce any amount of output. Economists have developed a rich phraseology for talking about costs, and the most important terms are explained in the box on p.70.

A particularly important concept related to firms' costs is that of marginal cost, which is the amount by which total costs increase when an additional unit of output is produced. A typical marginal cost curve is illustrated in figure 4.2 above.

There is a striking parallel between the graph of the marginal product of labour in figure 4.1 and the marginal cost in figure 4.2: when one goes up, the other goes down. There is no artistic license at work here, as in the

The cost of everything

Just as Eskimos are said to have hundreds of different words for snow, so economists have a hefty vocabulary for talking about costs. Here are the main terminological distinctions:

Total costs or simply "costs" – the total payments made by the firm to inputs it uses for production.

Fixed costs – the part of the total costs paid to fixed inputs. In the simplified version of the firm presented here, these are the payments made to keep and use capital, known as the *rental costs* of capital. Fixed costs are the "overheads" of doing business in the short run, which must be paid out no matter how much output the firm decides to produce. Note that in the long run there are no fixed costs as all factors of production are variable.

Variable costs – costs that accrue to variable inputs or, in the short run, wages paid to employees. Once the fixed costs have been dealt with, these are the costs of actually making things. In the long run there is no difference between variable and total costs because there are no fixed costs.

Average costs – in general these are costs expressed in *per unit* terms. So, if Boeing's annual total costs are $2 billion and it makes 1000 aircraft in a year, its average total costs are $2 million per plane. Similarly, average fixed or variable costs are then just the fixed or variable costs per unit.

Marginal costs – the increase in costs that results from producing one more unit. Because it's only possible to raise output by employing more variable inputs (employing more workers in the short run, adding more of anything in the long run), marginal costs are identical to the increase in variable costs from producing an extra unit.

A few of the most important costs are illustrated for a typical firm in **figure 4.3** (opposite above).

Note that lines representing both the average costs and the average variable costs intersect the marginal cost curve at their minimum points. This is no accident. To see why, think of average costs as a "running average" of how much each unit cost to make. If the next unit costs less than the pre-existing average – in other words, the marginal cost is less than the average cost – then the average costs must be falling. Likewise, if the next unit costs more to make than the pre-existing average – that is, the marginal cost exceeds the average cost – then the average must be rising. This means that at the only point where the average is neither falling nor rising – its minimum – the marginal cost must *equal* the average cost.

The argument for why the marginal cost curve crosses the average variable cost curve at its minimum is almost identical – just think of average variable costs as a running average of the variable cost required to make each unit of output, and the marginal cost as the increase in variable costs from producing one more unit.

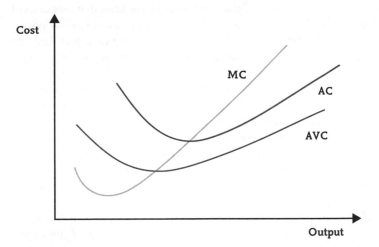

Figure 4.3: The marginal cost curve always intersects the average cost (AC) and average variable cost (AVC) curves at their minimum points.

short run the only way the firm can raise its output is by recruiting more workers. The less productive these workers are – the lower the marginal product of labour – the more workers will be needed to produce an extra unit of output, and hence the more expensive this will be – the higher the marginal cost. Since diminishing returns to labour set in once the workforce has reached a certain size, marginal costs will also rise beyond this point – as they do once output exceeds Q^* in figure 4.2.

Perfect competition

To recap: profit maximization means that firms set their marginal revenue equal to their marginal cost; the only way to increase output in the short run is to hire more workers; and the diminishing marginal product of labour means that marginal costs tend to rise beyond a certain level of output. It may not seem like it, but this is very nearly all that is needed to work out a firm's supply. All that's missing is an account of how the firm competes against its rivals in whatever industry it operates.

In this chapter, the firm will be taken to exist in a **perfectly competitive** industry where no individual firm has sufficient "market power" to exert any influence on the price output is sold at. All firms in the industry are assumed to behave like **price takers** – they take the price of output as

Firms in perfectly competitive industries have marginal revenues equal to the market price.

given and work on the basis that they can sell as much or as little as they like at that price.

In many industries, it's clear that firms do not act like price takers. Apple, for example, must realize that, as the sole producer of Mac computers, the more computers it makes, the lower the price will be at which it can sell all of them. **Chapters 7** and **8** consider types of industry where price taking is a poor assumption. However, for many industries, especially where the companies involved are small relative to the overall size of the market, price taking is a realistic approximation. For instance, a farmer's decision to plant an extra field of potatoes will have a negligible impact on the global potato price.

If firms are price takers, then the extra revenue they get from selling one more unit of output – in other words, their marginal revenue – is always just the market price, since that is what they sell the additional unit for. If, by raising their output, they cause the market price to change, then they'd also have to consider the fact that all of the rest of their output was worth a different amount when calculating their marginal revenue – but this is exactly what price taking rules out. The upshot is, therefore, that firms in perfectly competitive industries have **marginal revenues** equal to the **market price**.

A firm's short-run supply curve

A firm's **short-run supply curve** reports the relationship between the price of a good and the amount of it that firm will sell, assuming everything else holds as constant. Figure 4.4 opposite illustrates the derivation of a firm's short-run supply curve, using the assumptions that the firm maximizes profits and acts as a price taker. The argument proceeds in three steps.

The firm's **supply curve** is given by its **marginal cost curve**. This is the most important feature of a perfectly competitive firms' supply. Firms who have very little market power – who act as price takers – make the decision over whether or not to sell a particular unit of output by calculating whether making that unit is profitable *in isolation*. They don't worry about the effect of their decision on the overall market price. This means they produce a unit of output if the price they stand to receive for it – their marginal revenue – is greater than the marginal cost of making it. They continue producing up to the point where the marginal cost equals the price.

But there are two caveats. For one thing, the shape of the marginal cost curve means there can be two levels of output where price equals marginal

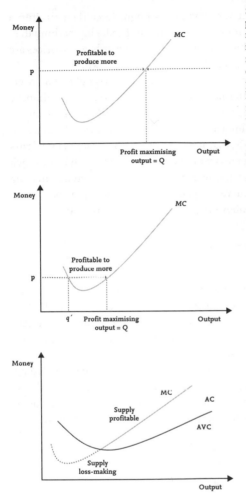

Step 1: As firms are price takers, price equals the marginal revenue. So if the price is p, then marginal revenue is higher than marginal cost at output levels of more than Q, so it would be profitable for the firm to produce less. Likewise, marginal revenue is less than marginal cost when the firm produces more than Q. So the profit-maximizing firm chooses to produce Q when the price is p.

Step 2: At a price of p, price equals marginal cost at both Q and q'. But price is higher than marginal cost at output levels just above q', so the firm increases its profits by moving from q' to Q.

Step 3: The firm is better off not producing anything when price is less than average variable cost. So its supply curve is given by the yellow line on the figure.

Figure 4.4: How to derive a firm's supply curve from its marginal cost (MC) and average variable cost (AVC) curves. The vertical axis of all three graphs is labelled "money", meaning it can refer interchangeably to prices or costs of the same magnitude.

cost. Which level does the firm choose? As the figure shows, a profit-maximizing firm will always choose the level where the marginal cost is sloping upwards – as if marginal costs were falling there would be opportunities to profit from producing more output. The conclusion: the firm's supply curve only includes **upward-sloping sections** of its **marginal cost curve**.

The second caveat is that very low prices might force the firm into a loss, and this in turn might mean it was better off producing nothing than whatever makes price equal marginal cost. In other words, when prices are low enough the firm might find it's best off **shutting down**.

Note, however, that in the short run the firm has to pay out certain overheads or fixed costs no matter how much output it makes, so it will make a loss equal to these fixed costs even if it does shut down. This means that it should stay open so long as it doesn't make a loss even bigger than this – so long, in other words, that it covers its variable costs. Now a firm's revenues exceed its variable costs whenever the price at which it sells each unit of output is greater than the **average variable cost** incurred in making them. So the firm's supply curve is equal to the upward-sloping part of the marginal cost curve that is above the average variable cost curve.

Short-run industry supply and price elasticity of supply

The short-run supply shows the relationship between the market price and the amount *all firms in the industry* will offer for sale, holding all other relevant factors constant. It is, therefore, simply the summation of the short-run supply curves of all the firms in the industry. Figure 4.5 below depicts a pair of typical short-run supply curves.

An obvious feature of both of the curves is that they are **upward-sloping**, so as the market price rises, the amount of output made in the industry also increases. This must always be true because each individual firm's short-run supply curve is also upward-sloping – since each firm will pro-

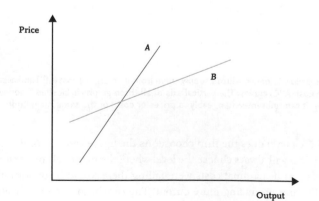

Figure 4.5: A pair of supply curves.

duce more as the price goes up, it must be that the *total* output of all firms also increases with the market price.

But although both curves slope upwards, curve A is steeper than B, meaning that output in industry B is more sensitive to changes in the market price than it is in A. This sort of thing can be of interest to businesspeople and policy-makers – for example, if a supermarket chain such as Wal-Mart or Tesco were to raise the price it paid for wholesale cheese, how much more could it expect the farmers who supplied it to churn out? And if a regulator raised the maximum price it allowed energy companies to charge consumers, would it trigger a sudden glut in the supply of electricity?

As with demand, economists tend not to measure this sensitivity using the slope of the supply curve directly, since this depends on the units of measurement (kilowatt-hours or mega–watt hours, pounds or kilos, etc). Instead they calculate the **price elasticity of supply** using the formula below:

$$Price\ Elasticity\ of\ Supply = \frac{\%\ Change\ in\ Quantity\ Supplied}{\%\ Change\ in\ Price}$$

Though the price elasticity of supply isn't quite the same thing as the slope of the supply curve, the shallower the supply curve is, the higher its price elasticity will be – the **more elastic** supply is, in the terminology. As the industry supply is built up out of individual firms' marginal cost curves, this means it's possible to deduce the price elasticity of supply from the slope of these curves.

In industries such as mining or nuclear power it can be difficult to raise output in the short run due to limits to the amount of capital installed – what are known as **capacity constraints**. The expense of producing more under these constraints means that firms' marginal costs ramp up very steeply, so the industry supply curve will also be very steep – i.e. supply will be inelastic. In other industries such as software or video-streaming, where the marginal cost of production barely increases at all with output, the shallowness of individual firms' marginal costs translates to a shallow – and therefore elastic – supply curve. In both cases, the general idea is that firms' responsiveness to a price hike depends on how many extra units of output are made profitable by the new price – and this depends on how quickly marginal costs rise with output.

Shifts in short-run supply

So far the discussion has centred on how changes in price affect the output of firms in the industry, holding all other relevant factors constant.

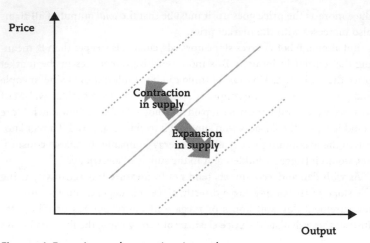

Figure 4.6: Expansions and contractions in supply.

But what happens if these "other relevant factors" change? Indeed, what are these other factors?

A change in something other than price that affects firms' output decisions will cause the supply curve to shift around, as it does in figure 4.6 above. Upward or leftward shifts in the supply curve – less industry output for any market price – are generally called **contractions** or **reductions in supply**, while downward or rightward movements are termed **expansions** or **increases in supply**.

As the supply curve is made up of firms' marginal cost curves, the most straightforward reason why the supply curve might shift is as a result of anything that affects the **marginal cost of production**. So, if wages were to go up, the cost of hiring the necessary workers to add extra output would rise, forcing marginal costs upwards – with the effect that supply would contract. On the other hand, a boost to labour productivity would mean it would take fewer workers to produce extra output, depressing marginal costs and thereby causing an expansion in supply.

A less obvious force behind shifting supply curves emanates from local and national exchequers. All countries levy **consumption** or **indirect taxes** – taxes such as VAT on the consumption of particular goods – on at least some commodities, with supposedly "sinful" products such as booze and cigarettes usually hit particularly hard. These taxes drive a wedge between the price consumers pay for a good – i.e. the market price – and the sum

Taxing coffee shifts the supply curve for this latte to the left (see figure 4.7 below).

that producers receive for it, which is the market price minus whatever tax is imposed. And it is this wedge that causes shifts in supply.

To see how this works, imagine coffee is initially untaxed and the market price is $2 per cup with q cups produced, but then a health scare leads a "concerned" government to impose a tax of $1 per cup. Before the tax was slapped on, producers were willing to accept $2 per cup in order to produce q cups, and the existence of the tax doesn't affect this – q remains

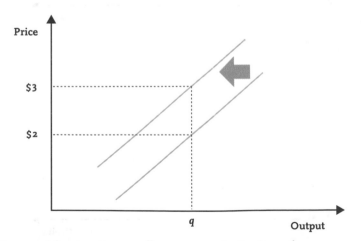

Figure 4.7: A $1 per cup tax on coffee causes a contraction in supply.

the total of all firms' profit-maximizing outputs when they get paid $2 per cup. However, after the tax is levied, the market price needs to be $3 in order for the producers to receive $2, so industry output will now be q only when the price is $3. The same argument applies for any given level of output – the price will have to be $1 more than it was before the tax in order for firms to produce the amount in question. The result is a parallel, leftward shift in supply as in figure 4.7 above. A similar story can be told for why **consumption subsidies** lead to expansions in supply.

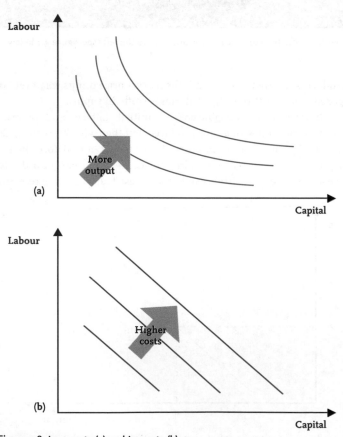

Figure 4.8: Isoquants (a) and isocosts (b).

Long-run production

Now turn to the long run, when a firm can vary the amount of capital and labour it uses as it sees fit. How does this affect the way it organizes its production?

To answer this, it's possible to use very similar tools to those used to analyse a rational consumer's demand for apples and bananas in **Chapter 3**. Much as one can draw a "contour map" of a consumer's preferences over apples and bananas, it's also possible to map the firm's production technology by relating each combination of inputs and the *maximum* level of output they can make with them. This is given in panel (a) of figure 4.8. Each "contour" (known technically as an **isoquant**) is made up of all of the "bundles" of capital and labour that can produce the same amount of output. The slope of an isoquant, the **marginal rate of technical substitution**, gives the rate at which firms can swap the two inputs while holding output constant. And this will equal the ratio of the marginal products of the two inputs.

A second contour-type map of natural interest to the firm tells it how much each combination of labour and capital costs. This is given in figure 4.8 (b). Just as the slope of the consumer's budget line was the market rate of exchange between apples and bananas, the slope of each of these curves – which are called **isocosts** – is the market rate of exchange

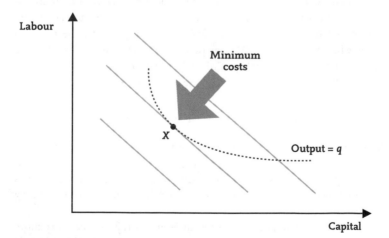

Figure 4.9: If the firm wants to produce q at minimum cost, it chooses the combination of output and labour given by X.

Drivers on le métro – French toast?

Measures such as a 35-hour week and strict conditions on firing employees make French workers among the most legally protected in the developed world. To para-phrase George W. Bush, it's almost as if they don't have a word for laissez-faire.

One might expect that such protection preserves workers' roles in the face of tech-nological advance, but, at least in the case of the Parisian métro, things have turned out to the contrary. While cities in nations with weaker labour laws, such as New York, London, and Berlin, continue to run metro systems operated by drivers, Paris has been a pioneer of automation. It started running driverless trains on one line in 2011, and has subsequently extended the system to others.

Why has Paris been the forerunner in adopting this technology? One explanation is that onerous labour regulation makes train drivers more expensive relative to capital in France than elsewhere – and this means the isocost curves faced by the Parisian authorities are less steep than those in other cities. The upshot – *quelle horreur* – is that the cost-minimizing way of producing métro journeys involves a higher degree of automation.

between labour and capital. This means that isocost maps always consist of straight, parallel lines as in the diagram.

Putting the two together, as in figure 4.9 below, one can see how a firm produces a given level of output at the lowest possible cost. This is where the **market rate of exchange** between labour and capital equals the **ratio of their marginal products**.

The basic idea is very similar to that behind a rational consumer choos-ing where the personal and market rates of exchange are equal. The market rate of exchange presents the "trades" between inputs that the firm *can* make, while the ratio of marginal products signals the "trades" that the firm is *indifferent between making*. Unless these two are the same, the firm can make itself a bit better off by trading one input for the other on the market.

Long-run costs and economies of scale

In the short run, a firm can only produce more by employing more work-ers, and with a fixed stock of capital these workers will gradually get less and less productive. As was shown earlier on, this means that the firm's marginal costs quickly escalate beyond a certain point, ultimately causing average costs to increase.

The story in the long run is rather different, as the firm can hire more workers *and* install more capital. This means, for example, that a bicycle company that operated a factory with fifty workers and produced 1000

The Kraft of good mergers

The 1960s saw the apogee of the American conglomerate. After a merger wave forged various large firms out of seemingly unrelated parts, many of the country's leading corporations straddled a broad spectrum of industries. The now-defunct LTV, for example, operated in sectors ranging from aerospace to meat-packing and sports equipment.

One of the forces behind the creation of these corporate behemoths was the belief among investors that large "diversified" firms would be more profitable than their constituent parts. Certain back-office and supply-chain functions could, perhaps, be shared while "synergies" – opportunities for different business lines to draw on each other's strengths – could also be exploited.

Whether this was a product of too much sex, drugs, and rock 'n' roll, one can only speculate. But clearly the arguments in favour of merging a meat-packer with a shipbuilder are far weaker than those for merging two companies in the same sector, where economies of scale and synergies are far likelier to exist. And, as it turned out, combining groups of very different businesses tended to drag the performance of the overall entity down, as its operations became unwieldy and difficult to manage. Diseconomies of scale thus prevailed, and around half of the mergers of the sixties were later unstitched.

For this reason, most of the "conglomerates" that exist in Western economies today, such as General Electric and Kraft, only tend to operate across related lines of business – say, foodstuffs or electronic equipment – where there are greater economies of scale.

Diseconomies of scale. In 1966 Ling-Temco-Vought were developing aerospace and aircraft products including this tiltwing Vstol prototype. At the same time they were also active in holiday resorts, golfing equipment, meat-packing and, numerous other sectors, buying up scores of companies.

bikes could, presumably, replicate this facility so it had two factories, one hundred workers, and turned out 2000 bikes. It would then have doubled both its inputs and its output, so its input cost *per bike* – i.e. its average cost – would be just the same for 2000 bikes as it was for 1000 bikes. In the long run, therefore, its average costs may not rise as it expands its production.

It might even be able to do better than that. Perhaps, instead of simply replicating its existing operations, it could build a larger factory with more efficient facilities that allowed workers to concentrate on more specialized tasks. This might mean that by doubling the amount of capital and labour it uses, it could more than double its cycle output. The firm's average costs would therefore *fall* as it got larger. As economists typically put it, the firm would experience **economies of scale** or **increasing returns to scale**.

Economies of scale crop up all over the place in everyday business, usually to the chagrin of smaller firms. Local cafés often complain that they are unable to compete with chains such as Starbucks, with their centralized management, branding, and supply chains (not to mention tax accountants), while independent grocers and bookshops struggle against supermarkets and larger online retailers.

In other industries, however, such economies of scale don't persist for very large amounts of output. Individual pubs, restaurants, and hairdressers seem to be able to compete effectively on a small scale with much

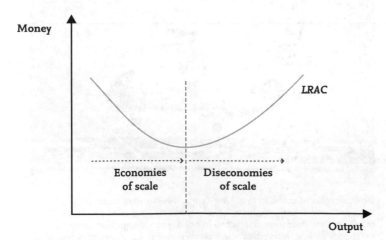

Figure 4.10: A typical long-run average cost (LRAC) curve.

larger chains, suggesting that big companies in these industries don't have a decisive cost advantage.

What's more, size can drag down performance, as larger companies are often harder to organize effectively, leading to **diseconomies of scale** where average costs increase with output. There can be many reasons for this: management may become less focused, with different divisions being run as personal fiefdoms rather than components of a profit-maximizing whole; large labour forces can unionize, forcing up wage costs; and in extreme cases the political attention that naturally follows very large companies can constrain what they do in a manner that doesn't apply to their smaller rivals. One could argue that all of these ills blighted the big American car manufacturers – General Motors, Ford, and Chrysler – before they were bailed out and slimmed down in 2009. The box, on p.81, discusses the way many of the conglomerates that grew up in the 1960s encountered diseconomies of scale.

The conclusion, then, is that in the long run average costs may fall as output increases, reflecting economies of scale, but that at some point diseconomies of scale set in, causing average costs to creep back up again. A typical long-run average cost curve is illustrated in figure 4.10 opposite.

Barriers to entry and exit

A firm's long-run supply curve can be derived in just the same way as its short-run supply was. The result is that the firm's supply is given by the upward-sloping section of its marginal cost that lies above its average cost curve.

At the industry level, however, things are complicated by the fact that, over the long run, established firms can close down and new start-ups can join the industry. The long-run industry supply is not simply the summation of a set number of individual firms' supplies – you need to take into account the possibility of **entry** and **exit** to and from the industry. The model of perfect competition assumes that firms can join and leave the industry as they see fit – in technical parlance, there are assumed to be **no barriers** to **entry or exit**.

As with the supposition that firms are price takers, the idea that there are no barriers to entry or exit does not sit well with reality for some industries. For example, in most of the world it is impossible simply to pitch up as a new weapons manufacturer because there are tight legal restrictions on who can operate in this sector. And even if you were allowed into the industry, competing effectively with established firms would require access to a huge amount of finance in order to exploit big economies of scale and a great deal of technological know-how, much of which is secret. Potential arms manufacturers thus face a veritable Maginot Line of barriers to entry. **Chapter 7** examines this kind of case. However, in other areas – think food, retailing, or basic manufacturing – the barriers to setting up or shutting down are fairly minimal – at best, little more than filling in a few forms – so the assumption is much more reasonable.

Firms enter an industry whenever doing so earns them economic profits, otherwise they stay out.

Given this, what circumstances would cause a firm to enter or leave the industry? **Opportunity cost** supplies the answer. If the firm's owners could earn more money doing something else, the opportunity cost of remaining in the industry would be greater than the money they were earning. And this would imply they were making an **economic loss**. If, on the other hand, being in the industry was the best possible use of the firm's resources, then the opportunity costs of it doing business would be less than the money it generated – so it would turn in an **economic profit**.

It therefore follows that a profit-maximizing firm will *leave* the industry whenever it makes an **economic loss**, otherwise it will continue trading.

What about entry into an industry? The argument is surprisingly similar. If firms in an industry were making economic profits, then their resources must generate more cash than they would do if put to the next-best available use. But then this means that firms in the "next-best" industry would be able to improve their profitability by moving their resources over into the sector with economic profits. So – if they were profit maximizers – the aroma of economic profits would entice them into the industry, while anything else would mean they stay put. Firms therefore enter the industry whenever doing so earns them economic profits, otherwise they stay out.

Long-run supply

Putting this all together, economic profits draw companies into the market while economic losses cause them to bail out. So whenever prices are high enough for firms to make profits, output will tend to go up, and whenever they are so low that firms make losses, it will tend to fall. If the market price just allows firms to break even, then there will be neither entry nor exit. And for this to happen, the price each firm receives for

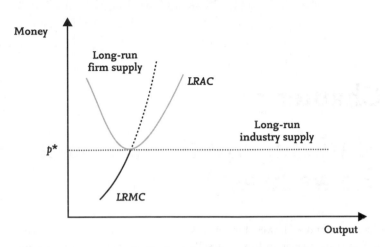

Figure 4.11: Long-run supply. The firm's long-run supply is given by the section of its long-run marginal cost (LRMC) curve above its long-run average cost (LRAC) curve (the dotted section of LRMC on the graph – see figure 4.4 for the argument behind this). Because entry will occur at any price above p^* and exit at any price below p^*, the industry supply curve is just the horizontal line at p^*.

each unit of output must be the same as the amount it costs, on average, to make. In the jargon, the **price** must equal the **average cost**.

Now, if you consider figure 4.11 opposite, you'll see that there's only one point on the firm's supply curve where this is true: where the price is p^*. At p^*, any number of firms can exist in the industry, all making zero economic profits. Any price above p^* and a stampede of entry causes output to rise without bounds; anything below and a wholesale exodus makes it collapse down to zero. The industry supply curve is therefore a horizontal line at p^*, as in figure 4.11.

A notable consequence of this is that the long-run supply curve of a perfectly competitive industry is as elastic as it could possibly be. Economists say such a supply curve is **perfectly elastic.** As will be shown in **Chapter 5**, this implies that there can only be **equilibrium** in the market with the price at this level.

Chapter 5

Markets, equilibrium and the welfare theorems

Chapters 3 and 4 showed how prices determine consumers' and firms' decisions over what to buy and sell in isolation from each other. But economists are primarily interested in what happens when, as in the real world, these decisions are made simultaneously in **markets**. In particular, economists want to make predictions about the amount of goods that are transacted in a market, the prices at which these transactions take place, and how this all might change in case supply or demand were to shift. What's more, they want to assess the desirability, from a social point of view, of these predicted outcomes: could we do better by abolishing markets and using some other mechanism, such as Soviet-style central planning, to allocate resources? These are the questions to which this chapter is addressed.

The answers are quite remarkable. Not only will prices tend to adjust to an **equilibrium** where supply and demand of all goods are balanced, but, under perfect competition, this equilibrium has the extraordinary property of being **efficient** in the sense that it is impossible to **reallocate** goods in a way that makes everyone better off. And to cap things off, market outcomes are, in principle, fully compatible with **equity**: one can achieve an egalitarian market equilibrium by redistributing people's wealth and allowing them to trade in competitive markets. These efficiency and equity properties of complete markets with perfect competition are the content of the **fundamental theorems of welfare economics**. (see p.91)

This chapter presents, interprets, and criticises these hugely influential results. The discussion begins in the context of a single market – at the level of **partial equilibrium** analysis – where it's possible to draw out some of the ideas behind the welfare theorems using supply and demand curves. It then progresses to the level of **general equilibrium** analysis, where all markets are considered together and the welfare theorems are described in detail.

Partial equilibrium

Consider the market for a single good, such as tea. Recalling **Chapters 3** and **4**, the demand and supply curves for tea can be drawn as in figure 5.1 below. A first question to ask is – how much tea will be sold in this market, and at what price?

As the demand curve slopes down and supply is either flat or upward sloping, then the curves will cross at a single point (if at all). On the figure, this is where the price of tea is p^* and the quantity sold is q^*.

Now imagine the going rate for tea – the **market price** of tea – was higher than p^*, say it was p'. As the figure shows, the amount of tea suppliers would offer for sale would be greater than the amount consumers would be willing to buy, so there would be an **excess supply** of tea. Clearly this is unsustainable: some firms, having produced tea in the expectation that they'd sell it for p' would be unable to do so. These teabag merchants would find themselves in seriously hot water. Desperate to shift their excess stock, one might expect them to offer discounts, forcing the market price for tea downwards.

It's a similar story for prices below p^*, such as p''. These prices lead to **excess demand** for tea, with some consumers unable to buy as much tea

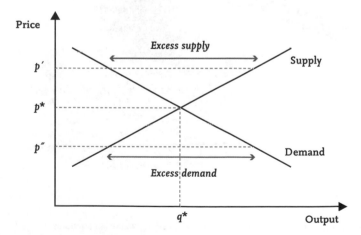

Figure 5.1: Supply, demand, and equilibrium.

Groping for an answer

Economists call the mechanism where prices "adjust" upwards or downwards in response to excess demand or supply *tâtonnement* – French for "groping". The terminology is due to one of the pioneers of equilibrium theory, Léon Walras (1834 –1910), who imagined a hypothetical auctioneer attempting to clear markets by a process of trial and error. This figure, now known as the *Walrasian auctioneer*, would grope his way to market clearing by announcing a set of prices for everything, observing supply and demand, and then cutting prices in markets with excess supply and raising them in markets with excess demand. Eventually he would fumble upon an equilibrium.

Though the general idea of adjustment is an intuitive one, describing the process in detail is a little problematic. Walras's auctioneer story suffers from the obvious flaw that no such auctioneer really exists. And the description of sellers offering discounts and buyers bidding against each other given in the text is hard to reconcile with the assumption that everyone is a price taker.

Going, going, gone. There is no such person as the Walrasian auctioneer

as they expected to. Frustrated by this, they might "bid" against each other for teabags, causing the price to rise.

Thus, whenever the price of tea is anything other than p^*, there is an unsustainable excess of either supply or demand. And these imbalances cause the price to drift back towards p^*.

By contrast, at p^* itself the supply and demand of tea are equal – the **market clears** – and there is no upward or downward pressure on prices: everyone who is inclined to buy and sell at p^* is able to do so. Economists call this the **equilibrium price** for tea – the word "equilibrium" refers to a point where there is no tendency for it to change – and say the market for tea is "in equilibrium" at p^*. Since the price always tends towards its equilibrium level and is stable at that level, it seems natural to predict p^* and q^* as the price and quantity one would expect to observe in this market.

Consumer and producer surplus

Now imagine that some particular market is in equilibrium. Is it possible to say anything about the desirability of this as an outcome compared to other possibilities?

To answer this question, it's helpful to think again about what the demand and supply curves represent. Up until now, demand curves have been interpreted as giving, for any price, the amount of a good consumers will buy. But you can just as well turn this around and think of them as giving, for any level of output, the price that ensures that amount is bought. This is illustrated in panel (a) of figure 5.2, which gives a demand curve for cakes.

In the figure, to sell one hundred cakes the price must be €1.50: any lower, and sales would rise above one hundred; any higher, and they'd fall below that level. €1.50 is thus the maximum amount of money that the buyer of the hundredth cake would be willing to part with in order to buy it: it reflects that customer's **willingness to pay** or the **marginal benefit** (measured in euros) from the cake.

If, as in panel (b), the market price is €1 per cake, then the consumer of the hundredth cake pays fifty cents less for it than she was willing to – meaning she receives a **surplus** of fifty cents from the transaction. Adding up the surplus of every buyer in the market, as in the shaded area in the figure, gives the **consumer surplus**: the total surplus gained by consumers as a result of participating in the market.

But what about producers? In **Chapter 4** it was shown that, in perfect competition, supply curves are the summation of firms' **marginal cost**

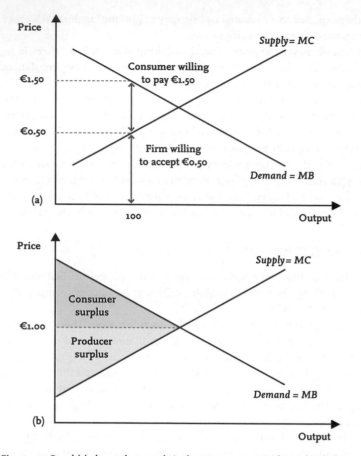

Figure 5.2: Panel (a) shows that supply is the same as marginal cost (MC); demand is marginal benefit (MB) (panel (a)). In equilibrium, consumer and producer surplus is given as in panel (b).

curves. This means that you can use supply curves to read off the marginal cost of producing each unit: in figure 5.2 (a), for example, the marginal cost of the one hundredth cake is €0.50. It also means you can measure the surplus firms receive from participating in the market by looking at the difference between the market price of each good they sell and its marginal cost. If the market price is €1, then the firm that makes the hundredth cake receives a surplus of fifty cents that it wouldn't have gained if it hadn't offered the cake for sale.

The overall surplus accruing to firms from participating in the market – known as the **producer surplus** – is simply the sum of the surpluses firms get from selling all of the cakes that are exchanged (the shaded area in figure 5.2 (b)). In the long run the producer surplus is the same thing as the total profit in the industry, but in the short run it is the difference between industry revenues and variable costs, since firms must bear fixed costs whether they participate in the market or not.

One way of judging the performance of the market for cake, or indeed any market is to tally up the **total surplus** – for producers and consumers – that it creates in equilibrium. This would, of course, be to ignore the potentially important question of how the surplus is distributed – whether it is evenly shared

> No other mechanism can outperform the market in generating surplus for producers and consumers.

between consumers and firm owners – but this is an issue that is best tackled from a general equilibrium perspective (social justice is about more than cake – just ask Marie Antoinette) and will be returned to later on. Figure 5.3 illustrates the total surplus in the cake market.

As the figure shows, the equilibrium level of output, q^*, yields a greater amount of surplus than any other. Amazingly, *no other mechanism can outperform the market* in generating surplus for producers and consumers.

Why is this so? The key is that buyers and sellers act in their own **self-interest** – only buying a good if the price is less than the consumer's marginal benefit and selling only if the price is more than the firm's marginal cost. This means that, if trading the good does generate a surplus – i.e. its

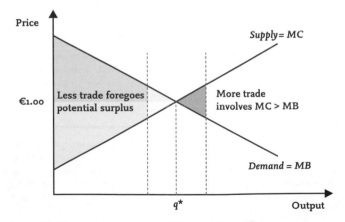

Figure 5.3: Total surplus is maximized at the market equilibrium.

The deadweight loss of taxation

As **Chapter 4** showed, consumption taxes and subsidies have the effect of shifting around the supply of a good, and this in turn will impact upon the market equilibrium. As an illustration, the impact of a tax of t pence per banana is depicted in the figure below. The figure shows that, unsurprisingly, taxing bananas causes the equilibrium price to rise and the amount sold to fall.

More subtly, the tax also affects the amount of surplus generated in the market. The existence of the tax means that the gains from trade are now split three ways – between banana consumers and producers as before, and also the government in the form of **tax revenue**.

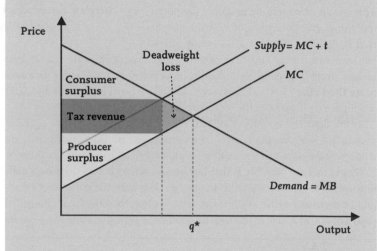

As a result of the government taking a slice of the surplus, the self-interested actions of producers and consumers alone no longer suffice to ensure that all gains from trade are exploited – in technical parlance, the tax is **distortionary**. The problem is that the tax drives a t-pence wedge between the price buyers pay and that sellers receive, so trade is impossible whenever the surplus it would create is smaller than t pence. The lost surplus that results from this is known as the **deadweight loss** of the tax.

Just as consumption taxes lead to too little trade, the same sort of argument shows that consumption subsidies lead to *too much* trade, with attendant deadweight losses. Does this mean, to misquote Benjamin Franklin, that nothing is certain except deadweights and taxes? Not in all cases: **Chapter 6** argues that consumption taxes and subsidies can be used to remove deadweight losses that arise for other reasons.

marginal benefit is higher than its marginal cost – at least one of the buyer or seller will self-interestedly want to trade. And as was shown above, in a market equilibrium, everyone who wants to trade does so. So the good must be traded in equilibrium.

If trading the good does not generate a surplus – its marginal cost is more than its marginal benefit – then it is impossible for both the buyer and the seller to self-interestedly wish to trade (the price can't be above marginal cost *and* below marginal benefit). Since trade only happens in markets if it's in both parties' interests, this means the good cannot be traded.

The fact that self-interest alone can ensure that all **gains from trade** in a market are exploited is the essence of the **invisible hand** argument associated with Adam Smith, which is examined in greater detail in the next section.

Competitive equilibrium and the welfare theorems

The analysis presented so far suggests market equilibria have some striking properties, but, by focusing on individual markets in isolation from each other, the story ignores the interconnections that exist *between* markets. For example, if the price of bicycles were to go up, consumers might switch their expenditure towards cars and owners of industrial capital might withdraw from the car market to set up more lucrative bike factories. If this were the case, both the supply and demand of cars would depend on the price of bicycles.

In earlier sections, the price in the bike market was assumed to adjust to its equilibrium level. But this adjustment will have knock-on effects on supply and demand in other markets, such as that for cars, which might set in train further price adjustments that affect the equilibrium in the bike market, leading in turn to more adjustments elsewhere and so on ad infinitum. Could such a process cause prices to evolve chaotically, never coming closer to a **general equilibrium**, where all markets clear? Indeed, is it even possible for supply to equal demand in all markets simultaneously?

Under the assumptions made about firms and consumers in **Chapters 3** and **4** – specifically the assumptions that their **indifference curves** and **isoquants** have the particular shapes depicted on p.51 and p.78 – it turns out that there always is a general equilibrium and that **tâtonnement** (see p.88) will always bring prices to it. So what about the **welfare** properties of this outcome: is it possible to say whether the institution of free markets leads to a better or worse social outcome than other arrangements? This is the question the fundamental theorems of welfare economics answer.

Before setting the theorems out, it's helpful to be more precise about the kind of market outcome they concern. A **competitive equilibrium** is a **general equilibrium** where:

▸ There are free markets for **all goods**.
▸ Everyone – consumers and producers – acts as a price-taker, that is, **behaves competitively.**
▸ Everyone has the same **information** about the goods that are traded.

Each of these three properties is dissected at length in future chapters. **Chapter 6** is addressed to (a); **Chapter 7** and much of **Chapter 8** concerns (b); and **Chapter 9** focuses on (c).

The first welfare theorem

A basic difficulty with assessing the "social performance" of the market is that the question of what is "socially good" is itself hugely contentious. What may seem utopian to a libertarian may be noxious to a communist.

However, one principle that many doctrines would endorse is that, whenever it's possible to make some people better off without making anyone else worse off, it would be desirable for such a change to be made. These changes – that benefit some people and harm nobody – are known as **Pareto improvements**, after the Italian economist Vilfredo Pareto (1848–1923) who introduced the concept to microeconomics. Whenever production and consumption are such that no reorganization of them leads to a Pareto improvement, the economy is said to be **Pareto efficient**.

One can think of a Pareto improvement as a **mutually beneficial trade** between a group of consumers and/or producers. A deal is struck where consumers in the group trade goods with each other, firms trade inputs with each other, and firms agree to make some changes to the goods they supply to consumers in return for some payment. Since nobody is left worse off by the deal and some people benefit, all members of the group would willingly sign up to the deal: it is indeed a mutually beneficial arrangement.

Intellectual Property Rights

Some economics textbooks credit Adam Smith with the original insight behind the first welfare theorem. But though his "invisible hand" analogy certainly fits the logic of the first welfare theorem, a closer reading of his work on markets suggests he wasn't really thinking in terms of equilibrium or efficiency when he claimed that self-interested individuals are led "without knowing it, [to] advance the interest of society, and to afford means to the multiplication of the species". Rather, his view seems to have been that unrestrained markets promote **economic growth** (of which more in **Chapter 16**).

Antoine Cournot (1801–1877) and Léon Walras's analysis of equilibrium in the nineteenth century and Vilfredo Pareto's 1909 mathematical proof of the theorem were far more important to the development of the material in this chapter. A further major advance, due to Kenneth Arrow (1921–) and Gérard Debreu (1921–2004), came in the 1950s, when the result was extended to include financial markets (see **Chapter 10**).

However, by the 1960s many economists agreed that the assumptions of the theorem must be false and that, as such, it was little more than a theoretical curiosity. This scepticism about the efficacy of free markets was reinforced by Richard Lipsey and Ronald Lancaster's 1956 **theory of second best**, which showed that if inefficiency was unavoidable in one market, the most effective cure may involve "adding" more inefficiency in another.

But just as this view was prominent in the era of widespread state intervention in Western economies, the theorem came back into fashion with the rise of the Thatcher–Reagan doctrine of deregulation and privatization in the 1980s (which, it must be said, placed much more emphasis on the word "free" than "market"). The section "Understanding the welfare theorems" explains why many of today's economists believe the result is important.

Pareto efficiency thus requires there to be no mutually beneficial trade "out there" that hasn't already been exploited: if there's a deal to be had, then people must make it. It is therefore an *extremely* exacting condition to require of an economy, and most certainly one that is never met in practice. And yet the first fundamental theorem of welfare economics says this:

- Production and consumption in a competitive equilibrium are Pareto efficient.

This is the insight associated with Adam Smith, and since refined and formalized by others. The logic of the theorem reveals the startling power of **self-interest** and the **price mechanism** in leading consumers and firms, as though guided by an invisible hand, to achieve the social goal of **Pareto efficiency**. It can be traced out in three steps:

❶ If consumers act like utility maximizers, it's impossible for them to make mutually beneficial trades of goods with each other – there is **efficiency in consumption**. As **Chapter 3** showed, self-interested consumers spend their income by choosing a bundle where their

The price of everything and the value of nothing

In his 2012 book, *What Money Can't Buy: the Moral Limits of Markets*, Harvard philosopher Michael Sandel criticizes the "corrupting" effects of markets on society. Trade in certain "goods", such as friendship, human organs, or sexual favours seems somehow to diminish either the traders involved or the good itself. If Steve pays Jim to be friends with him, doesn't this make Steve and Jim's "friendship" less valuable than it would be if no money had changed hands?

Almost certainly, but just because Steve and Jim's "friendship" is a contrived one, it's debatable whether there's anything wrong with allowing trade in quasi-goods such as "friendship" or "sex", provided everyone involved is willing to exchange these debased versions of the real thing at the terms proposed.

And even if you feel that these kinds of deal are simply morally wrong or have unacceptable social effects – ushering in what Sandel describes as a "market society" that encourages shallowness and avarice – Sandel acknowledges that this doesn't mean markets should be abandoned altogether. Does Alf's purchase of an apple from Gwen really morally demean Alf and Gwen or undermine the integrity of apples?

Socialyup.com sells five hundred Facebook fans in the form of "likes" for $30. What price (if any) for true friendship?

personal rate of exchange equals the market rate of exchange, given by market prices. In so doing they exploit **all possible gains** from trade on the market. But as everyone faces the same prices, this means that all consumers have the same personal rate of exchange, so as a result they also exhaust all possible gains from trade with each other.

> In a competitive equilibrium, personal rates of exchange equal ratios of marginal costs.

❷ Similarly, if firms maximize profits, it's impossible for them to exchange inputs with each other to reduce costs – there is **efficiency in production**. Profit-maximizing firms organize production so that the ratio of their inputs' marginal products is equal to the market rate of exchange between these inputs. This ensures they cash in on all available cost reductions from trading inputs on the market (see **Chapter 4** for the explanation). Once again, the fact that all firms face the same prices implies that all firms' inputs have the same ratio of marginal products, so firms must exhaust **all possible cost savings** from trading inputs with each other.

❸ Finally, in a **competitive equilibrium**, it's impossible for firms and consumers to change *what* is produced and consumed in a mutually beneficial way – there is **efficiency in the product mix**. This is because the **ratio of the marginal costs of two goods** is the same as the rate at which firms are willing to **shift production** from one good to the other. If, for instance, the marginal cost of a car is twenty times that of a bike, then in order to induce a firm that made both to produce one fewer bike and one more car, you'd need to increase the compensation it received for that unit of output by twenty times.

So, remembering that firms in perfectly competitive industries arrange their production so that the price of a good equals its marginal cost (see **Chapter 4**), it must be that the market rate of exchange between any two goods – i.e. the ratio of the goods' prices – equals the **ratio of their marginal costs**. And since consumers ensure their personal rates of exchange are also equal to the market rate of exchange, in a **competitive equilibrium** personal rates of exchange equal ratios of marginal costs.

And *this* means there must be efficiency in the **product mix**: put simply, the rate at which consumers are willing to exchange two goods equals the rate at which firms are willing to shift production between them, so it's impossible to change what is produced to firms' and consumers' mutual benefit.

The second welfare theorem

Pareto efficiency may be a desirable end to achieve, but it alone hardly amounts to a milk-and-honey vision of socioeconomic paradise. One instance of it might be where a single person controls *all* of the production and consumption in an economy. Here, though it may well be impossible to benefit anyone else without harming this plutocrat by forcing him to relinquish some of his wealth, that doesn't necessarily mean it wouldn't be a good idea.

You might therefore conclude that Pareto efficiency needs to be supplemented with other conditions – including, perhaps, some to do with fairness or **equity** – in order to describe an ideal economic state of affairs. The first welfare theorem says that free markets will always lead to *some* Pareto efficient outcome in equilibrium, but can things be arranged so that they lead to the *right* one, where all these other conditions are met? This is the question that the second welfare theorem answers.

In economic terminology, a person's **endowment** is made up of all of the things of economic value that she has control over. It includes her possessions, the cash in her bank account, the shares she owns in firms, and the value of her labour: in other words, it is her wealth, conceived of very broadly. One way of redistributing resources in an economy is by **reallocating endowments**: taking part of some people's endowments away from them through a form of **poll** or **wealth tax**, and then disbursing the proceeds to others. Note, this kind of taxation is **non-distortionary**: it does not interfere with the price mechanism (see the box on p.92).

The second welfare theorem says that, provided endowments can be reallocated at will, free markets can be used to achieve whichever Pareto efficient outcome one prefers. More precisely:

- Any Pareto efficient pattern of production and consumption can arise in a competitive equilibrium, given a suitable reallocation of endowments.

The logic behind the second theorem is really quite simple. If production and consumption are Pareto efficient, all mutually beneficial trades must have been exploited. This means that, if there are free markets, where people only do things that are beneficial to them, no more trades will be made. But this is just the same as saying consumption and production are in equilibrium – so if endowments are allocated so that consumers and firms behave in this way to begin with, nothing will change.

Understanding the welfare theorems

Hopefully the revelation that much of **Parts Three** and **Four** concern **market failure**, where the rosy conclusions of the two welfare theorems fail, won't come as too much of a spoiler. As those chapters will show, it is inconceivable that a real market outcome could ever be a competitive equilibrium. Does this mean the theorems are of no practical importance?

Most economists think not. For one thing, by establishing precisely what is needed for market outcomes to be Pareto efficient, the welfare theorems make it clear how markets might fail and what policymakers can do if this happens. Subsequent chapters look at this in detail.

Less straightforwardly, one can think of the theorems not merely as mathematical results, but as *stories* about how markets work. Looked at in this light, the logic of the first welfare theorem seems to carry two messages:

1. In markets, wheeler-dealing firms and consumers will exploit mutually beneficial trades spurred only by their own self-interest – there is no need for a **central authority** to coordinate everything beyond enforcing property rights. In other words, markets are **decentralized**.
2. Furthermore, in order to know what trades are available and thus to decide what to do, participants in markets only need to know the prices of everything – they *don't* need to know anyone else's endowment, preferences, or production technology. Markets thus do not demand that producers or consumers process very large amounts of **information**.

These two points suggest that markets are extremely effective mechanisms for facilitating mutually beneficial trade. To illustrate this, consider, as a counterpoint, the mechanism of central planning. Under this kind of regime, there is plainly a need for a central agency to cajole firms and consumers to do what it tells them to. And, what's more, this central bureaucracy would need to chew through vast reams of data about consumers and producers – much of which they would be reluctant to reveal – in order to work out what should be produced and who should get it. Organizing an economy in this way is therefore likely to be much more costly and, if the experience of the former Soviet bloc is anything to go by, far less successful than using markets.

As a final note, thinking about the first welfare theorem in this way highlights serious practical limitations of the second theorem. The latter envisions some sort of central authority reallocating endowments between people to ensure society's distributive goals are met. But in fact this is almost never seen in practice – land reforms in some developing countries are a rare example – and the two bullets above offer some clue why. In order to carry out this sort of policy, a government would need to know precisely what people's endowments were and be able to enforce transfers of them. But for most people, a large part of their endowment takes the form of **human capital** – what their skills are worth on the market. Gauging this and then forcibly redistributing it through some system of indentured labour requires an iron fist rather than an invisible hand.

PART THREE:

Market and government failure

Part Two set out models of demand, supply, and equilibrium where, provided a few assumptions are met, unfettered markets perform very well indeed. But there is an unfortunate catch: these assumptions will not be met in practice, and the result is inefficiency. In other words, real life market outcomes are characterized by **market failure**. How market failure might arise and what might be done about it is one of the main occupations of both professional and academic economists. And it is the principal focus of the chapters in this part of the book.

The first assumption required for markets to be efficient was that there was **free trade** in all goods. But some "goods", such as pollution, are never traded: they are merely dumped upon the victims by producers or consumers of other commodities. These non-traded goods are **externalities**: by-products of the trade of other goods that affect people "external" to this trade and are not themselves exchanged in the marketplace. **Chapter 6** shows how **missing markets** for externalities lead to inefficiency, and explores various ways that policymakers can address this problem, including taxes and "cap and trade" type systems.

A special kind of externality arises when a good is produced that can be enjoyed (or endured) by many people at once. In the market for these goods, which are known as **public goods**, opportunistic consumers **free ride** on the consumption of others, leading to inefficient levels of output. The last part of **Chapter 6** outlines the theory of public goods and considers how they can be produced efficiently.

Chapter 7 tackles the second of the assumptions required for market efficiency: that people behave competitively. In particular, it looks at **monopoly**, the most extreme case of uncompetitive producer behaviour there is. It explains why monopoly power leads to inefficiency and what can be done by **competition** or **antitrust** authorities to combat it.

Finally, just because it's broke, that doesn't mean it needs fixing. Although market failures are unwelcome, economists also worry about the possibility that governments' attempts to address them end up making matters worse. Such situations involve **government failure**. Both chapters will consider some examples of this.

Beyond the topics covered in this part of the book, there are other ways that the market can fail, including where the assumption that producers and consumers have the same information about goods is false. Discussion of this and other cases is postponed till later on in the book, after some more of the economist's toolkit has been developed.

Chapter 6

Externalities and public goods

The first way in which markets can fail is simply through their absence. Obviously, if there is a good that producers and consumers would like to trade but are unable to, then not all mutually beneficial trades will be made so there won't be Pareto efficiency. But why might this ever happen?

One reason could be the lack of well-defined **property rights** over the good: nobody legally "has the right" to that good, so it's impossible for it to be bought or sold on a market. For example, in many countries there's no legally enforceable way of buying or selling the right to pollute the air: it's just something that happens as a by-product of various activities. In this case, a problem arises because pollution affects people who are external to these "various activities" and, as such, their interests are not taken into account by the people involved in making the pollution. This is an example of an **externality**. Precisely what externalities are, why they cause a problem, and what to do about them are the first questions this chapter asks.

For some goods, the problem runs deeper than this. For example, if a broadcaster transmits a TV programme, then one viewer's "consumption" of the programme has no bearing on anyone else being able to watch it. This means that if someone pays the broadcaster to show the programme, she creates the externality of allowing anyone else who pleases to tune in without paying for the privilege. In other words, people can **free ride** on a single person's purchase. Goods such as TV broadcasts are known as **public goods** and tend to be underproduced in markets. They are the focus of the second half of the chapter.

Externalities

Let's go back in time to a point before smoking in public places was banned in many jurisdictions. Suppose you and some friends are sitting in your favourite pub enjoying a pint and each other's company. Someone on the next table then lights up a cigarette, and then another, and then another. The unpleasant smell of tobacco begins to waft in your direction. Your enjoyment begins to be seriously diminished. Economists call a problem like this an **externality**. The problem is that the smoker's actions impose a cost on someone else – in this case, you! – but there's no market for this cost. So the smoker does not take this cost into account when they decide whether or not to light up another cigarette. This leaves room for **Pareto improvement** in that it would be possible to make both smokers and non-smokers better off.

If only everyone could trade cigarette smoke, the problem would disappear. Imagine the world was such that the smoker "owned" the smoke he emitted – he had the legal right to produce smoke, and could sell to others an undertaking to limit his production of smoke. Then you and your friends could pay the smoker for a less smoke-filled environment. Provided you were willing to give up more money than the smoker would need to compensate him for not smoking so much, a Pareto improving deal could be struck. Similarly, if the world was such that non-smokers "owned" the clean air in the pub, which the smoker could pay to pollute, Pareto improvements may be possible. For just one cigarette, the smoker may be willing to give up more than enough money to compensate you and your friends for having to put up with the resulting smoke. This means that legal systems where

No smoking? Perhaps not if it had been decided this externality could be addressed via bargaining.

The efficient level of pollution

One of the conclusions of the economic analysis of pollution that some people sometimes find troubling is that the efficient level of pollution is rarely zero. Intuitively, if something is bad, like second-hand smoke, it should not be allowed. However, most pollutants are a result of producing something useful. The internal combustion engine pollutes, but has become indispensable as a means of transport and very few people actually believe it should be banned outright. This may be more difficult to appreciate with an activity like smoking which is known to be bad for the health of the smoker as well as those in close proximity to the smoker. But the smoker sees things differently and derives pleasure from smoking a cigarette, and that (to an economist) qualifies as something useful. This is an example of the non-paternalistic perspective that is at the core of economics (see the box on p.23 in **Chapter 2**).

In some countries, the existence of universal state-funded healthcare adds a complicating factor to these discussions as it creates an externality in all sorts of actions that would otherwise only affect the individual concerned. For example, living alone and smoking in the privacy of one's own home would not normally affect anyone else, so there would be no economic case for state intervention. However, many countries publicly fund healthcare, meaning that everyone else has to pick up the bill for treating the smoker for whatever ill effects this might have on him. But even this does not mean that the efficient level of smoking is zero! Smokers still derive pleasure from smoking and this must be traded off against the increased health costs of their habit that are shared by everyone. So there is an economic case for interventions designed to reduce smoking but not necessarily for a ban.

there is no trade – either where smokers can smoke as much as they want or there is an outright ban on smoking – result in Pareto inefficiency. But by assigning **property rights** and allowing trade, everyone can be made better off.

The terminology here is telling. Markets are efficient when all the benefits and costs of production and consumption are borne by people involved in the transactions. But this is not always the case. In the example above, the smoker trades cigarettes with a retailer, but then his consumption affects the welfare of third parties "external" to the transaction. The fact that you have no say, via the market, in how much he smokes, is why it is called an externality.

Broadly speaking there are two kinds of externality that can arise from a transaction: **positive externalities** where third parties benefit from the transaction and **negative externalities** where third parties are hurt by the transaction. The argument above shows that trading cigarettes can lead to negative externalities. As to the precise nature of this problem and what can be done about it, the following sections attempt to blow away the clouds.

Negative externalities

As well as cigarette smoke, a widely discussed example of negative externalities is pollution. The production of certain goods such as steel create waste products, which, if simply dumped into the environment, can harm the local population, perhaps by creating an eyesore or damaging the air or water quality.

The amount of steel – and hence the amount of waste product – produced will be determined, in the market, by the supply and demand for it. And as explained in **Chapter 5**, these respectively reflect the marginal costs to producers of steel and benefits to consumers. They are thus labelled the **marginal private costs** (MPC) and **marginal private benefits** (MPB) in figure 6.1 opposite.

However, not all costs associated with making steel are included in the marginal private cost. Each additional unit of steel creates some amount of the waste product, which imposes an **external cost** on the local community. The **marginal social cost** (MSC) of a unit of steel is the sum of the marginal private cost of making it and the marginal external cost of the pollution.

Not all costs associated with industrial manufacture are included in the marginal private cost. Pollution carries with it marginal external costs.

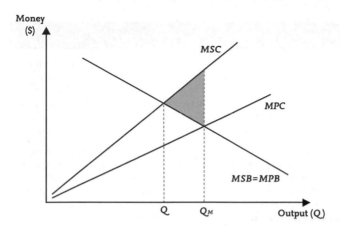

Figure 6.1: A negative externality leads to a deadweight loss equal to the shaded areas. There are no external benefits so the marginal private benefit (MPB) equals the marginal social benefit (MSB). (MSC = marginal social cost; MPC = marginal private cost.)

To find the **socially optimal** level of steel production, economists use marginal analysis:

▶ If the marginal social benefit is greater than the marginal social cost, then everyone who benefits from a bit more steel production can compensate everyone who loses and still be made better off. So increasing steel production could lead to a Pareto improvement.
▶ Conversely, if the marginal social cost is greater than the marginal social benefit, the people who are harmed by steel production could compensate those who benefit from it for a marginal reduction in steel output. Once again, this would lead to a Pareto improvement.
▶ So the only level of steel output where there is no potential Pareto improvement is where the social marginal cost equals the marginal social benefit. This is what economists consider the **social optimum**.

However, as the figure 6.1 shows, the market equilibrium output of steel, where private marginal benefit equals private marginal cost, is higher than the social optimum. The problem is that producers only take private costs – which they pay – and private benefits – for which they are paid by consumers – into account when deciding how much to produce. They have no economic incentive to worry about external costs and so ignore them, which leads to overproduction. The invisible hand of self-interest thus leads them astray, and there is a **deadweight loss** as shown in the figure.

Education – *cui bono?*

There are plenty of reasons to think that the "consumption" of education leads to positive externalities. For example, in democracies, more educated people will generally vote in better governments – something that benefits even the uneducated – and many believe that the presence of higher skilled – and thus more highly paid – workers in an economy tends to raise the aspiration of everyone. Or at least that's what the authors, who make a living out of university teaching, like to think.

The question of whether to subsidize university education is a contentious topic in many countries, and positive externalities offer one argument in favour of subsidy. For the same reason that negative externalities result in a good being overproduced, positive externalities mean output falls short of the socially optimal level. Decision-makers will equate private marginal costs and benefits, disregarding **marginal external benefits**. Could this be fixed with a subsidy?

Surprisingly, at least in England and Wales, seemingly not. The private benefits of a higher education are estimated to be huge: one study has shown that a university graduate in the UK can expect to earn £160,000 more over their career than someone who did not go to university. Set this against the £27,000 of debt that would come from a three-year course, and the net private marginal benefit of a university degree is still substantial. There are reasons to be sceptical about these numbers (**Chapter 9** presents a particularly big one), but at face value they suggest there is underconsumption of education even taking only private costs and benefits into account. One possible explanation is that there are supply constraints leading to rationing, in which case subsidy alone will be of little use.

Solutions to the problem of externalities

Economic solutions to problems posed by externalities come in several forms, but will typically share one thing in common: they will be attempts to **align the incentives** of decision-makers so that the effects of externalities on third parties are somehow accounted for.

▶ The government might "speak for society" in trying to achieve the socially optimal quantity. This could involve **taxing** activities with negative externalities or **subsidizing** those that produce positive ones; or alternatively the government might set **quotas** that impose the socially optimal levels of output on the relevant market.

▶ Or they may change institutions in order to **internalize the externality**, bringing affected third parties inside transactions so that they can represent their own interests. This might involve **creating the missing**

market in the externality or encouraging **mergers** between otherwise separate entities.

Taxes or subsidies

So far, consumption taxes and subsidies have been given a bad press: **Chapter 5** showed how they led to inefficient levels of output and deadweight losses. But some taxes and subsidies can be justified on the basis of externalities.

▶ If you get drunk you might place extra strain on public services, imposing a social cost on everyone else – so alcohol is taxed in many countries.

▶ If you insulate your home, you will consume less energy to heat it during the winter and reduce carbon emissions to the benefit of society – so loft and wall insulation are often subsidized.

The basic idea is that the government manipulates prices through taxes and subsidies in order to **price in** the external costs and benefits of these activities. This is illustrated in figure 6.2 below.

The left-hand panel of figure 6.2 shows an example of a tax correcting a negative externality. The negative externality means that marginal private cost lies below the marginal social cost. However when a per unit tax of t^* is imposed, the supply curve – which, remember, is just the marginal private cost – is shifted up so that it intercepts marginal benefit at the same point as marginal social cost. So in equilibrium, output ends up being at the socially optimal level. The right-hand panel shows the analogous case of subsidising goods that generate positive externalities. Figure 6.2 shows that where there are positive externalities, external benefits create a divergence between marginal private benefits and marginal social benefits; a subsidy of s^* reduces private marginal costs so that the socially optimal amount of the good is traded.

> It is ...possible for the State ... to remove the divergence in any field by "extraordinary encouragements" or "extraordinary restraints" upon investments in that field.
>
> Arthur Pigou, *The Economics of Welfare* (1932)

Despite the many boosters of these methods (see the box opposite), solving the problems of externalities using taxes and subsidies can be difficult in practice. Note that the tax or subsidy must be set equal to the marginal external cost or benefit at the *socially optimum quantity* if the intervention is to achieve the efficient outcome.

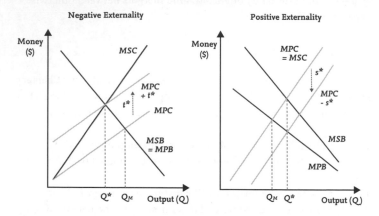

Figure 6.2: Correcting externalities with taxes and subsidies. Q_M represents market outputs; Q^*, socially optimal outputs. (MSB = marginal social benefit, MSC = marginal social cost, MPB = marginal private benefit, MPC = marginal private cost.)

Pigovian taxes and the Pigou Club

Per-unit taxes (and subsidies) such as those outlined in the text are sometimes called **Pigovian taxes** after the economist Arthur Pigou, who first suggested such an approach in 1920, later explaining:

> It is plain that divergences between private and social net product of the kinds we have so far been considering cannot... be mitigated by a modification of the contractual relations between any two contracting parties, because the divergence arises out of a service or disservice rendered to persons other than the contracting parties. It is, however, possible for the State ... to remove the divergence in any field by "extraordinary encouragements" or "extraordinary restraints" upon investments in that field. The most obvious forms which these encouragements or restraints may assume are, of course, those of bounties [subsidies] and taxes.

Arthur C. Pigou, *The Economics of Welfare*, 4th Edition (1932)

Many economists feel that greater use of Pigovian taxes should be made in order to reduce externalities, particularly greenhouse emissions, and improve the environment. In 2006, the Harvard economist Gregory Mankiw founded the "Pigou Club" of "economists and pundits" who have publicly called for greater use of Pigovian taxes. The club's membership includes such luminaries as the former Federal Reserve chairman Alan Greenspan, the Nobel prize winner Joseph Stiglitz, and Steven Levitt, one of the co-authors of *Freakonomics*.

Give the people what they want?

Efficiency isn't the only motive behind per-unit taxes and subsidies. The government may tax alcohol and tobacco because they believe these are goods people ought not to consume, or subsidize classical music and opera because they believe these are goods people ought to consume. The economic terms for goods like these are **demerit** and **merit** goods – and punitive taxes on demerit goods are known as **sin taxes**. The social morality behind this kind of intervention lies outside the remit of economics, so economists rarely think along these lines. However, not all policymakers are economists, and they may well have paternalistic motives.

A more cynical reason for slapping taxes on alcohol or tobacco is simply that this is a good way to raise revenue. Demand for these goods is inelastic, so that when the price rises, there is only a small drop in the quantity consumed. This makes them excellent goods to tax in order to raise revenue. When the tax raises the price there is only a small reduction in the number of units purchased and so the tax revenue the policymaker will earn from these goods can be set relatively high.

This may be difficult to measure beforehand, especially since the marginal external cost or benefit may well vary with the quantity being produced or consumed.

Quotas and "cap and trade"

As an alternative to tinkering around with prices, one very simple solution to negative externalities is to issue a decree that no more than the socially optimal amount can be produced. This is a **quota**. Provided you know what the socially optimum quantity is, it is possible to set that as the quota.

But imposing an efficient quota involves more than saying, "thou shalt not produce more than *x* tonnes of steel". For one thing, a quota should target the externality itself – carbon dioxide or soot, for example – rather than a product that gives rise to it. This allows companies to **innovate** – coming up with cleaner ways of making steel, for instance, or new products such as smoke-free cigarettes that serve the same purpose but without any externality. And, for externalities such as carbon dioxide, targeting a single product is ineffective anyway as the production of many different goods causes emissions.

A second, subtler difficulty with quotas arises when many firms produce the externality. If this is so, it seriously matters how much of the quota is assigned to each firm. To illustrate, imagine two firms, A and B, produce one hundred tonnes each of noxious gas, and the socially optimal amount of the gas is one hundred overall. Suppose that firm A can reduce its emissions of the gas much more cheaply than firm B can – it may, for instance, be able to clean up its production process relatively easily. This means that a quota regime that assigned fifty tonnes of emissions to each firm would be inefficient – it would be possible to produce the socially optimal amount of gas at a lower overall cost to the firms by asking firm A to reduce its emissions by more and B by less.

To ensure efficiency, the quota must be such that both firms face the same marginal cost of reducing or "abating" their emissions – in technical terms, their **marginal costs of abatement** must be equal. If firm B had a higher marginal cost of abatement than A, then the cost of asking A to abate a little more would be more than offset by allowing B to abate a little less: the same overall level of abatement would be achieved at a lower combined cost to A and B. The same logic applies if firm A had a higher marginal cost of abatement than B.

Designing an efficient quota can thus require an amount of information no real-world policymaker is ever likely to have. She must not only know the overall efficient level of the externality, but also the **marginal abatement cost curve** of every firm that produces the externality. Does this mean that they are of no practical interest?

Not with a slight tweak. If, instead of issuing each firm with an inflexible quota, the policymaker were to distribute **tradeable permits**, giving the holder the right to emit a certain amount of the externality, then the equilibrium result would be efficiency. Such schemes are known as **cap and trade** mechanisms; examples include the EU Emissions Trading Scheme (see the box opposite) for carbon dioxide and the US Acid Rain Program for sulphur dioxide. The logic of cap and trade is as follows:

► As permits are traded, a market price for them emerges.
► Firms will then have an incentive to sell permits whenever the money they raise from the sale is higher than the cost of not being allowed to pollute quite as much. In other words, firms will sell permits whenever the market price of permits is higher than their marginal cost of abatement.
► Similarly, they will purchase permits whenever this is cheaper than abating – so they will buy permits whenever the market price is lower than the marginal cost of abatement.
► So in equilibrium, all firms will trade permits such that their marginal cost of abatement equals the market price of permits. All firms therefore have the same marginal cost of abatement, so there is efficiency.

The argument shows the elegance of the market mechanism in ensuring that abatement is done at minimum cost, but remember that it all relies on a policymaker knowing what the socially optimal level is to start with. The box below highlights a few practical issues with cap and trade schemes.

Cap and trade meets realpolitik

The EU Emissions Trading Scheme (EU ETS) is the world's largest and best-known cap and trade scheme. Under it, large factories across the EU (plus a few other countries) must monitor their output of carbon dioxide and buy permits to cover whatever they emit. Leaving aside the inconvenient truths that not all CO_2 in the EU is emitted by large factories and not all countries that emit CO_2 belong to the EU, then provided the correct number of quotas are initially issued, the mechanism should deliver efficient abatement no matter how permits are doled out to factories to begin with.

But while the initial allocation of permits does not matter from the perspective of economic efficiency, it matters very much to the participants. The more permits a firm is initially assigned the better off that firm will be: even if they do not plan to use the permits themselves, they can boost their profits by selling them on. Within the EU ETS, the initial allocation is decided by the member states and different member states use different allocation mechanisms. For example, some of the UK's allocation is assigned to existing installations on the basis of historic emissions – a practice known, bizarrely, as **grandfathering** – while other parts of the allocation are auctioned. Given the stakes involved, when a scheme such as this one is proposed, potential participants will expend resources **lobbying** politicians to influence the way permits are allocated. From an economic perspective, resources expended in this way are entirely wasted. They represent what economists call **rent-seeking activities** that do not increase the total amount of gains to be had in the economy, but simply compete over their allocation. This does introduce some inefficiency.

Problems like this can also be opportunities. A clever assignment of the initial permits can be used to win the support of interest groups who would otherwise oppose the introduction of a quota completely. If the opposition of such groups would, for whatever political reason, be insurmountable, then acquiring their support could be the difference between implementing a quota scheme and not.

Internalizing externalities

The solutions to the externality problem discussed so far involve the government coming in and speaking for the third parties affected by an externality, either through taxation or quotas. But is this necessary? Couldn't these external parties be allowed to speak for themselves? Measures that force producers of externalities to take the third party's view into account – and thus **internalize the externality** – do just this.

Externalities were introduced earlier on using an example where a smoker in a pub irritates a group of friends. It was argued that the **missing market** for clean air means that Pareto improving deals, either involving the smoker paying the friends for the right to pollute or the friends paying the smoker for clean air, go begging. Creating this market by assigning property rights is the essence of the **bargaining** solution to externalities.

To see precisely how it works, consider another example. Suppose there is a toy factory that, as part of the process of making toys, pollutes a river used by a fishery. The toy factory produces so that its private marginal cost equals the market price of toys (see **Chapter 4**) but it disregards the external cost it inflicts on the fishery. This, as already witnessed, leads to inefficiency.

A policymaker may not have any idea what the true external costs are or what the socially optimal level of pollution is – meaning that she would struggle to solve the problem using taxes or quotas. As an alternative, she might create the missing market by giving either the factory or the fishery property rights to clean water and allowing them to bargain with each other. This could work in one of two ways:

(1) If the fishery is given the right to clean water, then the factory can "bribe" it to pollute the water up to a certain level. You can think of it as buying the "units" of the pollution from the fishery at a given price per toy.

- What price will the fishery set? The fishery gains from selling pollution whenever the price it receives is greater than the marginal cost of pollution on its operations and it loses whenever the price is smaller than the marginal cost. So it will set the price equal to the marginal cost and trade up to the point where it has exhausted all gains. As the marginal cost of pollution to it is just the same as the marginal external cost, this means the pollution price equals the external cost of toymaking.
- How will the factory respond? It will want to continue making toys up to the point where the marginal benefit of doing so equals the marginal cost. The marginal benefit is simply the price it sells the toy for, while the marginal cost is the private cost of production plus the price of a unit of pollution that it must pay the fishery. And since the latter is the external marginal cost, it will produce where the price

equals the sum of the private and external marginal costs – that is, where **price equals social marginal cost**. And so there is efficiency.

(2) If the factory is given the right to pollute the water as it sees fit, then the fishery can pay it to abate its pollution and thus reduce its production of toys. The logic is nearly identical to the other case. At whatever the price is, the fishery will buy permits up until the point where the pollution price equals the external marginal cost of pollution. And this means the factory will make toys where the toy price equals the marginal private cost of making them plus the pollution price, which is equal to the external marginal cost. The result, once again, is toy production set where the toy price equals the social marginal cost – and thus efficiency.

The toy factory example suggests that solving the externality problem is child's play. Simply assign property rights and let self-interested parties negotiate their way to Pareto efficiency. The fact that it doesn't even matter (from an efficiency point of view, at least) who is assigned the rights to pollution is an instance of the **Coase theorem** after Ronald Coase (1910–2013), who first proposed it. Coase was awarded a Nobel prize for this, amongst other insights; and remarkably, he remained active in research publishing a book

Toys vs. fish. A theoretical externalities dilemma that might be solved just by allocating property rights and triggering negotiation over price.

Mergers

Another way of solving the problem of the factory and fishery and, quite literally, internalizing the externality is to simply bring the two firms under common ownership. Merge the two firms and the merged entity will take into account all of the costs one department imposes on the other. The cost of the toy factory's pollution for the fishery is now an internal matter and the merged entity will seek to minimize this impact as part of their profit-maximizing activity. Once again, however, the process of merging is likely to involve transaction costs.

with Ning Wang on China at the age of 102. His longevity might be attributed to a lack of stress resulting from his laid-back and indeed elegant attitude to problem solving, which can be summed up as creating the conditions where the problem solves itself.

However, the description of the fishery and factory glosses over an important issue. As anyone who's ever been to a Moroccan souk will testify, bargaining can itself be a costly process. Haggling over the gains from trade in pollution incurs costs without any societal benefit, especially if the firms get their lawyers involved. The costs the parties incur in doing deals are known as **transaction costs**, and were emphasized by Coase in his work. They are likely to be particularly severe if there are more than two parties at the table – for instance, if there was a fleet of independent fishermen using the same river.

Public goods

Remember when you first moved out of your parents' house? You probably shared a flat or a house somewhere with friends. If your friends were anything like your authors', then you will have all drunk a lot of tea and coffee and simply deposited the used mug near the sink to be "washed up later". Again if your friends were anything your authors', that "washed up later" would be postponed and postponed. The used mugs, plates, pots and pans just continue to pile up... And then someone cracks and does the washing up – hopefully.

The person who cracks first is providing a **public good**; they bear the cost (actually doing the washing up) while everyone enjoys the benefit (a cleaner kitchen). Note the similarity with positive externalities: the washer-up makes his decision based on his private interests, but the other housemates are also affected – they get to **free ride** on the washer-up's cleaning. Indeed, public goods can be thought of as goods with very widely dispersed positive externalities. While the problem of who does the washing up is a relatively localized example, this is a problem that can have global consequences. Greenhouse gas abatement can be thought of as a **public good** between nations, one which no nation is yet providing (see the box below).

A public good has one key property that makes it different from other goods – it is **non-rival.** Non-rivalry means that one person's consumption of the good does nothing to reduce the amount available for someone else to consume. Think of television broadcasts. If Anne and Bob both live within range of the transmitter and Anne sets up her receiver, this does nothing to stop Bob from setting up his receiver. The amount of television broadcasts Anne's receiver picks up does nothing to reduce the amount of television broadcasts Bob's receiver can pick up.

A **pure public good** has an additional property: it is **non-excludable.** This means that it is impossible to stop someone else from using the public good. So while television broadcasts are public goods, they are not pure public goods. It is possible to deny them to people who have not paid to receive them. TV broadcasters do this by encrypting their transmissions and giving their customers the technology to decode them.

It's getting hot in here...

Carbon dioxide emissions have already been mentioned as an example of a negative externality. But, from the point of view of economic theory, there's more to it than this. The negative externalities associated with CO_2 emissions are truly global in scope and scale. They will affect everyone, including the people who belch the stuff out. Anyone who reduces their own carbon footprint bears the full cost of this but only reaps a tiny fraction of the benefit – less than one eight billionth, taking the unborn beneficiaries into account.

CO_2 emissions thus impose non-rival, non-excludable external costs on the whole of humanity. They are an example of a **pure public bad**, also known as a **non-depletable negative externality.** In this sense, taking action to reduce one's emissions is a public good.

The public good aspect of the problem of climate change shows why nation states have been so reluctant to engage in unilateral cuts in carbon emissions: they'd much rather free ride on the actions of others. The best way to solve the issue would therefore be through some kind of international treaty that enforced reductions on all countries. Unfortunately, so far the difficulties in haggling over the terms of such an agreement have been too much for self-interested governments to overcome.

On the other hand, the washing up in a shared house discussed above is a pure public good: it is non-rival as all house sharers benefit from the clean kitchen and it is non-excludable as it is impossible to stop one housemate from enjoying the clean kitchen. Military protection is another example of a pure public good. All Americans and Russians were "protected" by the threat of Mutually Assured Destruction during the Cold War. Neither country could point out the house of a citizen and inform the other side that this house was "fair game" as that citizen was behind on their payments to maintain the nuclear deterrent.

Efficiency and public goods

What is the efficient level of production for a non-rival good? As with externalities, the efficient quantity of a public good will be where the marginal benefit to society of the last unit is the same as the marginal cost to society of providing the last unit. This is another application of that marginal analysis argument. The interesting issue with public goods concerns exactly what is the marginal benefit of the last unit produced. Think about an extra hour of radio programming playing music. The marginal benefit of this extra hour for the most avid music fan might well be very high, so that should be part of the social marginal benefit of this extra hour. But it doesn't stop there. The most avid music fan consuming this extra hour of radio broadcast does nothing to stop the next most avid music fan consuming it as well. So the marginal benefit this person derives from the extra hour of broadcast should also be included in the marginal social benefit of the extra hour. The same reasoning applies to the third most avid music fan, and the fourth, and the fifth...

So for a public good, the marginal social benefit of producing an extra unit is the sum of the marginal private benefit derived from that unit by every member of society. For efficient provision of a public good, this is what should be equated to the **marginal cost of provision**.

Can the market provide public goods?

Suppose a pure public good is provided through a market where there are three potential consumers. This is illustrated in figure 6.3 below, where the downward sloping individual private marginal benefit curves represent each individual's demand for the good.

In a free market, each individual will purchase the public good until the marginal private benefit is equal to the price they have to pay for it (which is equal to its marginal cost). For person number one, this is at Q_m in the figure. However, once Q_m has been purchased, the two other individuals can use person one's consumption – remember the good is non-rival. At this level of output, their marginal benefit is less than the marginal cost, so they won't bother contributing any more of the good. Instead, they **free ride** on person one's consumption.

Compare this to the socially optimal level of output, where the marginal social benefit equals the marginal cost. This is Q^* in the figure – so clearly there is underproduction. As with normal externalities, the reason is that none of the consumers takes into account the external benefit their own purchase has on others. And as everyone from a flat share will know, this can result in the build-up of a lot of dirty dishes before a public good is provided.

How can public goods be provided?

If public goods cannot be provided by the market, can they be provided by the government? Indeed, in some ways the name would suggest they should be provided by some sort of public authority. However, this is actually much more difficult than it sounds.

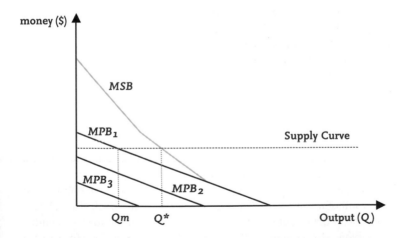

Figure 6.3: Attempts to provide a public good. The marginal social benefit of a public good (MSB) is the summation of all of the marginal private benefits (MPB). The market level of production Q_m is less than the social optimum, Q^*.

Suppose a government is considering providing a new road link between two cities. The road will be treated as a public good – there is no road charging and there are no toll roads in this country. They know how much it will cost to build the road (which they will recoup through taxes). In theory, if they know the value each individual places on being able to use this road to travel between the two cities, then they know the social benefit of the road. They should then be able to tell whether the benefit is greater than the cost and so whether they should build the road.

The problem is that the government is not psychic. They do not know the value everyone places on being able to use the road; they have to find that out. They could try to find it out by asking people and conducting a survey. But would people tell the truth? In fact, they would have an incentive to lie.

Suppose the person conducting the survey knocks on Milton's door one evening. Suppose further that Milton's use of the road will mean that he will only just benefit from the road's construction after he is taxed his share of the cost. Will Milton admit that he only just benefits from the construction of the road? Not if he's *homo economicus*. Instead he'll massively exaggerate the road's benefits to him, therefore increasing the chances of it being built. People who only narrowly value the road less than what they'd pay for it will likewise exaggerate how much the road will hurt them.

So the government cannot simply ask their citizens. If people are to tell the truth about which public goods they want to pay their share for and which they do not, then they need to be provided with incentives. Fortunately there is a mechanism that will do just this, called the **Clarke-Groves mechanism** after the economists who suggested it. Their key insight was to see that **pivotal agents** were the key to ensuring honesty.

A pivotal agent is an agent whose report changes the outcome. Suppose the sum of the valuations for the road without Tom's report is positive, implying the road should be built, and then Tom's reported valuation is so negative that once it is included the overall valuation comes back negative. Tom's valuation has changed the result and that makes him a pivotal agent. The Clarke-Groves mechanism proposes that Tom is taxed as a result of being pivotal. The size of the tax should be the "harm" Tom has done to the rest of society – the net valuation of the road as reported by everyone else without Tom's valuation. This is the net benefit everyone else would have got before Tom stuck his oar in. Under this regime it is in Tom's interests to report truthfully as, if he exaggerates, he faces the

Governments are not psychic, making it hard to identify the benefits of public goods such as new motorways.

prospect of paying a pivotal agent tax which is greater than the amount by which the construction of the road, and the ensuing tax, would hurt him. If he tells the truth, the only time that Tom pays the pivotal agent tax, is when he would prefer paying the pivotal agent tax to seeing the road get built. Similar arguments can be made about people who would prefer to see the road get built as well.

As you probably suspect given it is never used in practice, there is a problem with this solution. The money collected in tax from pivotal agents cannot be spent on anything useful. If it were, that would give people an incentive to misrepresent their preferences so as to increase the tax paid by other agents who are pivotal. This would defeat the object of the exercise. So while public provision of public goods can ensure that the efficient quantity of the public good is provided, this will be at the expense of inefficiencies elsewhere.

Market and government failure

The topic of this chapter has been market failure and how the government might best intervene to put things right again. However, as has been repeatedly emphasized, there are serious pitfalls to all of the policy options described. Economists would be foolish if they forgot that governments can fail too. Even the most well-intentioned government attempting to correct a market failure may make a mistake. Such mistakes could include:

► Basing an intervention on the wrong information – taxing an externality without good estimates of the marginal external cost, imposing quotas without knowledge of the social optimum, or providing the wrong amount of the public goods because of bad information on social marginal benefits. This might be a result of dodgy data or the impact of lobbying on the political establishment.
► Losing sight of the original purpose of the intervention due to political pressures. An externality tax might end up being inflated by moral judgements that the good should not be consumed or the government's desire to raise as much revenue as possible. Or it may go the other way, with the government reducing the tax so as not to reduce consumption too much and thus harm revenues.

The second bullet highlights that policymakers should be wary of the **law of unintended consequences**, which holds that even the best-intentioned policy intervention can have unanticipated negative effects.

Moreover, whenever the government is making decisions in the economic realm, those decisions will have a large impact on numerous groups of people. This gives people incentives to engage in the kind of **rent-seeking activities** described on p.213. The resources directed to rent-seeking activities are entirely wasted from the perspective of economic efficiency. The best way to mitigate rent-seeking problems is to reduce the private incentive to engage in rent-seeking by reducing the chance that such activities will be successful. This would require that government decision makers be supported by a talented and well-informed bureaucracy – although that bureaucracy would then have interests of its own to protect.

There is a large scope for government failure, and government involvement creates the incentives for wasteful rent-seeking behaviour even if the government ends up making all the right decisions! However, just as **Chapter 5** argued that market failure does not mean that markets should be abandoned altogether, the possibility of government failure doesn't mean that all state intervention is futile.

Chapter 7
Monopoly

In March 2009, the UK Competition Commission required the British Airports Authority (BAA) to sell three of their airports. The Competition Commission claimed that BAA's control of the vast majority of the airports in the UK was uncompetitive and led to a bad deal for customers. In the United States, firms have even been split up into separate entities for fear that their control of the market leads to a bad deal for consumers (Standard Oil in 1911 is one example). One might think that the risk of being broken up into smaller companies was a disincentive for pursuing growth and profit. So why might governments break up large companies? The answer lies in the fear of **monopoly**, where a single firm dominates a market. Monopolies, unlike the competitive firms considered so far, have an incentive to reduce the quantities of the goods they put on the market in order to increase the price. Low quantities and high prices represent a bad deal for consumers and society as a whole.

> Monopoly implies the absence of alternatives and thereby inhibits effective freedom of exchange.
>
> Milton Friedman,
> *Capitalism and Freedom*
> (1962)

This chapter begins with a simple explanation of why monopolies lead to inefficiency and what governments can do to prevent this. It then looks in depth at one particularly intractable case of monopoly – known as **natural monopoly** – that can arise in industries such as transport and power transmission. In natural monopolies it is impossible or inefficient to introduce competition, making them tricky to deal with. The scope for government failure is, as usual, depressingly broad, so a good deal of the chapter discusses the pitfalls of the various policy options.

What makes a monopolist behave differently?

One of the defining features of a competitive equilibrium is that firms act as **price takers**: they assume they can sell as much or as little as they like at the prevailing market price. As noted in **Chapter 4**, this makes sense in industries such as agriculture where individual producers make up a tiny proportion of the total output: an extra tonne or so of tomatoes supplied to the market will have no discernible impact on the equilibrium tomato price. As figure 7.1 shows, price taking means that each firm faces a horizontal demand curve for its output. The **marginal revenue** a firm makes from selling an extra unit of output is therefore just the market price at which it is sold. This is shown by the purple shaded area in the left-hand panel in figure 7.1.

But where the industry is controlled by a single firm – a monopolist – the assumption of price taking behaviour looks far less tenable. The monopolist faces the *entire* industry demand curve, which slopes downwards, and therefore knows that, as it increases its own output, the equilibrium price has to fall. This means that there are *two* components to its marginal revenue. First, just as in competitive industries, selling an extra unit means the monopolist's revenues go *up* by the market price, shown as the purple shaded area in the right-hand panel in figure 7.1. But in addi-

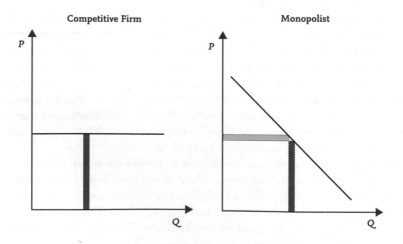

Figure 7.1: Marginal revenue for a competitive firm and a monopolist.

Monopolies: lacking a certain x-factor?

Monopolies are not only inefficient in *what* they produce, but they also tend to fall short of competitive firms in *how* they produce it. If the manager of a competitive firm does not seek constantly to innovate and improve on production methods, they will fall behind and go out of business. If, by contrast, the manager of a monopoly does not seek constantly to innovate and improve on production methods, then profits will be a little less fat and, quite possibly, nobody will notice anyway. The incentives of the manager of the competitive firm are stronger and more personal than those of the manager of the monopoly. The resulting tendency for monopolies to drift along unproductively is known as **x-inefficiency**.

tion to this, putting that unit on sale lowers the equilibrium price – and thus depresses the price it receives for whatever it was already selling. The monopolist's revenues thus also goes *down* because it ends up selling its existing output – known as its **inframarginal units** – for less. This **inframarginal effect** is illustrated by the yellow shaded area on the right-hand panel of figure 7.1.

How does this seemingly technical observation translate into a major public policy issue? To see this, remember that profit-maximizing firms always set their production where marginal cost equals marginal revenue. If price equals marginal revenue, as it does for competitive firms, this means that supply is given by the marginal cost curve (see **Chapter 4**). As the left-hand panel of figure 7.2 shows, competitive firms then produce all units where the marginal benefit (as given by the demand curve) is greater than the marginal cost. The result, as shown in **Chapter 5**, is efficiency.

However, for the monopolist, marginal revenue is *not* the same as price, owing to the inframarginal effect. So its supply curve is not the same as its marginal cost curve. Instead, the monopolist has a downward-sloping marginal revenue curve, reflecting the fact that, the more it sells, the larger the number of inframarginal units whose price will fall if an extra unit is dumped on the market. It sets its supply where its marginal cost equals the marginal revenue, as in the right-hand panel of figure 7.2.

As the figure shows, this level of output is inefficiently low. There are some units where the marginal benefit to consumers is greater than the marginal cost to the monopolist, but the monopolist chooses not to put them on sale. The result is a **deadweight loss** as in the figure.

It may seem puzzling that the monopolist would refrain from putting these units on sale. After all, consumers are willing to pay more than the marginal cost of making them, so the sales, taken in isolation, would be

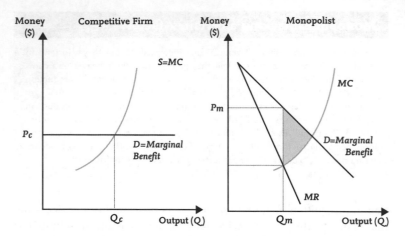

Figure 7.2: Output decisions for a competitive firm (left) and a monopolist (right). The deadweight loss of monopoly is the green area – the surplus of marginal benefits over marginal costs. P_c and P_m are the respective competitive and monopoly prices, with Q_c and Q_m the respective quantities.

mutually beneficial. The problem, however, is that the monopolist's horizons are broader than this. Though the sales, in isolation, are profitable, making them causes the market price to fall; this inframarginal effect means that they reduce the overall profit for the monopolist. And since consumers have nowhere else to go, the Pareto-improving deals are not made in monopoly.

Price discrimination

The previous section showed how the inframarginal effect holds monopolies back from making sales that would be profitable in isolation. You see the same sort of reasoning in many everyday settings: "I'd love to give you a special discount/pay rise/extra large portion of chips, but if I did I'd have to do the same for everyone else". But what if a monopolist could give a consumer a discount *without* having to do the same for everyone else? Then the inframarginal effect would disappear, or at least be mitigated. This is the essence of **price discrimination**.

The purest form of price discrimination is known as **first-degree price discrimination.** Monopolies charge each individual consumer a different price equal to their marginal benefit, and will therefore want to sell every unit where the consumer's marginal benefit is greater than the marginal cost to the monopolist. The consumers may get a raw deal, but because the inframarginal effect disappears, the result is efficiency. Unfortunately, first-degree price discrimination is almost impossible to implement in practice. The monopolist needs to know consumers' marginal willingness to pay: information they'd be hugely reluctant to reveal given that the monopolist would then sting them for the full amount.

By contrast, **third-degree price discrimination** is very widely practised. Student or senior citizen discounts are examples. The logic here is that, by splitting up demand into various sub-groups, monopolists can trade a bit more with one group – for instance, offering student discounts – without having to lower the price for *everyone*. This moderates the inframarginal effect, allowing monopolists to make more Pareto-improving deals and come closer to efficiency. Note that third-degree price discrimination is great for students and pensioners – they receive discounts that would not otherwise be offered – but can be bad news for everyone else, as it allows the monopolist to raise "normal" prices without losing as many sales as it would without price discrimination.

Last but certainly not least is **second-degree price discrimination.** The logic behind this is essentially the same as that behind third-degree price discrimination: it's all about splitting up the market and so dampening the inframarginal effect. But instead of doing this on the basis of observable characteristics such as student ID cards or senior citizen bus passes, it works by inducing consumers to **self-select** into different pricing categories.

The classic example of second-degree price discrimination is first and second class travel by train and by air. Some people are willing to pay much more for their travel than others: airlines and train operators would therefore like to separate their consumers into groups of people with "high" and "low" willingness to pay. But how would they ever get someone to identify themselves as having a high willingness to pay? The answer travel firms have come up with is that they sell slightly different goods. They offer one form of travel with plenty of space and comfort and peace and quiet – "First Class". On the same vehicle they offer another form of travel where the passengers are crammed in like sardines – "Standard" or "Economy Class". The firms then allow customers to choose which kind of travel they will buy. The extra space and comfort of first class travel doesn't normally cost the firm that much extra to provide, but some travellers are willing to pay a very high premium for it. Those who would have been willing to pay a lot more for travel anyway will tend to buy first class tickets, while those who are willing to pay only a little for travel end up buying standard class tickets in the sardine-can-like section.

The travel and electronics industries are rich sources of examples of second-degree price discrimination. For example:

▶ The 486 central processing unit of PC-compatible computers came in an expensive, fast DX version and a slower, cheaper SX version.
▶ IBM produced two versions of the same laser printer: a cheap version with a slow print speed and a more expensive version with a high print speed.
▶ As well as offering first and second class travel, train companies sell tickets at different prices for travel at different times of the day, charging more for travel in peak hours when commuters who are less price-sensitive have to travel.

While these are all examples of second-degree price discrimination, in each case there is something else going on. What made the 486DX faster than the 486SX was that the DX had a component called a maths co-processor which made certain mathematical functions faster. It wasn't that the SX chip did not have a maths co-processor, but that the maths co-processor on the chip had been disabled. So it wasn't that the DX was an improved version of the SX, but rather that the SX was a sabotaged version of the DX. Similarly, the slower laser printer offered by IBM was just like the faster printer, but it had extra microchips added in order to deliberately slow down the print speed. In these examples, second-degree price discrimination gives firms the incentive to deliberately make their low quality offering worse in order to scare people who are on the borderline between choosing the high or low priced offering into choosing the high priced option. Deliberately reducing the quality of the low priced option in this way is known as **product crimping**. This phenomenon was brought to the attention of economists by Raymond Deneckere and Preston McAfee in their paper "Damaged Goods" published in the *Journal of Economics and Management Strategy* in 1996.

Peak and off-peak services on trains are an example of second-degree price discrimination. But what can train operators do about that first off-peak train of the day? How can they stop people who might be tempted by a peak time train from seeing the first off-peak train as a potential substitute? A system of graduated prices getting cheaper through the morning would just be too confusing and too difficult to enforce, so varying the price is not a great option.

One UK train operator's solution to this problem on their trains from London to Oxford may have something to do with the number of carriages. The peak services leaving London in the morning have eight carriages (as do a number of the later off-peak services), but the first off-peak service in the morning – which is the closest substitute to the peak services – will normally have at most five carriages, and sometimes as few as two. But the number of commuters is not all that different, creating severe overcrowding on that first off-peak train. This makes the train much less comfortable and so commuters on the verge of selecting a peak train may well be tipped over the edge and pay the extra expense to avoid the overcrowding.

Monopoly and policy

If monopoly results in inefficiency, what should be done about it? The saying goes that an ounce of prevention is worth a pound of cure, and so it is with monopoly. The best thing to do about monopoly is to stop a monopoly arising in the first place. Most countries have **competition** or **antitrust** authorities and one of the things those authorities will do is "approve" or "block" mergers. They will block a merger if they fear that the merged entity will have "too much" market power and might be able to monopolize a market.

For international firms attempting to merge, this can mean approval is needed from multiple competition authorities. In 2001, the European Commission blocked a proposed merger between General Electric (GE) and Honeywell – two American companies – whose merger had already been approved by the US Department of Justice. Both GE and Honeywell did so much business in the European Union that the EU also had a say on whether the merger should go ahead or not.

Where prevention has failed, and a monopoly has resulted, these authorities will not shy away from "cure". In the past monopolies have been broken up into several firms to try and make a market more efficient. The break-up of Standard Oil in the USA in 1911 and the decision of the UK Competition Commission to force the British Airports Authority (BAA) to sell several airports are two such examples.

An additional example from the United States concerns AT&T, which was eventually broken up by the US Justice Department in 1984. AT&T was a vertically integrated firm selling local phone services, long distance phones services, and telephone equipment. The firm had a dominant market share in each of these areas, which, in the early part of the twentieth century, had been considered a **natural monopoly** (see p.132). However, by the 1970s, technological change meant that competition was now thought to be more appropriate in the long-distance market and the market for equipment, whereas the provision of local services was still thought to be a natural monopoly. The concern was that if one firm controlled the supply of local services, but also competed in the other markets, then they could leverage their control of local services to tilt competition in their favour. So in 1982, in order to end a lawsuit that had been running for eight years, AT&T agreed to divest itself of the local phone services where the natural monopoly lay.

Naturally, a lot of lobbying will surround competition cases. When Microsoft was fighting an antitrust suit in the 1990s, it paid for adverts that took the form of an open letter to President Bill Clinton signed by 240 economists (the economists in question did not know that the advertising space had been paid for by Microsoft). The authors decried the effect of antitrust cases brought against successful companies as a result of complaints by their competitors rather than by consumers. The Microsoft case was among those cited. Given that Microsoft paid for the adverts, the complaint in the letter that "more of the energies of firms are directed to politics, less to production and innovation" would seem to have been borne out, albeit in a somewhat circular way.

This is not to suggest such machinations didn't, or don't, take place. The second investigation into the supermarket industry conducted by the UK Competition Commission, which began in 2006, resulted from a complaint to the OFT in 2004 by, among others, the Association of Convenience Stores. When the Office of Fair Trading (OFT) initially decided there were no grounds for a referral, the Association of Convenience Stores launched the legal challenge against that decision which eventually led to a referral. Of course, all of this lobbying is nothing more than wasteful rent-seeking behaviour by those involved.

This inter-corporate mudslinging also highlights something about economists' attitudes to competition and efficiency. Competition should be a process of firms struggling to cut their costs and outdo each other in bringing the best possible offering to the market – but it is not a process anyone is ever supposed to win outright! Like the perpetual wars of Orwell's dystopian world in 1984, no side should ever be able to land a "knock-out" blow against their opponents and achieve permanent dominance. That being said, being able to achieve dominance in a market for some time is a powerful incentive to innovate and come up with new products to offer consumers. And while one competitor might be temporarily removed from the game, that is less of a concern if others are able to take their place.

Patently ridiculous?

Many monopolies owe their existence to **barriers to entry** preventing rivals from competing against them (see **Chapter 4**). One seemingly obvious anti-monopoly policy would therefore be to prevent these barriers from being erected wherever possible.

The patent system, however, is an example of a policy that does the opposite. Anyone who dreams up a new product or manufacturing process may apply for a patent, which, if granted, entitles them to a legal monopoly over their innovation for a number of years. Why would anyone want to legally enshrine inefficient monopolies in this way? The reason lies in providing incentives for research and development. If the moment an entrepreneur develops a new product, other firms can backward engineer what the entrepreneur has done and then compete with the entrepreneur in offering the product, the entrepreneur will receive no return on their effort expended in coming up with their innovation. There will be no incentive to bother inventing the product to begin with. So while patents create **static inefficiency** by allowing products to be supplied by a monopolist instead of a competitive industry, they provide **dynamic efficiency** by providing incentives to develop new products.

However, some economists have started to raise questions as to whether the patent system, as actually practised, provides the right incentives for innovation. One disadvantage is that it provides an incentive for people to become **patent trolls**: owners of patents who have not implemented them in business products and who have

no intention of doing so. Patent trolls simply sit back and try to make money by suing anyone who brings a product to market that looks, or uses a component which looks, remotely similar to their patent. During the various smartphone and tablet wars, Apple and almost all of their competitors have been accused of being patent trolls.

Professor Paul Klemperer of Oxford University has pointed out in an article in the *Financial Times* that some of the patents being granted are "less than startlingly inventive". Klemperer cites "one-click shopping" as something that is hardly the kind of brilliantly innovative idea that patents are supposed to be protecting, and yet Amazon were able to use their patent to drag Barnes & Noble into a costly legal dispute. To many economists, the expensive legal actions and court battles in many of the recent patent wars look more like rent-seeking activity than a properly functioning institution to provide incentives for innovation.

For example, Apple's dominance in the market for tablets may have been costly for consumers in terms of Apple having (for a time) enjoyed near monopoly power. However, Apple's competitors are now catching up and consumers have benefitted overall since. If Apple had had no prospect of dominating the market in the way that they did, they would have had no incentive to develop these products in the first place.

Determining when monopoly power is a temporary reward for innovation or is something that might last too long to the detriment of consumers is one of the most difficult tasks faced by professional economists. It will necessarily involve a certain amount of "crystal ball gazing" to predict how long a monopoly might last.

Natural monopoly

Sometimes, monopoly might be the only show in town. In figure 7.3 below, a firm has very large fixed costs and minimal marginal costs. As a result, its average cost curve slopes downwards – in other words it experiences **economies of scale** – even as it raises its output to serve the whole market demand. Water or electricity companies, where there are steep upfront costs in constructing a distribution network but low marginal costs of transmission, are likely to fall into this model.

In this situation, a competitive industry simply cannot supply the market, as setting price equal to marginal cost implies that price is lower

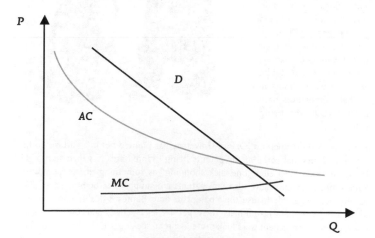

Figure 7.3: Average cost (AC), Marginal cost (MC), and demand (D) in a natural monopoly.

Saving the banks and securing for the workers

As with so many other policies, a lust for efficiency is not the only reason governments often nationalize firms. One recent wave of nationalization occurred in the wake of the financial crisis of 2007–8, where many banks were bailed out in return for government stakes. The reasons for this are examined in **Chapter 18**.

A second, more historically influential reason to nationalize companies is the idea that the profits from production should be owned in common and accrue to the public rather than to shareholders. Clause 4 of the UK Labour Party constitution used to commit the party:

"To secure for the workers by hand or by brain the full fruits of their industry and the most equitable distribution thereof that may be possible upon the basis of the common ownership of the means of production, distribution and exchange, and the best obtainable system of popular administration and control of each industry."

This text was seen as committing the British Labour Party to nationalization of key industries. At the heart of this idea is a distrust of the market mechanism as a means of allocating resources in favour of a more centrally planned approach.

than average cost (see the figure below). So all firms supplying the market would make a loss. What's more, given the extensive economies of scale available, having more than one firm in the industry would mean everyone was producing at inefficiently high cost. Imagine if a house were served by multiple water mains and electricity networks – clearly this would involve inefficient duplication of infrastructure.

Breaking up a natural monopoly is therefore not a viable policy option for providing the good or service in an efficient way. There are really only two alternatives available: **nationalization**, or **price regulation**.

Nationalization

Nationalization means that the government owns a controlling stake in the firm, owning more than fifty percent of the shares with voting rights. This enables the government to hire and fire the firm's management and set the management's objectives. When they do so, they do not run it with the aim of profit maximization. They run it with the aim of maximizing social welfare: setting price equal to marginal cost (and thus exploiting all Pareto-improving trades), and running the enterprise at a loss. If, for whatever reason, it is politically unacceptable for the firm to incur losses, they will set price equal to average cost, and so trade as much as they can while remaining in the black.

Up until the 1980s, nationalization was the predominant way of dealing with natural monopoly in Western economies. Across Europe and North America, water, electricity, gas, and rail networks were largely state-owned and operated. Over time, however, it became evident that nationalized industries are particularly susceptible to **x-inefficiency** (see the box on p125). Revenues tend to flow to the state's coffers rather than managers' pay packets, blunting their incentives to cut costs. As a result, most nations **privatized** these sectors in the 1980s and 1990s, relying instead on price regulation to deliver efficiency.

An obvious way round the problem of x-inefficiency in nationalized firms would be to reward managers according to their performance, mimicking the incentives that the market would offer them. However, perfect measures of managers' performance in maximizing social welfare can be difficult to come by, and using imperfect measures can often have destructive effects. For example, Colonel Rawls in the HBO TV series *The Wire* insists on policing to targets. To meet his targets, Rawls engages in time-consuming arguments over where murders took place, attempting to ensure that difficult-to-solve murders are counted as being under someone else's jurisdiction and thus affecting someone else's targets.

In the UK, the National Health Service (NHS) has a target that ninety percent of patients should be treated within eighteen weeks of being referred by their doctor. In February 2012, an NHS administrator told *The Guardian* newspaper how she had been ordered to cancel the operations of patients who were already over the eighteen-week target and fill those slots with the patients who were closest to breaching the limit. This kind of thing was not the intention of the policymakers who set the eighteen-week target, but when the target is present and managers' financial compensation will be affected by missing the target, it is easy to see how such a thing might happen. It's another case of the **law of unintended consequences**, mentioned in **Chapter 6**.

Price regulation

An alternative to nationalization is price regulation. In order to ensure that the firm produces at minimum cost, and does not exploit their monopoly power by restricting output, the government imposes a **price cap**. If the firm cannot raise prices above a certain level, they will have only one way to increase profit – by reducing costs. The profit incentive remains, as the firm will be able to increase their profit with any cost-reducing innovation they may invent. They are simply prevented from using their monopoly power in a manner that might reduce economic efficiency.

The complication in any such system comes from the question: where to set the price cap? The price cap should ideally be set at the marginal cost of the natural monopoly (with the resulting losses met by a subsidy from government). However, marginal costs are notoriously difficult to measure. They do not appear on the accounts of firms whose data recording systems are set up to comply with statutory accounting requirements rather than economic logic. As a result, average costs are usually used instead. These can be relatively easily calculated from the total costs of the firm and the total output.

However, even here there are problems. The person who wants to know the average cost is the regulatory body charged with setting the price cap; the person who knows the average cost is the firm whose price will be capped. The regulator should be sceptical about any answer they get if they simply ask the firm "what is your average cost?" Complicated (and

Gamekeepers turned poachers?

When trying to free hostages, police are wary of Stockholm Syndrome, where hostages come to sympathize with the goals of their captors. **Regulatory capture** is a similar phenomenon in regulated industries: the regulator comes to see issues from the perspective of the firm they are supposed to be regulating and begins to defend the interests of the firm to the general public rather than vice versa. The UK rail minister Theresa Villiers was recently mocked for claiming that steep fare rises "make life better for commuters". Under regulatory capture, this sort of world view can become endemic.

Why might regulatory capture occur? One reason is that the firm has a greater incentive to influence the regulator than any one customer of the natural monopoly. The firm's incentive comes from the (potentially large) monopoly profits they can extract from all individuals, whereas the individual's incentive comes from the (relatively modest) monopoly profits extracted from them. So a regulated firm will pay lawyers and economists to make representations to influence the regulator. For consumers, by contrast, activities directed at influencing a regulator represent a public good which no one will have a strong incentive to provide (see **Chapter 6**).

Another reason for regulatory capture concerns the people who work for the regulator. They will build up a lot of industry-specific skills and knowledge: what might be termed industry-specific human capital. The only potential alternative employer to whom such skills and knowledge might be useful is the regulated firm. So the people within the regulator will, quite naturally and subconsciously, seek to avoid too much confrontation with the people within the firm they seek to regulate. You never know who might be working for whom at some point in the future.

therefore costly) legal and accounting procedures are needed to ensure the information revealed is correct. And the whole process is prone to the phenomenon of **regulatory capture** (see box below).

Government and market failure

The above discussion highlights a number of potential ways in which government policy towards monopolies may go amiss. The suggested strategies to correct market failures due to monopoly give an indication of how a government might fail and make things worse when trying to alleviate the inefficiency of monopoly.

▶ A regulator might become overzealous in enforcing antitrust rules and so break up companies unnecessarily. This would result (ironically) in firms being too cautious at pursuing rivals' customers.

▶ The regulator might be lobbied into allowing an unnecessary monopoly on spurious grounds of "innovation", as with patent trolling.

▶ Regulatory capture might lead to a monopoly being allowed excessive price rises.

▶ Performance targets intended to maximize welfare may backfire with unintended adverse effects.

As with externalities, the possibility of government failure in dealing with monopoly does not mean that the government should never intervene in the economy. However, it does mean that the government should do so cautiously. Field-testing of new policies through randomized controlled trials would help to identify unintended consequences of a policy before the policy is adopted more widely. Wider consultation of economists before policy implementation might also help. Even when a policy has little direct impact on the economy, economists have a particular way of thinking about incentives, which makes them more likely to anticipate unintended consequences of policy options. (The authors would like to take this opportunity to state that their consultancy rates are very competitive!)

PART FOUR:

Further topics in microeconomics

Parts Two and **Three** covered the material that all good microeconomists can reel off by heart. But modern microeconomic theory has developed beyond this core in a variety of interesting directions. This part of the book presents some of the most influential offshoots.

The model of decision-making presented in **Chapter 2** then applied in **Parts Two** and **Three** describes agents choosing from alternative actions in order to maximize either profit or utility. But in many cases, the best action for one agent depends on the decision taken by others – people must choose strategically on the basis of what they expect others to do. This kind of strategic decision-making is the subject matter of game theory, which is introduced in **Chapter 8**. One area within game theory that is of particular interest to economists is strategic decision-making by firms in oligopolies –– industries that lie between the polar opposites of perfect competition and monopoly, where there is competition between a few firms. The second half of **Chapter 8** presents different models of oligopoly, considering whether such industries will produce efficient outcomes.

One of the assumptions required for a competitive equilibrium to be efficient set out in **Chapter 5** was that everyone has the same information about goods. But market interactions are often affected by asymmetric information, be it over the quality of a used car or the amount of effort a prospective employee intends to put in if she is hired for a job. How asymmetric information can lead to market failure, and what may be done about it, is the topic of **Chapter 9**.

Finally, **Chapter 10** introduces the economics of finance. It considers the role of the financial sector, what the prices of assets such as shares and bonds should be, and whether behavioural finance can explain seemingly irrational phenomena such as asset bubbles.

Chapter 8

Game theory and oligopoly

At the height of the Cold War and especially during the Cuban Missile Crisis of 1962, President John F. Kennedy and his counterpart Nikita Khrushchev had to make very big decisions. Both Kennedy and Khrushchev wanted to avoid thermonuclear war, but they also wanted to avoid making too many concessions to the other side. The extent to which each would be satisfied with the outcome would depend not only on their own decisions, but also on the decisions made by their opposite number.

Candidates in elections have to decide where to campaign, how much advertising to buy, and in which markets. They want to use their time and campaign money to sway opinion and mobilize voters in crucial areas, but also want to avoid spending money unnecessarily. If their opponents don't bother appearing or advertising in an area, it hardly makes sense to spend millions on advertising and schedule hundreds of appearances there. They might reason that the lack of competition means a few thousand spent in advertising and one appearance by the candidate should be enough to win – that is, they might take the actions of their rivals into account when deciding what to do. In other words, they might think **strategically** when planning their campaign.

This interplay between one's best decision and the decisions taken by others is known in economics as **strategic interdependence**, and it comes up in any number of situations. Strategic interdependence exists in matters of high statecraft and low street politics. It exists in war between opposing generals (and even between generals who are supposed to be on the same side!) and in sport between opposing players and coaches. The formal analysis of situations of strategic interdependence is known as **game theory**, and any situation of strategic interdependence is referred to as a **game**. This chapter presents an introduction to this field, which has come to span economics, politics, and even evolutionary biology.

One key economic application of game theory is to strategic competition between firms. In this kind of competition, firms are large enough that their decisions concerning output will affect the market price, but they are not so big as to totally control the market – mainly because of the (to them) inconvenient presence of the other firms. This kind of market structure, which lies in between the competitive model of **Chapter 4** and that of monopoly in **Chapter 7**, is known as **oligopoly**. The second part of this chapter uses the game theoretic tools developed in the first half to explore this topic.

Game theory

An important distinction between different kinds of games is the distinction between **simultaneous move games**, where everyone moves at once, and **sequential games** where some players might get to move at different times. The method used to analyse the two games is somewhat different in each case, so they are presented in turn below.

Simultaneous move games

Almost all game theory explanations start with the **Prisoners' Dilemma** and there is no reason this *Rough Guide* should be any different. A verbal description of the Prisoners' Dilemma might go something like this:

The police have caught two criminals who have pulled off a jewel heist. There isn't enough evidence to convict the thieves of taking the jewels, but they can be convicted of a more minor crime, breaking and entering. Breaking and entering carries a maximum sentence of three years at the discretion of the presiding judge. The jewel heist would carry a sentence of two–eight years, again, at the judge's discretion. The police lock the criminals in separate cells and tell each of them that the judge will "throw the book at them" over the breaking and entering charge and hand down the maximum sentence. However, if they confess to the jewel heist and implicate their co-conspirator, the judge will go easy on them and only hand down a two-year sentence (while maximizing the punishment of the criminal who failed to confess). If they both confess, they will end up doing about six years each. Each criminal knows that the same deal being offered to them is being offered to their co-conspirator.

Coming up with predictions of how strategic interactions such as this will be resolved is the main occupation of game theorists. Their approach is to condense each situation down to its essential details, leaving it in a form that can be worked through analytically. In the case of the crime novella outlined above – and indeed any **simultaneous move game** where decisions are taken without knowledge of what other people have done – these basic details might be summarized as Who? ,What?, and Why?

► Who is making decisions? In this case, it is the prisoners, so they are referred to as the **players** of the game. In the Prisoners' Dilemma, the players are the two prisoners – in the description of the game, no one else is making decisions.

► What are the decisions they have to make? These are referred to as the **actions** of the game. A choice of an action for each player determines the **outcome** of the game. In the Prisoners' Dilemma, each player is choosing between whether to confess or keep quiet, so those are the actions.

► Why do they choose what they choose? Or to put it more dramatically, what is their motivation? In game theory, the players' motivations are summarized by their **payoffs**, which are expressed as utilities (see **Chapter 2**). A player's payoffs capture that player's preferences over outcomes: the higher the player's payoff from some outcome, the more the player prefers that outcome. In the Prisoners' Dilemma, it is natural to suppose that the prisoners prefer to spend as little time in prison as possible, so the payoffs for each prisoner from each outcome are captured by the number of years they'd spend in prison, with a "minus" sign in front.

When playing a game, each player's goal is to choose an action which will bring about the outcome that gives them the highest possible payoff.

A simple way of representing these bare bones in a two-player game is in a table, which is called the **payoff matrix,** as shown in figure 8.1. Prisoner 1 is playing in the position that is sometimes referred to as being the **row player**. The rows of the table are labelled with the actions available to prisoner 1. Prisoner 2 is playing in the position that is sometimes referred to as being the **column player**. The columns of the table are labelled with the actions available to prisoner 2. So prisoner 1's choice determines a row of the table and prisoner 2's choice determines a column of the table, and together these choices determine an outcome, and every possible outcome is represented by a cell in the table. Each cell in the table records the pay-offs to each player that would result from that outcome. The eight years that prisoner 1 would spend in prison if he kept quiet while prisoner 2 confessed are recorded by the -8 in the bottom left of that cell, while the two years that prisoner 2 would spend in prison if that were the outcome are represented by the -2 in the top right of that cell.

		Prisoner 2	
		Keep Quiet	Confess
Prisoner 1	Keep Quiet	-3 -3	-2 -8
	Confess	-8 -2	-6 -6

Figure 8.1: The Prisoners' Dilemma. Prisoner 1's payoffs from any set of actions are given in the bottom left of the relevant cell and prisoner 2's in the top right.

As in **Chapter 2**, a basic assumption of game theory is that the players are **rational** – that is, whatever action they take, they take because they believe it's the best alternative available to them. In other words, it is assumed players will always choose a **best response** to what they believe the other players will do.

The assumption that players are rational and the way of representing the game via the payoff-matrix together make it easier to predict what the players will do, or as game theorists would say, "solve" the game.

▶ Suppose for a moment that prisoner 1 somehow "knew" that prisoner 2 would keep quiet, what would be the best thing for prisoner 1 to do? For prisoner 1 to keep quiet would then result in a payoff of -3, but confessing would lead to a payoff of -2. So the highest (least negative) payoff comes from confessing.

▶ Now suppose that prisoner 1 somehow "knew" that prisoner 2 would confess: what would be the best thing for prisoner 1 to do now? For prisoner 1 to confess himself would now produce a payoff of -6 instead of the payoff of -8 from keeping quiet. So the highest payoff comes from confessing.

So the best thing for prisoner 1 to do, which will maximize prisoner 1's payoff whatever prisoner 2 does, is to confess. In this case prisoner 1 is said to have a **dominant strategy**, a strategy that is the best thing for prisoner 1 to do whatever prisoner 2 does. It is not difficult to see that prisoner 2 also has a dominant strategy in confessing. Where both players have a dominant strategy, the game has a **dominant strategy equilibrium** and that would be the prediction of game theorists as to how the game would be played.

This prediction of play can seem perplexing. If only both the thieves could keep their mouths shut, they'd end up with only three years each in jail – as opposed to the six years they get from rational play. How could this be rational? Here, it's a simple case of there being no honour among thieves: even if the other guy keeps quiet, it's still best to squeal.

Playing rationally in the Prisoners' Dilemma means more time behind bars for the prisoners than if both were to keep quiet.

As well as making games easier to solve, payoff matrices allow game theorists to see how, by changing the names of the players and actions, the same analysis can be applied to a wider range of settings. The Prisoners' Dilemma turns out to be particularly amenable to this. For example, **Chapter 6** described public goods, where everyone benefits if everyone chips in but each individual would prefer to free ride on the contributions of others. As shown later on, competing oligopolists face a similar problem. Other Prisoners' Dilemma-esque situations that crop up in this book include in monetary (**Chapter 16**) and trade policy (**Chapter 17**).

Nash equilibrium

Life wouldn't be very interesting if rationality always led to a single outcome – especially if you were an economist. But thankfully it's clear that there are plenty of situations where not all players have dominant strategies. Consider the following tale:

> Ross likes Rachel and Rachel likes Ross (indeed, you could say they were *friends*) and they enjoy spending time together. On Saturday night they could either go to the Natural History Museum or the Fashion Show. Ross would like to go to the Natural History Museum, but Rachel would like to go to the Fashion Show. However, they both prefer to meet each other on Saturday evening compared to spending the night alone. Ross and Rachel must simultaneously decide where to go on Saturday evening, but, due to the sudden outbreak of a computer virus, they are unable to communicate by phone, text message, Twitter, Facebook, or email.

Since both Ross and Rachel would like to coordinate their decisions so they end up at the same destination, this kind of game is known as a **coordination game**. The added frisson arising from Ross's preferred destination being different to Rachel's means this particular example is called a **battle of the sexes game**.

Stripping the story down as before, the payoff matrix to this game would look something like figure 8.2 below. The description above doesn't spell out exactly what the payoffs are, but the payoffs recorded in figure 8.2 are consistent with the description of Ross's and Rachel's preferences over the possible outcomes of the game. As before think of the payoffs recorded in the payoff matrix as Rachel's and Ross's utilities from the various possible outcomes. Naturally, they try to get the highest utility they can.

It's clear from the matrix that neither player has a dominant strategy.

▶ If Ross "knew" Rachel was going to go to the Natural History Museum, that would also be the best thing for Ross to do.

▶ But if he "knew" Rachel was going to go to the Fashion Show, then the best choice for Ross would now also be the Fashion Show.

		Rachel	
		Go To Natural History	Go To Fashion Show
Ross	Go To Natural History	3 4	1 1
	Go To Fashion Show	0 0	4 3

Figure 8.2: The battle of the sexes

This way of thinking is actually describing Ross's **best response** to the actions Rachel could take. The best choice for Rachel similarly depends on what she believes Ross will choose. Just assuming the players are rational doesn't, therefore, get you far in solving this game – depending on what each player believes about the other's intentions, anything could happen.

Economists, however, are often interested in finding **equilibrium** outcomes – where none of the players, having seen what everyone else chooses, wishes they'd done something else. One way of thinking about equilibria is as possible long-run outcomes of a game: what might happen once everyone's learnt how the game is played. In equilibrium, not only will everyone play a best response to whatever they believe their opponents will do, these beliefs about each other's actions will also be correct. In other words, each player will play a best response to what everyone else does. Such a set of actions, all of which are **mutual best responses** to each other, is known as a **Nash equilibrium**.

In the battle of the sexes, there are two Nash equilibria highlighted in the payoff matrix in figure 8.2: either both players best respond to the other by going to the museum; or they best respond to each other by going to the fashion show.

Nash's great contribution – and the reason why the concept bears his name – was to show that every game has at least one Nash equilibrium. However, as shown above, some games have more than one Nash equilibrium. In games where there are multiple equilibria some sort of refinement of a Nash equilibrium is needed to arrive at a clear prediction of what will happen.

A trip to skeletons at the Natural History Museum is one of the two possible Nash equilibria of the coordination game.

One such refinement, suggested by the Nobel Prize winning economist Thomas Schelling, is that some equilibria might, in some way, act as **focal points**. The idea behind focal points is that players' expectations about how the other will play a game are important. What is more, players from the same cultural and social background are likely to share common expectations.

For example, in a chauvinistic society it might be that couples such as Ross and Rachel always do what the man wants. Therefore they will both think it obvious that the other will turn up at the Natural History Museum, and so each selects their best action based on this belief: going to the Natural History Museum. By contrast, in a matriarchal society, it might be that couples like Ross and Rachel always do what the woman wants and so they will expect to play the equilibrium where they go to the Fashion Show. (In an equality driven society, they might take turns and so if they did something that Ross preferred last weekend, they might expect to go to the Fashion Show this weekend.) In each of these cases, because of the context, there would be a common expectation among the players as to which equilibrium would be played. That common expectation acts as a focal point. With no such common expectation, Ross and Rachel might well "mis-coordinate" – indeed, they might both try to be altruistic and

John Forbes Nash Jr

John Nash was awarded (jointly with John Harsanyi and Reinhard Selten) the 1994 Nobel Prize in Economics for his "pioneering analysis of equilibria in the theory of non-cooperative games". The contribution for which Nash is famous (and which now bears his name) was put forward as his PhD thesis at Princeton University, where he had been admitted as a graduate student largely on the basis of a five word letter of recommendation: "This man is a genius." Nash was the subject of the book and film *A Beautiful Mind*. The film, where he was played by Russell Crowe, mainly deals with his mental illness (Nash was diagnosed with paranoid schizophrenia) but also includes a sequence where the idea behind the Nash equilibrium dawns on him. In the film, Nash and three of his fellow graduate students are in a bar when five women walk in: an incredibly attractive blonde and four less attractive but still beautiful brunettes. This sparks discussion among Nash and his colleagues as to which of them should get to hit on the blonde. One of the students, citing Adam Smith's suggestion that the best result for the group is achieved when each individual acts in their own interest, says they should all have a go and may the best man win!

Nash points out that this solution will lead to none of them "getting lucky" (which economists would model as a sudden surge in utility) later in the evening. If they all hit on the blonde, they will "crowd each other" and she won't be attracted to any of them. If they then try their luck with one of the brunettes, they will be spurned, as no one likes being second choice. Instead they will do better if they each go after one of the brunettes from the start. Then they can all get lucky. Instead of staying to test his theory (as any good scientist should), Nash promptly thanks the blonde woman for the insight she has given him and leaves the bar to write up the theory.

Quite apart from the inherent sexism of the scenario and the singularly questionable premise that four nerdy male graduate students can charm beautiful women to bed at will, there is one problem with this depiction of Nash's contribution. The solution Nash suggests is not a Nash equilibrium! Under Nash's proposed approach, none of the students would be pursuing strategies that were best responses to the actions of the other graduate students. To see why this is not a Nash equilibrium, think of the situation as a simultaneous move game (it is simpler to ignore the way in which the early stages of chatting up the women will reveal each graduate student's strategy and allow them to adapt). Suppose that any graduate student who "gets lucky" with a brunette gets a payoff of 1, any graduate student who gets lucky with the blonde gets a payoff of 2, and a graduate student who does not get lucky gets a payoff of zero. The graduate students are choosing between the two actions: chat up the blonde; or chat up a brunette.

Any graduate student who chats up a brunette will get lucky and get a payoff of 1. If one graduate student chats up the blonde, he will get lucky and get a payoff of 2; but if more than one graduate student chats up the blonde, neither will get lucky and all graduate students who tried to chat up the blonde get a payoff of zero. The strategy profile suggested in the film is not a Nash equilibrium because if every other graduate student were chatting up the brunettes, a graduate student's best response would be to chat up the blonde and get a payoff of two rather than one.

end up with Ross at the Fashion Show and Rachel at the Natural History Museum.

Thomas Schelling advised the Kennedy administration and saw the Cold War as a game with two potential equilibria. In one equilibrium, there would be tension, but not actual military confrontation. In the other there would be thermonuclear exchange, where whichever party fired first would be the most likely "winner". Schelling was very keen that common expectations be built up in the East and West that the former equilibrium would prevail rather than the latter.

Sequential Games

Not every game involves both players choosing without knowledge of what others have done: sometimes players move **sequentially**, observing all past decisions. For example, suppose that one player – let's call him Stalin – is playing a game against another player, called Hitler. They have to divide a cake. Whoever plays as player 1 proposes a division, and then whoever plays as player 2 accepts it or rejects it. Acceptance results in the instantaneous enactment of the proposed division. Rejection makes the cake disappear and neither player gets any. It is assumed that both players like cake.

Whoever acts as player 1 will propose a division where they get virtually all of the cake and the other player gets only enough to keep them from rejecting the division out of spite. So who gets to move first can dictate how much cake they end up with – this is why games like this are called **dictator games**.

This example illustrates a crucial point about games where one player gets to choose their action after witnessing what their opponent does: timing matters. It matters in games with a more obvious economic interpretation too, as the following **entry deterrence game** shows.

Entry deterrence games have two players who are both firms: an "incumbent", a monopolist who controls a market, and an "entrant", who decides whether to set up in the incumbent's market. The action takes place in two stages. In the first stage, the entrant decides whether or not to enter the market. If the entrant chooses not to enter, the game ends and the incumbent keeps the monopoly profit – a payoff of $10m – while the entrant gets nothing. If the entrant decides to enter, the game moves on to the second stage, where the monopolist has to decide whether to accommodate the entrant or to engage in a price war. Accommodating the entrant means sharing the monopoly profit, in which case the incumbent receives $5m and the entrant receives $4m. If the incumbent engages in a price war with the entrant, then the incumbent will receive a payoff of $1m while the entrant will lose their sunk cost investment to enter the industry and lose $1m.

As before, the first step in analysing a game like this might be to represent it in a payoff matrix. This is given in figure 8.3. There are two Nash equilibria in this game shown by the highlighted cells: one where the entrant joins the market and the incumbent best responds by accommodating him; and another where the incumbent initiates a price war and the entrant stays out. It's easy to check that both players are responding optimally to each other's choice in both these cases.

However, there is something unsatisfactory about the prediction that the entrant may stay out if the incumbent threatens a price war. Put simply, the threat of a price war is not a credible one. Were the entrant ever to enter, it would become plain to the incumbent that a price war is not in their interests. Once the entrant has, in fact, entered, they cannot be deterred.

		Entrant	
		Enter	Stay Out
Incumbent	Accommodate	4 5	0 10
	Initiate Price War	-1 1	0 10

Figure 8.3: The entry deterrence game.

The problem with the payoff matrix form of the game used in figure 8.3 is that it strips away too many details: it takes no account of the timing of the game. A better way of describing sequential games such as this is as a kind of tree diagram, known as an **extensive form** representation. This is given in figure 8.4 overleaf.

The arrows in the extensive form represent the timing of play: first the entrant makes their decision; then, if they enter, the incumbent gets to

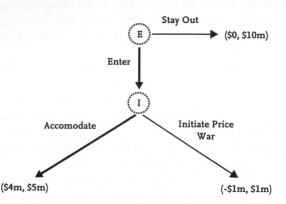

Figure 8.4: The entry deterrence game in extensive form. Payoffs are recorded in the form (payoff to entrant, payoff to incumbent).

decide whether to accommodate or initiate a price war. The tree diagram makes it possible to solve the game by reasoning about what each player would do at each point that they may have to make a decision:

▶ Consider the incumbent's decision if they are ever called to move.
  • The payoff from accommodating is $5m.
  • The payoff from a price war is $1m.
  If they are rational, they will choose to accommodate.
▶ Knowing what the incumbent will do if they are called on to act, the entrant should now realise the payoffs from each of their choices.
  • The payoff from staying out is $0.
  • Knowing that the incumbent will accommodate entry, the payoff from entering is $4m.

If they are rational, the entrant will choose to enter. This method of "solving" games by starting from the last choices made in the game and working backwards is known as **backwards induction**. The beauty of this approach is that it takes into account what each player would actually do if called on to act: it therefore rules out the incumbent bluffing the entrant into staying out with the **non-credible threat** of a price war. The solutions arrived at by applying backwards induction are known as the **subgame perfect Nash equilibria** of the game. These refine the Nash equilibrium solution concept by ruling out non-credible threats.

Chess does have a subgame perfect equilibrium outcome, but luckily for the millions of people who enjoy playing the game, it is too complex to "solve" even with the use of computers

This all sounds very neat and tidy, but there are still problems. Chess is a game which, in principle, could be solved by backwards induction and so it should have a subgame perfect equilibrium. However, it is simply too vast and complex to draw out the game tree and solve by backwards induction. After each player has taken only one move, there are four hundred possible positions in which the board could be. After only three moves each, there are more than a million possible positions. The computational power to "solve" chess simply does not exist. This may be bad news for game theorists, but is excellent news for millions of people who still enjoy playing the game.

Oligopoly

A large number of industries are neither perfectly competitive as in **Chapter 4** nor a true monopoly as in **Chapter 7**. Firms do not act as price takers, but neither are they completely without competitors. Take Starbucks in the UK as an example: given their market share in the coffee industry they can set their own prices, but they also face fierce competition from, among others, Costa. **Oligopoly** is the name for a market structure such as this somewhere between the perfectly competitive ideal and a monopoly. The analysis of oligopolies is one of the most important applications of game theory in economics.

Perhaps the most obvious way to think about oligopoly is to imagine the firms competing by setting different prices. Consumers, being rational, will want to buy from the firm that is charging the lowest price. This is what the French mathematician Joseph Louis Francois Bertrand (1822–1900) did and the resulting model of competition between oligopolists is known as the **Bertrand model**.

Price setting oligopolists – the Bertrand model

In its simplest form, the Bertrand model is just a game with two players – i.e. firms in an industry – who each decide how much to charge for their output. Think of Starbucks and a small independent coffee shop, which for the sake of argument will be called Central Perk, competing to sell coffee to the local twenty-something New Yorkers. Each firm's sales depend on how the price it sets compares to its rival's.

► If it sets the higher price, no rational consumer would ever buy coffee from it.
► If it sets the lower price, everyone will buy coffee from it.
► If the two firms' prices are equal, each will end up serving half the market.

The firms' payoffs are just the revenues from whatever they sell minus costs, which are $1.50 per cup.

What would an equilibrium look like in this game? The way to work this out is to look at each firm's best response to any action its rival might take and then find a pair of actions that are mutual best responses: this will be the Nash equilibrium. To begin with, then, suppose that Starbucks are charging $2.50 for a coffee. What is Central Perk's best response to this?

► Any price greater than $2.50 would be silly because they wouldn't sell any coffee.
► Any price less than $1.50 would be even sillier as Central Perk would make a loss on every coffee they sold.
► Every price between $1.50 and $2.50 will see Central Perk make a profit on each coffee they sell.

And, of course, of all these profitable prices, the most lucrative choice is $2.49: this is Central Perk's best response. In fact, it's clear that in most cases, Central Perk's most profitable action is to undercut Starbucks by a single cent: that way it serves the whole market at as high a price as possible. The only exceptions are if Starbucks charges more than the monopoly price (which is by definition the most profitable price one can charge), or if they charge $1.50 or less, in which case undercutting would be loss-making. All the same reasoning applies to Starbucks – so its best responses are symmetric.

At what prices are both coffee shops playing a best response simultaneously? Clearly not when either of them charges less than $1.50, as this is never a best response. And also not when anyone charges more than $1.50 – as their rival's best response would be to undercut them, and the best response to that would be to undercut in retaliation. So the only possible equilibrium price is $1.50 – equal to marginal cost, where neither firm makes any profit. As **Chapters 4** and **5** showed, this is also the same efficient price that prevails in perfect competition.

If this equilibrium is an accurate prediction of real life competition, then it is seriously good news for coffee-drinkers everywhere. Only two firms are needed in an industry to ensure profit margins thinner than a skinny cappuccino, with prices brought down to their efficient level. Unfortunately, however, Bertrand's assumption that a firm can capture the whole market by cutting prices by a cent is a bit extreme: what if the firms differentiated their products, so some people were willing to pay a bit more for Starbucks? And what if the firms were **capacity constrained** – in that they were physically unable to serve the entire demand for coffee in New York?

The case where firms are able to differentiate their products in some way was examined in a famous model by Harold Hotelling (1895–1973), which is now called the **Hotelling model**. Suppose that consumers differ in how bitter they like their coffee. Take the extreme cases of Chandler and Monica, where Monica likes her coffee as bitter as possible, but Chandler likes his coffee to be bland. Monica and Chandler are just the extreme cases: there are millions of New Yorkers whose coffee tastes are distributed evenly between those of Monica and Chandler. Consumers like to pay as little as possible for their coffee, but there is a cost to consumers of consuming a coffee which is not their ideal strength.

If Starbucks sells the bland coffee that Chandler likes best and Central Perk sells the bitter coffee that Monica likes best, then both firms can make a profit and the equilibrium price of coffee will stay above the efficient level. For Central Perk, it is no longer necessarily the best strategy to just undercut Starbucks – it won't allow them to steal all of Starbucks customers. It may well be better to charge a higher price and make more profits from the customers whose preference is so close to that of Monica; that they are not likely to go anywhere else for their coffee.

But this is not the only insight of the model. Suppose now that Starbucks and Central Perk can change how bitter their coffee is: should they continue to serve coffee at opposing extremes? Sadly for Monica and Chandler, they won't. There will always be an incentive to target the taste of the coffee more towards the centre as doing so will attract new custom-ers, while the old customers with more extreme tastes will have few alter-natives. This model has been adapted to political competition to show why political parties have incentives to compete for the votes of those in the centre of the political spectrum. So there may be something in voters' complaints that "politicians are all the same these days". They have to be, but it is the voters who force them to be.

Allowing for complications such as capacity constraints and product differentiation means equilibrium prices will be higher than their effi-cient level. Furthermore, the next two sections give reasons to imagine they might be higher still.

Quantity setting oligopolists – the Cournot model

Another way of looking at oligopoly behaviour is to see firms choosing how much to sell rather than what price to sell it at. Focusing on these output decisions is the approach of the **Cournot model** of oligopoly, first set out by Antoine Cournot (1801–77).

Firms choosing quantities is not as silly as it sounds. Think about Starbucks and Central Perk in the example above. Both coffee shops must decide how many coffee machines to have; how much coffee to keep in the store at a time; and how many baristas to employ so as to keep the line of people waiting to order their coffee moving quickly. All of these decisions will constrain their price decision – very few New Yorkers would buy coffee at $1 a cup if they had to stand in line for two hours to get it.

In its simplest form, competition is modelled as a game between two firms who choose their quantities in order to maximize their profits. The choice of quantities is made independently and simultaneously. The market price is then determined based on the total quantity produced by the two firms.

The Nash equilibrium is where:

▶ Each firm is producing the best quantity for themselves, given their anticipation of the quantity the other firm will supply; and
▶ Each firm has correctly anticipated the quantity the other firm will supply.

So to find the Nash equilibrium, start by considering what the best quantity for one firm to produce would be given an expectation of the quantity the other firm will choose.

▶ If Central Perk don't expect Starbucks to produce any coffees at all, then the best quantity for Central Perk to produce would be the monopoly quantity.
▶ As the quantity that Central Perk expect Starbucks to produce increases, that implies a lower market price for coffee and so a smaller incentive for Central Perk to produce coffee themselves. Therefore the amount Central Perk would produce would decrease.
▶ As the quantity Central Perk expect Starbucks to produce increases, there will come a point where Central Perk would optimally choose to produce nothing in response. To find this point, just think about the price that would result in the market if just the quantity from Starbucks was produced. Wherever this is above the marginal cost of producing an extra coffee, there is an incentive for Central Perk to produce a coffee. So the point where Central Perk have no incentive to produce coffee is where they expect Starbucks to produce the same quantity that a competitive industry would, which will result in the competitive price being equal to marginal cost (see **Chapter 4**).

The symmetry of the problem means that exactly the same reasoning applies to Starbucks as to Central Perk. These best-response relationships – known as reaction functions – are sketched in figure 8.5 overleaf.

Take Central Perk's red reaction function. For the purposes of this reaction function, what matters is the quantity they expect Starbucks to produce, so that could be what is measured on the vertical axis of figure 8.5. But for the purposes of any equilibrium, their anticipation of Starbucks' quantity cannot be wrong, so the vertical axis might as well measure the quantity that Starbucks actually produce. Starbucks' reaction function can also be graphed by the purple line.

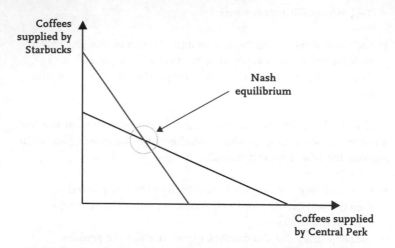

Figure 8.5: Best responses in the Cournot game. Central Perk's best response is in red and Starbucks' best response is in purple.

As the graph shows, the Nash equilibrium of the game is where these best responses coincide – with each firm selling somewhat less than the monopolistic output. How, then, does the total industry output compare with other industry structures described in the book? It turns out that total quantity will be between the monopolistic and perfectly competitive levels. This can be proven mathematically, but the intuition is a lot simpler. Recall the breakdown of marginal revenue from the discussion of monopoly in **Chapter 7**. When a firm produces an extra unit:

▶ its revenue increases by the price for which that extra unit was sold; but
▶ its revenue also decreases as the price that will be fetched by all the units the monopolist was already producing falls – an effect called the **inframarginal effect**.

The inframarginal effect is the key difference between the monopolist and a competitive firm. Competitive firms take no account of it as they are selling such a small quantity relative to the size of the whole market that it is completely unimportant for them, but monopolists consider the entire effect. This is why monopolists produce less than competitive industries (see **Chapter 7** for the detailed argument). By contrast, a duopolist in the Cournot model produces half of the industry quantity and so feels half of the inframarginal effect. As a result, a Cournot duopoly will make more than a monopolist but less than a competitive industry. Cournot's conclusion that output in duopoly is somewhere between the level under monopoly and that in perfect competition seems more sensible than Bertrand's idea that it is the same as in perfect competition. However, the initial assumption behind Cournot competition is less intuitive

The inframarginal effect is the key difference between the monopolist and a competitive firm.

than Bertrand's. It is much more natural to think of firms competing by choosing their price than their quantity. This intuition doesn't really stand up to detailed scrutiny. In the example of Central Perk and Starbucks, the decision over what size of coffee bar to have places a limit on how many drinks they can serve in a day. Anyone who expects New Yorkers or Londoners to stand in line for an extra hour in order to get coffee that is slightly cheaper has never been to New York or London!

Competition and the Prisoners' Dilemma

Whether through prices or output, the process of duopolistic competition has a lot in common with the Prisoners' Dilemma. With price competition, if both firms were to maintain high prices they could earn half the monopoly profits each. But if one firm did charge a high price, their competitor would benefit from undercutting him – much like the ability of one prisoner to get an extremely lenient sentence by confessing while the other keeps quiet. The result is that it is a dominant strategy for the firms to compete by charging a low price. Figure 8.6 illustrates this.

| | | Starbucks | |
		High Price	Low Price
Central Perk	High Price	$10m $10m	$1m $18m
	Low Price	$1m $18m	$4m $4m

Figure 8.6: Competition as a Prisoners' Dilemma

Explicit collusion

Another possibility is for firms to club together in a cosy **cartel**, collectively behaving like one big monopolist and then sharing out the profits. This leads to higher prices for consumers and higher profits for the firms – $10m each in the example instead of $4m. As both the firms would benefit from such an arrangement, one might, therefore, expect them to agree to abandon competing in favour of **colluding**. Authors going back as far as Adam Smith have been keenly aware of this possibility.

> People of the same trade seldom meet together, even for merriment and diversion, but the conversation ends in a conspiracy against the public, or in some contrivance to raise prices.
>
> Adam Smith, *The Wealth of Nations* (1776)

Towards the end of the nineteenth century, scepticism in the USA concerning the activities of big businesses led to the Sherman Act of 1890. Big businesses had been using a legal vehicle known as a **trust** to create legally binding agreements between firms as to prices and output. The Sherman Act and similar legislation elsewhere effectively prohibit such agreements between firms in the same industry.

This is a formidable problem for potential cartels. A legally binding agreement offers the best possible assurance that a competitor will keep their word and charge a high price and the best possible commitment to do the same. Without it, there may be no way out of the most pessimistic predictions of the Prisoners' Dilemma.

Tacit collusion and the Prisoners' Dilemma (revisited)

There is, however, a twist in this tale. As any parent will know, one of the best ways to induce good behaviour today is through the threat of punishment or the prospect of reward tomorrow. This idea has been used to suggest how oligopolists might be able to cooperate and share the monopoly profits between themselves without binding agreements.

An important aspect of competition that the Prisoners' Dilemma misses out is the fact that it usually takes place over a protracted period. Criminals don't just conspire once and for all and leave it at that; there may be opportunities for them to work together again that they would forfeit if they squealed. Similarly, firms don't set prices once and for all, but revise them every day, week, or month. The game is not played once, but **repeatedly**.

When the game is repeated, the rival coffee shops can come to realize that their interests are not so diametrically opposed over the long term. Without ever explicitly communicating, they might teach each other that low prices will trigger a painful response.

To be specific, suppose that Central Perk decided to keep its prices high, provided Starbucks did likewise; but to charge a low price forever more if it ever saw Starbucks cutting its prices. This sort of play is known as a **grim trigger strategy** as any price cut by Starbucks triggers a "grim" response (low prices forever) by Central Perk. It turns out that, provided they are sufficiently patient, a best response to this strategy would be for Starbucks to play a similar strategy themselves. This means there's a Nash equilibrium where both coffee shops keep their prices high.

Why is patience an issue? Playing the grim trigger strategy involves foregoing the benefits of cutting prices while one's opponent keeps them high for one play of the game (in this example $8m) in return for keeping prices high in all future plays (worth $6m every time the game is played). In other words, a firm that is colluding passes up the opportunity to make extremely large profits in one period in order to enjoy a stream of profits in future periods. This means that the colluding firms have to be patient.

Although the firms can't enforce this kind of collusion in the courts, the understanding that any "deviation" will be punished is enough to keep the agreement going. This is why economists refer to such behaviour as **tacit collusion**. Of course in the real world grim trigger strategies might not be the best way to go. There is too much room for a profitable cooperation to be lost forever due to a mistake or a misunderstanding, or one side failing to correctly interpret the price signals of the other. The important thing is that the punishment last long enough to wipe out any potential gains from deliberately cheating.

Collusion can be incredibly harmful to consumers because it generates the same inefficiencies as monopoly. The only difference is that the two separate firms mean the monopoly behaviour is harder to spot. This is why even tacit collusion is illegal in many jurisdictions, with hefty penalties for miscreants. In the UK, for example, collusive activity is prohibited and punishable with fines of up to ten percent of turnover for the companies involved, with potential jail sentences of up to five years for the individuals involved.

> Collusion can be incredibly harmful to consumers because it generates the same inefficiencies as monopoly.

In order to encourage firms who have been engaged in illegal cartel agreements to come

A Virgin's rap sheet

In 2006, Virgin Atlantic took advantage of whistleblower incentives when they reported their collusion with their main UK rival, British Airways, to the UK's Office of Fair Trading (OFT). Individuals at Virgin Atlantic were granted immunity from prosecution and the airline was not fined. A similar agreement was reached with the American authorities. By contrast British Airways were fined by the OFT who also brought a criminal prosecution against several BA employees.

The OFT's leniency programme came in for some criticism when the criminal trial of BA staff involved in the price-fixing arrangements collapsed due to the OFT's failure to present all of the evidence in a timely manner. Critics of leniency programmes claim that the full cooperation clauses encourage prosecutors to rely too much on the whistleblower in conducting the investigation. Whilst this may be a valid concern and something prosecutors should be wary of, leniency programmes do help to change the incentives and make it more likely that cartel members will turn themselves (and their co-conspirators) in.

forward, many competition authorities (including those in the US and EU nations) offer **leniency programmes**. Under the terms of these programmes individuals who have been involved in cartel agreements may be offered immunity from prosecution in return for coming forward, and firms may have their financial penalties substantially reduced or even waived entirely. There is a notable similarity between the incentives created by these leniency programmes and the original Prisoners' Dilemma game. These provisions are sometimes known as **whistleblower incentives**.

Chapter 9

Information and contracting

Contracting is the process of spelling out all the terms and conditions of a transaction. Don't worry, a chapter of *The Rough Guide to Law* has not been included by mistake. Economists are interested in contracting because sometimes it is impossible to include everything the parties care about in an **enforceable** contract. For example:

► Thomas is buying Steve's car. Thomas would pay more for a more reliable car, but only Steve knows how reliable his car is. No court can enforce a contract that sets higher prices for more reliable cars.
► Rebecca is hiring Sarah to do a job for her and wants Sarah to work hard, but no court will be able to measure Sarah's effort and enforce a contract that made the wages depend on Sarah's effort.

It doesn't matter how much Steve raves about how great his car is or how earnestly Sarah promises she will work her socks off: these promises are just words. The same words could easily be said by someone who sold an old banger or someone who spent all their time at work looking at Facebook and Twitter. It would be entirely understandable if Thomas and Rebecca got cold feet and pulled out. This might happen even though there is some trade between Thomas and Steve and between Rebecca and Sarah which would make both of them better off. Put in the language of **Part Three**, there might be Pareto-improving trades that don't take place, implying a **market failure**.

The key issue facing the parties to the potential contract is one of **asymmetric information**. One party to the transaction knows whether they'll be able to keep their word, but has no way of *proving* it to the other side. The uninformed side of the bargain then pulls out for fear of being ripped off.

There are, broadly speaking, two kinds of asymmetric information:

▶ **adverse selection**, where uncertainty surrounds something that happened before contracting; and
▶ **moral hazard**, where the uncertainty surrounds something that will be done after contracting.

Adverse selection and moral hazard are huge problems in all sorts of markets, and some such as insurance markets or labour markets are unfortunate enough to suffer from both problems! This chapter will examine both of these issues and the institutions that allow trade to take place in spite of them.

Adverse selection

The best way to illustrate adverse selection is the way that George Akerlof did in his article (see opposite) – by reference to the used car market. Good used cars, which will carry on running forever, are referred to as **peaches**; bad used cars that are likely to breakdown and need expensive repairs every couple of months are referred to as **lemons**. Suppose there is a market where the people who currently own cars place a value of $10,000 on a peach and $3000 on a lemon. The people who do not own cars place a value of $12000 on a peach, but $4000 on a lemon. Clearly there are gains to trade in this market.

▶ The owners of peaches should sell them to people who do not currently own cars at some price between $10,000 and $12,000.
▶ The owners of lemons should sell them to people who do not currently own cars at some price between $3000 and $4000.

The people who own cars would prefer to have the money to having the car. The people who do not own cars would prefer to have the car rather than have the money.

However, there is a problem. Only the people who currently own a car know whether it is a lemon or a peach. Suppose that roughly half the cars are lemons and half the cars are peaches, and that this is **common**

A lesson for aspiring economists – persistence pays

This entire area of economics was virtually invented by the Nobel Laureate George Akerlof (1940–) in 1970 when he published his paper "The Market for Lemons" in the *Quarterly Journal of Economics* (*QJE*). Akerlof had apparently sent the article to three other journals before sending it to the *QJE*, and had been rejected by all of them! Akerlof's persistence really did pay off, as the paper earned him a Nobel prize.

knowledge among potential sellers of cars and potential buyers. Then, on average, a buyer will place a value on a used car, the type of which they do not know, of $8000. Can second-hand cars be traded in a market for $8000? Unfortunately the answer is no. At a price of $8000, the owners of peaches are not willing to part with them, so they will not put them on the market. Buyers should realize this and so assess that anyone willing to sell a car for $8000 does not own a peach, but rather they own a lemon. So the maximum a buyer should be willing to pay for such a car is $4000. Thus the only cars that will be sold in the second-hand market are lemons at a price between $3000 and $4000. Economists, ever aware of the opportunity to pun, say that the bad cars drive out the good.

The presence of lemons might lead to no trade at all! Suppose that owners of lemons develop an emotional attachment to their old banger and in fact valued them at $5000. Then the presence of the lemons would still prevent the peaches from being traded, but there would be no Pareto improving trade in the lemons and the second-hand car market would

The inability of the buyer to distinguish the true value of a used car leads to adverse selection and can crash the second-hand car market.

completely collapse. The mere presence of lemons is enough to prevent any trade in cars. For potential buyers and the owners of peaches, it is enough to leave a bitter taste in the mouth.

The essence of the problem is that if good cars were ever going to be sold in the market, the owners of bad cars would have a strong incentive to sell their car as though it was a peach. Buyers are not stupid and so steer clear of any car advertised as a peach, no matter how persuasive the seller's patter. Once the price is low enough, it is only the sellers of the worst cars who are willing to sell – hence the name: **adverse selection**.

The interesting thing about this problem is that it is generated by the **asymmetry of information** rather than the lack of knowledge. If the buyers were suddenly to become as informed as the sellers, then the problem would disappear. Peaches would be sold at some price between $10,000 and $12,000 and lemons would sell at some price between $3000 and $4000.

What's more, if sellers were suddenly, somehow, to become as *uninformed* as the buyers, that would solve the problem too! Sellers, not knowing whether they have a peach or a lemon, would be willing to sell for $6500 or more. And buyers, not knowing whether they are buying a peach or a lemon would be willing to buy for $8000 or less. So trade would take place at some price between $6500 and $8000 and the cars (of unknown type) would end up with the people who value them more.

Why can't lawyers solve this problem? Why not just write a contract which says that the seller is selling a peach, and if the owner of a lemon ever tried to pass their car off as a peach allow the buyer to sue them for the price difference? Such a contract would be practically impossible to enforce. The quality of a car is extremely difficult to define legally and can only really be found out by driving the car around for a few months. Just imagine how expensive it would be to pay two opposing sets of lawyers and a judge to do that!

Signalling

In practice, there *is* a second-hand car market, and insurance and other markets prone to adverse selection do operate. In fact, many of the quirks of second-hand markets, insurance markets, and even employment markets exist as solutions to the problems of adverse selection.

For example, in the market for used cars, sellers often offer guarantees that they will pay for any repairs the car requires in the next year. Putting a guarantee like this in a contract is a relatively simple matter and *can* be enforced by the courts. But more to the point, such a guarantee is cheaper for the sellers of peaches than it is for the sellers of lemons. So a willingness to offer such a guarantee is a clear **signal** that one is selling a car that is a peach and not a lemon.

Another example of signalling concerns education. This was the idea put forward by Michael Spence in his article "Job Market Signaling", published in the *Quarterly Journal of Economics* in 1973, for which he shared the Nobel prize with George Akerlof. Spence suggested that it was cheaper for naturally productive people to get an education than it would be for people who are less productive. Even if education is subsidized to the point of being free, productive people will take less time to grasp key concepts and will be able to use that extra time to spend at leisure or work. Less productive people must spend more time studying and so have less leisure time or time to work.

Suppose that the labour of a productive person is worth $20 an hour and the labour of a less productive person is worth $10 an hour. Suppose that the industry is competitive so firms have to pay workers the value of their labour. It is common knowledge that approximately half the population is productive and the remaining half not so productive. So the average productivity of workers is $15 an hour. If it is impossible to tell productive workers from less productive workers when they apply for a job, both groups of workers will be paid $15 an hour.

However, if workers have the option of going and doing a degree, things might change. For productive workers, let the cost of taking time out from working in order to study for the degree be equivalent to a $6 an hour wage cut when they finally do enter the workplace and get a job. For less productive workers the cost is equivalent to an $11 wage cut when they enter the workplace.

One possibility is that if an employer sees a worker with a degree, they believe that worker is productive. If an employer sees a worker without a degree, they believe that worker is less productive. So workers with degrees will be offered wages of $20 an hour and workers without degrees will be offered wages of $10 an hour. Productive workers will find it in their interests to get a degree, because:

- ► If they don't they will have a wage of $10 an hour, but
- ► If they do, they will have a wage of $20 an hour at a cost equivalent to $6 an hour for a total payoff equivalent to $14 an hour.

However, less productive workers have no incentive to imitate their productive colleagues. For less productive workers:

▶ Not getting a degree leads to a wage of $10 an hour.
▶ Getting a degree leads to a wage of $20 an hour, but at a cost that is equivalent to $11 an hour, giving the less productive workers an effective wage of $9 an hour – so they are better off not getting a degree.

So the employers' initial beliefs would turn out to be correct and no one has an incentive to change their behaviour, making this an equilibrium. An equilibrium such as this one where the different types of workers do different things, making it possible to distinguish one from the other, is called a **separating equilibrium**.

The employers' initial beliefs need not be that all workers without a degree are not productive. While they might believe that a worker with a degree is productive, they might not expect that productive workers will bother to get a degree and distinguish themselves. So a worker without a degree is thought to have a fifty-fifty chance of being productive and an expected average productivity worth $15 an hour.

▶ If a less productive worker were to get a degree, they might get a salary worth $20 an hour, but at an effective cost of $11 an hour for getting the degree. Their net payoff from getting a degree would then be worth $9 an hour.
▶ Their payoff from not getting a degree is worth $15 an hour.

So less productive workers are better off without a degree. Similarly, productive workers have no incentive to get a degree.

▶ Not getting a degree gets them a payoff worth $15 an hour.
▶ Getting a degree will get them a wage of $20 an hour, but getting a degree will effectively cost them $6 an hour for a net payoff of $14 an hour.

No one has an incentive to do anything different, and the actions of the workers confirm the employers' initial beliefs, so this is an equilibrium. An equilibrium such as this one where different types of workers do the same thing and remain indistinguishable is called a **pooling equilibrium**.

The potentially frightening point here is that the *only* thing that changed between the two examples was employers' prejudices about people who did not have degrees. These prejudices can effectively determine whether a pooling or separating equilibrium prevails, and so employers' beliefs can in some ways be **self-fulfilling**.

The consequences of educational signalling for student funding

Michael Spence's signalling model of education makes uncomfortable reading for those who argue that more of the cost of higher education should fall on the taxpayer and less on students. Note that in Spence's model set out above, all of the time spent in education is entirely wasteful from the perspective of society. If you follow the logic, the output of each worker is the same before and after they get their degree, so society's output would be even higher if no workers got degrees and everyone just got a job. Indeed, both productive and less productive workers enjoy higher payoffs in the **pooling equilibrium** (see above) with no education than they do in the **separating equilibrium**.

Of course it is overstating the case to suggest that education is *entirely* wasteful and has zero impact on productivity, but to concentrate on this is to miss the point. The point is that even if education did nothing to productivity, there would still be an incentive to invest in it as a means of showing off. This highlights a general tendency to over-invest in education, whether the social benefits of that education outweigh the costs or not.

All too often, politicians and journalists cite higher salaries of university graduates as evidence that education is a good investment and that it should be subsidized. They argue that more education would lead to greater productivity. But this is the common error of confusing correlation with causation. It is possible that education could make workers more productive, but as Spence shows, it is also possible that education is a wasteful signalling device, and this would result in exactly the same correlation between education and earnings. If education increases productivity, a subsidy may be justified, but if productivity causes people to get educated, a tax might be the better response!

In either case, there is certainly a case for sending politicians and journalists who fail to see the difference between correlation and causation back to school.

Screening

Signalling is one kind of market institution to overcome the problems of adverse selection; **screening** is another. Whereas signalling relies on the informed party doing something to differentiate themselves, screening involves the uninformed party finding ways to extract the relevant information. Some screening mechanisms involve offering choices to the informed party, which will make them reveal their information through the choice that they make. Numerous examples of screening can be found in financial markets.

In credit markets, the borrower knows more about their ability to keep up the repayments on a loan than the lender. Suppose that the purpose of the loan is to start a business; entrepreneurs come in two types:

▶ "Safe hands", because of their conservative business practices, are more likely to see their business take off and repay the loan.
▶ "Buccaneers", because of their habit of leaping before looking, are more likely to drive their business into the ground and default on the loan.

On the application, banks can't tell one from the other.

In the market for car insurance, there may be broadly two categories of drivers:

▶ "Tortoises", who are not in a hurry and so take their time and drive carefully; as such, they are not likely to get into an accident.
▶ "Hares", who are hurrying everywhere and see it as everyone else's job to get out of their way; as a result, they are prone to accidents.

Of course it isn't the case that entrepreneurs and drivers come in these neatly divided "high risk" and "low risk" categories, but this simplification helps to show how adverse selection works. In the credit market, the buccaneers are willing to pay higher interest rates than the safe-hands because the buccaneers know they have a higher chance of defaulting, and so they'd be less likely to pay the interest on the loan anyway. But it is the presence of the buccaneers in the market which makes the banks charge a higher interest rate, so the market may well unravel in exactly the same way as the market for used cars unravelled. Bad credit drives out good credit.

Similarly, when it comes to car insurance, the hares and tortoises know their respective probability of getting into an accident. So the hares will be willing to pay higher premiums to insure themselves against accidents than the tortoises. Of course, from the perspective of the insurance company, it is the presence of the hares in the market which increases their expected losses and so increases the premium they want to charge, potentially above the premium that tortoises are willing to pay. The market unravelling process is a possibility again and bad drivers discredit good drivers.

Of course successful banks and insurance companies will know a bit more than nothing about their customers. When a bank is approached by a new loan customer, they will **credit score** that customer. This involves

Drivers of sports cars reveal information about their driving style to insurers.

looking at their credit history to see how good they have been at paying their debts in the past. This credit history and other socioeconomic data about the customer are then used to estimate whether the customer is likely to be a low risk or a high risk customer.

Insurance companies also gather vast amounts of data about their customers and use it to see which customer characteristics are most frequently associated with claims. They can then offer different prices to customers who differ in the most important characteristics. This is known as **customer segmentation**. So next time someone driving an expensive sports car cuts in front of you too close, don't resort to expletives – smile to yourself at how the choice of sports car will have revealed to his insurance company how badly he drives and raised his premiums.

Problems of adverse selection in insurance markets have also brought about government intervention. For example, in many countries having an insurance policy is a legal requirement in order to drive. This **compulsion** prevents the least risky drivers from opting out of the insurance market and so prevents the deterioration of the risk pool that insurers must cover.

Some sophisticated screening mechanisms rely on **self-selection**, where the different types of loan customer select different packages, thus revealing their type. For example, the system of credit scoring only imperfectly distinguishes high- and low-risk customers. Sometimes credit scoring will mistakenly label a high-risk customer as low risk, and if this hap-

An unhealthy expense

Healthcare costs in the USA are widely perceived to be among the most expensive in the world and millions of Americans lack health insurance. To an economist, adverse selection figures strongly in any diagnosis of what is wrong with the system. At any price, the healthiest people would have an incentive to drop out of health insurance and pay for medical treatment as and when they need it. This raises the risk profile of those people who are still buying insurance and so raises the costs for insurance companies, which leads to increased premiums. The increased premiums will only encourage more of the healthiest people still insured to drop out of the insurance market as well. The market keeps unravelling until only the least healthy people are buying insurance at sky-high premiums.

The Patient Protection and Affordable Care Act (2010), which was upheld by the Supreme Court in 2012, goes some way towards resolving the problem through the individual mandate. The individual mandate means that people must buy a health insurance plan or pay a penalty. Such **compulsion** should prevent the market from unravelling – while the healthiest Americans will be paying over the odds for their healthcare, millions more will be able to get healthcare at affordable prices as the risk pool of insured people will be improved.

pens too often, there will still be adverse selection within the different customer segments identified by credit scoring. However, credit scoring does mean that there is a cost to the customer from defaulting on the loan – their default will show up on their credit history and they will have more difficulty getting loans in future. High risk customers would be willing to pay more for insurance against this eventuality.

An insurance product that pays the customer's debts in the event something happens that leaves them unable to is called **creditor insurance** or **payment protection insurance**. So one solution is to sell an expensive creditor insurance product with the loan. Since the bank is already taking the credit risk by making the loan anyway, the insurance premium is almost pure revenue for the bank. Customers who pay a high price for the insurance are effectively self-selecting into a higher interest rate.

Moral hazard

The classic example of **moral hazard** concerns the shareholders of a firm hiring a Chief Executive Officer (CEO) to run the firm on their behalf. Suppose that there are only two possible outcomes: the profits of the firm can be high ($100m), or low ($10m). The effort of the CEO makes high profits more likely. Once hired, the CEO can choose whether to exert effort or not. The problem is that no court will ever be able to confirm whether the manager exerts effort or not; the shareholders may not even be able to confirm the manager's effort.

For the manager, exerting effort is costly; he prefers to slack off, "taking meetings" on the golf course or having "brainstorming sessions" during country retreats. Even when in the office, he might prefer to try and beat his highest score on "Angry Birds" rather than work to improve the profitability of the company. If profit goes down on his watch, "challenging market conditions" or "turbulence in global markets" can always be blamed. The manager does not need to admit that he blew off the crucial meetings in order to get that elusive third star on level 26.

The fact that the CEO's effort cannot be monitored means that whatever the promises made before he was hired, the moment pen has been put to paper the manager's inclination might be to slack off. The owners might well be willing to compensate the CEO for exerting effort, as they will find the increased profitability makes it worthwhile. But they cannot police whether the CEO has actually put in that effort once the contract has been signed and the CEO has been paid. In the language of **Chapter 8**, the manager's promises of hard work before he was hired lack **credibility**.

Once a CEO's contract has been signed there is the risk of moral hazard and unnecessary golf course meetings.

To an economist the solution is simple: give the CEO what management consultants would call **skin in the game**. The idea is to make the CEO's salary dependent on the profit of the firm. This can be done in such a way that the CEO finds it in his or her own interest to exert effort and maximize the firm's profit. This is the idea behind the **performance related bonus**.

The general pay structure in these examples involves paying a basic salary and paying a performance related bonus on top of that salary when profits are high. The idea is that the performance related bonus is large enough to incentivize the manager to put his shoulder to the wheel and bear the cost of effort. So the CEO is better off if they exert effort than if they do not, as the expected benefit of the bonus they would get if they work hard is greater than the cost of putting their shoulder to the wheel. Under these circumstances, economists say that the **incentive compatibility constraint** is satisfied. The CEO is also better off taking the job than not taking the job. So economists say that the **participation constraint** is satisfied. Bonus systems like this can work quite well, in theory. However the bonuses must only be paid out when the firm's performance has been good, and profits have been high. Paying out bonuses when profits are low will only encourage low profits in the future.

That is all very well when the CEO doesn't care about the uncertainty surrounding their pay, but in reality most people are **risk averse** (see **Chapter 2**), and performance related bonuses can make the CEO's pay quite uncertain. The CEO might work his or her socks off, but genuinely challenging market conditions might frustrate all the CEO's efforts and result in relatively low profits. The shareholders, being many, are better suited to taking on risk as they can spread that risk among their membership. This is not strictly speaking a problem, as the CEO can be compensated for bearing risk (through a higher salary and a correspondingly higher bonus). The more risk the CEO is exposed to, the more they must be paid on average, but in order to make sure they work, the CEO must be exposed to some risk in their salary. This is the essential **insurance–incentive** trade-off that is at the heart of all moral hazard problems. If the incentives are not sharp enough, the CEO will not exert effort; if the incentives are too sharp, the CEO will need to be paid too much on average. Then the CEO might need to be paid so much that it is not worthwhile to get them to exert effort in the first place.

Another problem with performance related bonuses concerns the metrics used to measure success. CEOs may have opportunities to make high profits for the company today at the cost of lower profit opportunities

Bankers' Bonuses

Bankers' bonuses have been the subject of controversy since the 2007-8 financial crash. They are seen to have incentivised the short-termist attitude to which many of the financial problems are attributed. But what has attracted most of the anger is that they still seem to be paid, even when the firms concerned are doing badly.

> Official statistics reveal that, in the financial year to April [2008], City workers took home £16bn, almost exactly the same as in 2007. The period covers the Northern Rock nationalisation and the UK employees hit by the Bear Stearns implosion. During the period, banks across the world were forced to make huge write-downs on investments linked to US subprime mortgages.
> *The Independent Online Edition*, Saturday 18 October 2008

In circumstances such as this, one can see how bonuses might come to be seen as being a reward for failure as much as anything else. From the outside, they seem to be coming up with the rations, rather than providing any kind of incentive. If that is happening, then bonuses will not provide the incentives to exert effort that shareholders would hope for.

Part of what is going on here may have something to do with the performance benchmarks used to determine bonuses. These are often based around performance relative to the rest of the market rather than absolute performance. This explains why, when the entire industry goes to hell in a handcart, the entire industry continues to pay bonuses: firms are rewarding their employees to the extent that they have kept the firm in a cooler part of the handcart.

However, when it comes to senior management pay structures, there may be an element of some firms having been effectively captured by the senior management and run for their benefit rather than that of the shareholders. The problem is that among shareholders, keeping an eye on the management is a **public good**. While the CEO will manage to keep one hundred percent of the profits he haggles from the shareholders in his pay packet, if there are a thousand shareholders, then each shareholder only keeps one thousandth of what they haggle from the CEO. There is a surprising weakness that comes from being part of a larger group.

tomorrow. While these actions may well not be to the benefit of long-term shareholders, if the CEO plans to retire shortly, the reduced profit opportunities of tomorrow will be someone else's problem. So a bonus structure such as this, dependent on current profits, may well encourage short-termism which would not be in the interests of shareholders. This is why bonus arrangements should ideally include some kind of "claw-back" arrangement so that bonuses can be recouped if long-term profitability falls.

Moral hazard in insurance

As well as facing problems from adverse selection, insurance markets also suffer from **moral hazard**. Take the example of home contents insurance. If Alison buys home contents insurance so that she is fully insured against the possibility that her house is robbed, she might be indifferent over whether her house gets robbed or not. The insurance company will replace her belongings anyway.

This means that Alison will have less of an incentive to take the actions she can take to avoid getting robbed. These actions, such as buying and installing proper locks or remembering to hide away valuables when leaving, are costly for Alison, so she won't do them unless she has an incentive.

The insurance company can include clauses in the contract that render the agreement null and void if Alison fails to take certain actions. For example, most home contents insurance contracts will include clauses that say they will only pay out if the insured party fits proper locks and uses them. These actions are contractible, but other actions are not contractible: how could an insurance company ever prove that Alison had left her stolen belongings "on display" the day she was robbed?

Problems of asymmetric information lead to serious issues that cause market failure in the sense of foregone trades.

Alison might promise to take these actions until she is blue in the face the day she signs the insurance contract, but the insurance company will never find these promises credible. Just as a potential CEO might promise to work his socks off but shareholders won't believe him unless he has skin in the game.

The partial solution is to give Alison something like skin in the game. Most insurance policies specify an **excess**. The excess is the amount of the loss, if it happens, that an insurance company will not cover. This might be anything from a couple of hundred to a thousand dollars, and if Alison is robbed she has to bear that amount of the loss. The larger the excess, the greater incentive Alison has to take care and take all those non-contractible actions which reduce the probability of being robbed. But it is also true that the larger the excess, the more risk Alison is exposed to. This is exactly the same insurance–incentive trade-off the shareholders had to deal with when hiring a CEO.

These problems of asymmetric information lead to serious issues that cause market failure in the sense of foregone trades. Many of the institutions in these markets are actually ways around the problem of asymmetric information that the market participants have instituted themselves.

Chapter 10
The economics of finance

To some of the uninitiated, making money on the stock market is what economics is all about. Hopefully the fact that your authors are not typing this book from a hammock in the Caribbean should be enough to convince you that this isn't true. However, **financial economics** – the study of financial markets from an economic point of view – is an important area. This chapter presents a selection of the major topics it covers, putting to use many of the tools from the previous nine along the way.

To begin with, the chapter addresses the fundamental questions of what financial markets are and why we need them. It then turns to the issue of **asset pricing** – how stocks, bonds, and other securities are valued – and presents the **capital asset pricing model (CAPM)**. It concludes by asking whether, given the findings of **behavioural finance**, asset prices really are as the CAPM suggests, considering Milton Friedman's **arbitrage** argument for **the efficient market hypothesis** en route.

The elephant on the trading floor is the **financial crisis of 2007–8**, which is not discussed in any detail here. Making sense of it requires a decent grounding in macro- as well as microeconomics, so this is left until **Chapter 19**.

Financial markets

In the long and painful aftermath of the credit crunch, readers would be forgiven for wondering whether society would be better off without financial markets. But, when they function properly, they can be of enormous benefit to their users. This section briefly explains why.

One issue that firms and individuals must contend with when they organize their finances has to do with **time**: their income and outgoings rarely match up contemporaneously. For example, workers' earnings generally increase over the course of their careers before plummeting to nothing at retirement. But most people like to keep their level of consumption relatively stable throughout their lives: if possible, they'd like to spread out the peaks and troughs in their income so their standard of living is constant. In technical terms, they want to carry out **consumption smoothing**. Similarly, firms often need to stump up significant sums of money to install new capital or build new premises. These investments rarely pay off overnight, instead generating a return over a number of years. Firms therefore need a way of financing these purchases in order to reap the future profits they generate.

A second issue that bothers people is **risk**. As **Chapter 2** explained, individual decision-makers are generally **risk averse** – they'd never take on a "fair-odds" gamble just for the hell of it – but most people's lives are beset by risk. A person may lose her job, crash her car, or suffer a debilitating illness. Individuals would like to **insure** against these risks: paying out money in the good times in return for protection in case something should go wrong.

Entrepreneurs can also face problems with risk. Suppose, for example, that one spots an opportunity to invest in a new brand of bikinis: the initial investment is of $500k and it yields profits of $1.5 million in the instance a major retailer agrees to stock it – something that will happen with a probability of fifty percent – but nothing otherwise. The "average" profit ($750k) is greater than the upfront costs ($500k), so the investment looks to be a good bet. But the sums involved could be daunting for a single entrepreneur: a $1 million net gain in case the bikini investment goes swimmingly, but a hefty loss of $500k if it doesn't. For this reason the project may be too risky for one person to take on alone.

Financial markets can mitigate problems related to risk and time. Their essential role is to allow people to trade "promises" that pay out money at different times or events. Examples might include:

▶ A worker nearing retirement gives a lump sum to an entrepreneur in return for a promise of a share of his future profits. This removes the timing problems described earlier by allowing the entrepreneur to finance an investment and providing the saver with an income when he retires.

▶ A group of people who are all worried about the risk of a house fire

Bonfire of the vanities?

The discussion in the text emphasizes the social value of financial markets, but what about the **banks** and other **financial institutions** that dominate them? These, after all, were the entities propped up by public funds in the wake of the credit crisis rather than the markets themselves. Could we have financial markets without banks?

Banks play the role of **intermediaries** in financial markets: they take a supply of funds from savers and channel them into various securities on their behalf. And there are several reasons why – in principle at least – having intermediaries in the realm of finance is a good idea.

One is that organizing your own finances, much like organizing your own health-care, is a difficult and important task that many people prefer to entrust to experts. Another is that securities markets are riddled with **asymmetric information** (see **Chapter 9**). For example, an entrepreneur applying for a loan will typically know more about her company's true prospects than a lender will (leading to **adverse selection**) and, if she secures her loan, she may then have the incentive to blow it on a fleet of company Jaguars rather than work hard to pay it back (so there is **moral hazard**). With all their expertise, banks can minimize these problems, **screening** applications for finance and structuring securities so that borrowers' incentives are correct. This makes it possible for more mutually beneficial deals to be done.

Of course, none of this is to say that institutions that perform these roles incompetently should be rescued. Indeed, you might think it obviously socially desirable for banks to fail if they are poorly run. **Chapter 19** considers why Western governments decided otherwise in the midst of the financial crisis of 2007-8.

agree to pay into a "pot" in return for the promise of compensation from the pot should any of their houses burn down (this is known as **risk pooling** – it's one way insurance policies work).

▶ The swimwear entrepreneur described above asks outside investors to pay ninety percent of the start-up costs of the investment in return for a promise of ninety percent of the potential profits – that is, she sells a ninety percent **equity share** in the enterprise (perhaps she'd do this by floating on the **stock market**). This means that she ends up with a $100k profit if things go well and a $50k loss if they don't, so the magnitude of the risk she faces is greatly reduced, and she may now be willing to proceed with the investment. This practice is known as **risk sharing**.

The promises exchanged in financial markets go by the general name of **securities** (also **financial assets**) and include **shares**, **bonds**, and **insurance**

Classes apart

Even by the standards of economics, the literature on finance is a minefield of jargon. In particular, there are markets for what can seem an impenetrable array of different types of securities (or **asset classes**, or **instruments**). Here are three important classes:

• **Debt** instruments are **bonds** issued by firms and governments. They promise to pay out a fixed amount – the **coupon** of the bond – in all circumstances unless the issuer goes bust, in which case they **default** on their debt.

• **Equity** instruments are shares in a firm (also known as stocks). These entitle the owner to a share in the firm's profits, paid out in the form of **dividends**. Since shareholders only receive dividends from whatever is left over after bondholders have been paid, shares tend to be riskier than bonds but they offer a higher potential return.

• **Derivatives** offer insurance against changes in prices. For example, **futures** contracts guarantee the holder the price of a commodity such as a barrel of oil or tonne of grain at some predetermined point in the future. This means they'll certainly be able to buy this commodity at that time, no matter what happens to its price. Other derivatives insure against changes in exchange or interest rates.

You can think of the value of a firm – its **enterprise value** – as just being the value of the money it will earn in the future. Since this money will end up in the pockets of either shareholders or bondholders, to work out the enterprise value of a firm, simply add up the value of its debt (the total value of its bonds traded on the market) and its equity (the value of its shares – also known as its **market capitalization**) and subtract the value of the cash it has in the bank (this money has already been earned). The ratio of the value of a firm's debt to its equity is known as its **leverage ratio**.

contracts. Facilitating their trade, which is what financial markets do, allows people to exploit Pareto-improving deals as in the examples above. In this sense, they are just a special type of market, with all the attendant benefits as outlined in **Chapter 5**.

Asset pricing using CAPM

Theories of **asset pricing** attempt to explain how the prices of securities are determined in markets. They thus try to shed light on questions such as why, at the time of writing, the **enterprise value** (see the box above) of Tesco was roughly $50bn and that of Facebook approximately $55bn even though Tesco's projected 2014 operating profits are $5bn while Facebook's are only $3bn.

One such theory, outlined in this section, is the **capital asset pricing model (CAPM** – pronounced "cap em"). The model is by no means definitive and some of its more outlandish assumptions are flagged in what follows. But despite its limitations, it does offer some important insights into valuation and is very widely used in industry.

Risk and return

To get started, remember that a security is just a promise to pay out money at various points in time, the amount contingent on various events occurring.

> **A security is just a promise to pay money at various points in time, contingent on various events.**

So one way of thinking about it is as a **stream of uncertain future cashflows**. The task of valuing a security is that of finding out what this stream of cashflows is worth. CAPM does this on the basis of two features of the cashflow: the amounts paid out – the **expected return** of the security; and the **riskiness** of the expected return – assumed to be measured by its standard deviation (a statistical measure of variability).

Economists generally express the expected return of a security as an **annual rate of return**: that is, the security's **average return per year** given as a **percentage of its price**. Using the average annual return is helpful because it allows one to compare securities that pay out money over different timescales. For example, **growth stocks** including (arguably) Facebook shares are expected to deliver most of their return far into the future whereas returns from shares in mature companies such as Tesco are more weighted towards the present. Note that future returns are always **discounted** since investors generally prefer to receive their money sooner rather than later (see **Chapter 2**).

The reason for expressing a security's return as a percentage of its price is also to make comparisons more reasonable. A security that costs €50 and returns €5 per year is surely no better or worse than one that costs €100 and returns €10 (you could buy two of the former securities and get the same return for the same price as the latter!). This is reflected in the fact that both offer a rate of return of 10%. Another advantage of working in terms of rates of return is that there is a one-to-one relationship between the rate of return offered by a stream of cashflows and the price of the underlying asset. So, for instance, any theory that says the rate of return of a security paying out €10 per year should be 10% implicitly says that the price of that security should be €100. This is precisely what CAPM will do.

The capital market line

CAPM assumes that everyone in the market has the same beliefs about the expected return and riskiness of any asset, so it's unproblematic to talk about "the risk" and "the expected return" of securities. And it takes it for granted that there is a special security known as the **risk-free asset**, which generates returns with absolute certainty. In reality, some **government bonds** might come close to being risk-free in this sense, though at the time of writing it's probably best not to chance on any examples.

Buyers of securities construct **portfolios** by dividing up the money they invest between the assets that are available for sale. One portfolio choice would be to buy each security in proportion to the value of it traded on the market, constructing what's known as the **market portfolio**. The market portfolio is akin to index-tracker funds that are sold to investors – if, say, Exxon Mobil shares make up 5% of the value of the Standard & Poor 500 at current prices, then a S&P 500-tracker would invest 5% of its money in Exxon Mobil shares. The difference is that index trackers tend to focus on specific subgroups of assets, such as shares listed on the S&P 500 index, whereas the market portfolio encompasses all securities available for sale.

The risk and expected return for the risk-free asset and the market portfolio are graphed in figure 10.1 below.

In the figure, the market portfolio is assumed to carry some risk. This will certainly be true in practice: if, for example, the global economy booms then the market portfolio will pay out more than if it crashes. But

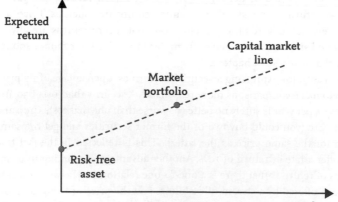

Figure 10.1: The risk-free asset, market portfolio, and capital market line.

it also offers a higher expected return. This must be so in order for anyone ever to hold the market portfolio instead of the risk-free asset: investors are risk averse, so they'll only tolerate extra risk if they are compensated with a higher expected return.

By combining the risk-free and market portfolios, investors can expose themselves to any amount of risk they like. If they ploughed 50% of their money into the risk-free asset and 50% into the market portfolio, the resulting portfolio would be half as risky as the market portfolio and offer an expected return halfway between the risk-free and market rate. If, alternatively, they **shorted** the risk-free asset (see the box below) and poured the proceeds plus all their money into the market portfolio, they'd end up with a portfolio that was *even riskier* than the market portfolio, with a correspondingly higher expected return: effectively they'd be borrowing money in order to invest it in the risky market portfolio. The line on figure 10.1 – known as the **capital market line** – shows all the **risk-return** combinations that investors could attain by mixing the risk-free and market portfolios in this way.

The long and the short of it

"Going long" on an asset is a financial idiom for buying it. So **shorting** or **going short** on an asset is, by analogy, somewhat akin to selling it. But whereas with physical commodities, it's usually impossible or illegal to sell something that doesn't belong to you, in securities markets it's common for traders to go short on assets they don't own.

If this sounds like the sort of practice that got the world into trouble in 2007, consider one investor selling Coca-Cola shares to another at the prevailing market price of $1 per share. The buyer hands over $1 to the seller in exchange for the promise of uncertain future money that a Coca-Cola share stands for. But this transaction is still possible even if the seller doesn't own any shares. In principle, there's nothing stopping her writing down "I hereby promise to pay the bearer whatever Coca-Cola shares pay", and transferring that piece of paper to the buyer instead of the share: exactly the same stream of uncertain future cashflows is changing hands. The seller receives $1 and is now liable for the cashflow that these stocks generate: she has taken a short position on Coca-Cola equity.

In practice, this would work slightly differently, but with exactly the same effect. The investor wanting to short Coca-Cola would borrow stock from a third party and then sell this to the buyer. She receives the Coca-Cola share price from the buyer, but is now on the hook for Coca-Cola shares from the person who lent them to her. This is great if Coca-Cola's share price goes down – she can "repay" the loan by buying the lender some shares for less than she sold them for – but if the price goes up she'll make a loss.

Asset pricing

So what does all of this imply about expected asset returns (and therefore prices)? CAPM answers this question when security markets are in **equilibrium** – when supply equals demand for all securities.

A first point is that, in equilibrium, whatever an asset's riskiness is, it could not offer a better expected return than the corresponding mixture of the risk-free and market portfolios. In other words, if you were to plot its risk and expected return, it could not lie above the capital market line. This is illustrated in figure 10.2 below.

In panel (a) of figure 10.2, shares in Gazprom lie above the line. This means that, by same logic used to draw the capital market line, it would be possible to draw a further line of the risk-return combinations one could get building portfolios out of Gazprom shares and the risk-free asset. This is the dotted line in the figure. As panel (a) shows, whatever level of risk an investor felt like taking on, she could always get a better expected return from a mixture of Gazprom shares and the risk-free asset than she could from any market/risk-free mix.

This, however, is impossible in equilibrium, as it would mean nobody ever bought the market portfolio. There would be excess demand for Gazprom shares and excess supply of all other risky securities. So the price of Gazprom shares would have to rise – pushing its expected return down – while other risky security prices would fall – causing their expected returns to go up and the capital market line to pivot upwards, as in panel (b) of the figure. (Remember the one-to-one relationship between prices and expected returns.) Eventually the risk-return profile of Gazprom shares would have to lie on or below the capital market line.

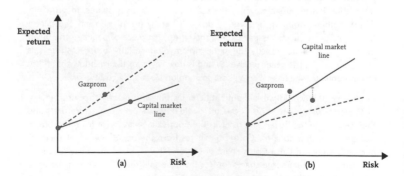

Figure 10.2: Equilibrium in financial markets.

So where, exactly, would it end up? This will depend on how the risk associated with Gazprom shares is correlated with the risk of the market portfolio. Any risk that is *not* correlated with the market risk can be **diversified**. For instance, if Gazprom bids against Shell for a mining concession, the uncertainty over who wins makes Gazprom's shares risky, but this is not market risk since the risks to Gazprom and Shell perfectly offset each other: Gazprom's loss is Shell's gain and vice versa. A canny investor could "diversify away" or **hedge** this element of risk in Gazprom's shares by holding shares in both Gazprom and Shell – eliminating risk without sacrificing return. As always, in equilibrium all these optimizing trades will be made.

Gazprom Tower, Moscow. Ultimately the risk-return of this company's shares would have to lie on or below the capital market line.

However, some risk in Gazprom's shares will be correlated with the risk of the market portfolio, and this cannot be diversified away. The technical measure of this undiversifiable risk is given by the security's **beta**: the correlation between Gazprom shares and the market portfolio multiplied by how risky Gazprom shares are. In order for anyone to buy Gazprom's shares – and thus for the demand for them to equal supply – investors must be compensated for bearing this risk in the form of a

CAPM in business

CAPM is widely used by businesses considering whether to undertake risky investment projects. By working out the project's beta, they can find out what expected rate of return would be available on the security market for the same level of risk. This rate of return is their **cost of capital** – it's the opportunity cost of investing money in the project instead of the security market. Unless their project offers an expected return at least as good as the cost of capital, they'd be better off putting their money elsewhere.

better expected return than that offered by the risk-free asset. And *this* is the proposition of CAPM:

► In equilibrium, an asset is priced so that the difference between its expected return and that of the risk-free asset is proportional to its beta.

The efficient market hypothesis and behavioural finance

In a world described by CAPM, security prices adjust to their **fundamental value**, where an asset's expected return reflects its undiversifiable risk. Investors in such a world must be content to hold a portfolio that performs no better than those on the capital market line. But if this is really true, then a lot of money, time, and newsprint are wasted on efforts to "beat the market". Is this all a delusion cooked up by self-serving asset managers and investment gurus? The **efficient market hypothesis**, which claims that asset prices do reflect their fundamental value, suggests that it could be.

However, just because CAPM supports the hypothesis doesn't mean it's true. One questionable aspect of CAPM is the idea that all market participants **rationally** assess the risk and return of all securities and invest accordingly. This has come under fire from economists working in **behavioural finance**, who point to a range of biases and mistakes to which investors are prone, including framing and loss aversion (see **Chapter 2**), and extrapolative expectation formation (see the box opposite). One might suspect that the presence of irrational traders in securities markets undermines the efficient market hypothesis, meaning there are profits to be had for more level-headed investors.

In fact it's not so simple. It's true that if, for example, a flock of irrational investors were to buy Toyota shares, forcing the firm's share price above its fundamental value, there may be an opportunity for more sophisticated traders to profit. All they would need to do would be to find a **substitute** security for Toyota shares – any other asset that depends on the same risks in the same way. An example of a substitute for Toyota shares might be shares in Volkswagen as both are affected in the same way by "good" and "bad" news for the global motor industry.

If shares in Toyota and Volkswagen were substitutes for each other and Toyota shares were overpriced, a rational investor could cash in by shorting Toyota shares and using the proceeds to buy shares in Volkswagen.

Toil and trouble? Asset price bubbles

Going back at least to "tulipmania" in seventeenth-century Holland, through to the 1920s US stock market boom and the dot-com bubble at the turn of the millennium, asset price bubbles have been a sporadic feature of financial markets over the ages. As the name suggests, they occur when the price of a type of asset gradually inflates over a period of time before suddenly bursting – often with socially dislocating consequences.

One explanation of bubbles from behavioural finance rests on irrational investors forming **extrapolative expectations** about prices: in other words, they base their expectations of how the price of an asset will change on how it has changed in the recent past. If share prices went up last year, such investors expect them to go up again next year – no matter what their fundamental value might be – and will thus want to buy more of them. Interestingly, given that irrational traders will respond to a share price rise by buying more shares, rational traders might *also* want to buy more shares. They know that the further increase in share prices that will result from everyone buying will only make irrational traders want to buy even more, so even if shares are already overvalued they'll be able to sell them on for a profit. Thus it may be that everyone – rational or not – has an interest in running with the herd in such times: hence the name economists give this phenomenon – **rational herding**. The bubble will therefore inflate until going short becomes overwhelmingly lucrative.

Other economists regard extrapolative expectations as a step too far away from rational decision-making – it doesn't take Isaac Newton to realize that asset prices must respect some laws of gravity. They note that, during bubbles, plenty of serious people believe steep price rises are justified by fundamentals. Just three days before the 1929 Wall Street crash, one of the most eminent economists of the time, Irving Fisher, opined that "stock prices have reached what looks like a permanently high plateau". As J.K. Galbraith notes in *The Great Crash* (1954), he even put his money where his mouth was, and lost around $8–$10 million when the market turned against him.

Tulipmania is one of the earliest recorded speculative bubbles. After the flower was introduced to the Netherlands in the sixteenth century, its price soared – according to some sources, exceeding the price of a middle-class house in Amsterdam at its peak in 1636.

Since the two securities are substitutes, the risks of shorting one and buying the other cancel out, so the investor would expose himself to no risk. And as the return from overpriced Toyota shares (for which the investor is liable) must be lower than that from fairly priced Volkswagen shares (which he would receive), the investor could expect to make a profit. So, without staking any of his own money (remember, he funded the Volkswagen shares by shorting Toyota), the investor would reap a risk-free return. As the British magazine *Private Eye* would put it, trebles all round! A money-for-nothing trade such as this is known as an **arbitrage**.

Before picking up the phone to your broker, note that there's a catch to this story. As investors don't need to stake any of their own money to carry out the arbitrage, there's no limit to the amount they would short Toyota and buy Volkswagen. The slightest deviation of Toyota's share price from its fundamental value would whip up a torrent of arbitrage. And since shorting Toyota shares effectively increases the supply of these securities, in order to reach equilibrium Toyota's share price would have to fall. Very quickly it would therefore return to its fundamental value.

So even with irrational investors, arbitrage means the efficient market hypothesis could still be true. This elegant argument in favour of the hypothesis, originally set out by Milton Friedman in 1953, and a lack of evidence to the contrary meant most economists up until the 1980s supported the hypothesis.

But since then, economists have begun to question the argument more closely. What if *both* Volkswagen and Toyota shares were overpriced? Or what if they weren't really substitutes? (In reality Volkswagen is more exposed to European markets than Toyota is, and Toyota is more exposed to the USA.) In these circumstances an arbitrage may not be available, in which case asset prices might not be forced to their fundamental value. And there is some evidence that this happens in reality: for example, a stock's inclusion in an index such as the FTSE 100 or S&P 500 appears to boost its price, even though this seemingly cannot have any effect on the level or riskiness of its future profits.

Given investor irrationality and the fact that arbitrage isn't always possible, the efficient market hypothesis is likely to be false. However, be warned: it does not follow from this that clever investors can use their expertise to consistently outperform the market. A far better way of doing this is to invest other people's money and charge them for the privilege – just look at what the experts do.

PART FIVE:

Macroeconomics – "the economy"

What does someone mean when they say something like "the economy should pick up this year"? What is the "the economy" in this context? What "the economy" is and whether it will "pick up" this year or the next are some of the questions that macroeconomists try to answer.

Normally when someone refers to "the economy" and its prospects for growth, they are referring to **gross domestic product** – GDP – the total value of all goods and services produced in the economy. For better or worse, GDP is often used as the litmus test of whether "the economy" is growing or shrinking, and so is also used as the ultimate arbiter of whether the government's economic policies are successful or not. That GDP should be the arbiter of whether we are better or worse off is not uncontroversial. What GDP is, what it measures, and perhaps more importantly what it does not measure will be the subject of **Chapter 11**.

Chapter 12 discusses what determines GDP in the long run – showing how investment in the economy's capital stock drives GDP growth, and that this in turn depends on technological progress and the quality of an economy's legal and political institutions. **Chapter 13** then examines the economy at a greater level of detail, setting out the "classical model", which was the dominant paradigm before the Great Depression of the 1930s At its heart, the model supposes that a country is endowed with certain fixed levels of labour and capital (the inputs to production) and a fixed technology for converting those inputs into outputs. An uncharitable interpretation of the classical model would say that it assumes that we live in the best of all possible worlds and the economy is always in equilibrium and always producing as much output as can be produced. A more charitable interpretation would be to say that the classical model is concerned with equilibrium because that is the simplest way of thinking about the vastly complex set of interactions that make up an economy. Needless to say, during the Great Depression of the 1930s the classical model was widely felt to lack either validity or relevance (depending on whether one were being charitable or not).

Chapter 14 outlines how John Maynard Keynes thought about how output in the economy was determined. Keynes's ideas allowed for the possibility of prolonged involuntary unemployment, something that would not happen in the classical model. Keynes also made recommendations as to what governments could do to end periods of prolonged unemployment and restore the economy to full employment. He advocated an active role for the government in ensuring macroeconomic stability through the use of **fiscal policy** (the tax and spend powers of the government) and **monetary policy** (the government's ability to control the money supply) in a process of "fine-tuning" the economy.

"Events dear boy, events." So said Harold Macmillan, a British prime minister, when asked what was most likely to blow the government off course. One might give a similar reply to the question of what is most likely to lead to the replacement of one dominant strand of macro-economic thought with another. In the post-war era, governments of all political colours in the West followed policies that might be described as having been inspired by Keynes. However, several of these countries began to experience economic problems in the 1970s to which standard Keynesian fiscal and monetary responses appeared ineffective. It was at this point that the monetarist ideas of Milton Friedman started to be considered and used by governments around the world. Those ideas are the subject of **Chapter 15**. In explaining all of these models and how they work, it is an expedient simplification to suppose that the economy is "closed" meaning that there is no international trade, no imports and no exports. **Chapter 16** relaxes this assumption and looks at what happens when the economy is open to international trade.

Chapter 11

Basics of national income accounting

Most people who know a little bit about economics will know that GDP is important. What is GDP? What are its shortcomings as a measure of how well off a country is? The conclusion to which most economists would subscribe is somewhat surprising. Most economists feel about GDP the same way Winston Churchill felt about democracy when he quipped that: "Democracy is the worst form of government... apart from all the others that have been tried from time to time." That is to say that economists generally think that GDP is a pretty bad measure of how well off people are, but that doesn't stop it being the best measure available. This chapter will describe the advantages and shortcomings of GDP as a measure of national wellbeing. But before discussing, how well off a country is and how it might be made better off, it is necessary to establish how such things *can* be measured. This is what national income accounting is all about – measuring things like how well off a country is, and by extension, the people who live in that country.

An important distinction in the measurement of everything from physical systems to financial ones is the distinction between **stocks** and **flows**. For example, a person's wealth is the value of the things that they own; their income is the amount of money they receive in a given period. This chapter starts by looking at how distinctions like this affect various items in the national accounts.

Stocks and flows

In all accounting, an important distinction needs to be drawn between **stocks** and **flows**. A stock measures how much of something exists at a particular point in time; for example, the money in Simon's bank accounts at 1pm on

31 December 2013 is a stock. A flow measures how much of something moves per unit of time; for example, Simon's annual income is a flow.

GDP is a flow variable as it measures the value of the output produced in an economy. The corresponding stock variable would measure the value of all the assets in the economy, seeing GDP as the return on those assets in the form of physical and human capital. The value of those assets would depend very much on the expected future flows of income that can be expected from them. This is why national income and national wealth are very closely connected.

This distinction between stocks and flows does not just apply to income and wealth. Many of the components of GDP are flow variables with important related stock variables. For example, investment is a flow that tends to increase the size of the capital stock in the economy. In any scenario, and regarding any statistic which might have a bearing on how well off people are, there is a need to be aware of whether it is a stock or a flow: an example where this is important concerns debts and deficits (see p.192). Whether a stock or flow is the most relevant statistic depends on the context and the comparison that is being drawn.

> **GDP is a flow variable as it measures the value of the output produced in an economy.**

Output, expenditure and income

Gross domestic product has, for all its faults (of which more later), become the metric by which national income is measured. GDP is defined as the total value of all goods and services in the economy – in other words it is the value of the economy's **output**. In almost every country, there is a statistical agency charged with measuring GDP. There are, broadly speaking, two ways of measuring it.

► The **expenditure method**: measuring the amount of money people spend buying goods and services from firms; or
► The **income method**: measuring the amount of money firms spend buying labour services from workers and repaying households for the use of capital machinery.

Suppose someone buys an MP3 music track for $1. That is an extra $1 of expenditure in the economy, but, for other people, it will also be an extra $1 of income. That $1 of income will be split in some way between the

Debts and deficits

There is an old joke about an employer interviewing a mathematician, a physicist, and an economist for a job and asking the question, "What is two plus two?" While the mathematician and physicist answer four (with the physicist making some allowance for measurement error), the economist immediately gets up, draws the blinds and switches on the radio at high volume. He then leans in and whispers in the interviewer's ear: "What do you want it to be?

Shifting the focus between stocks and flows is one way that economists can help politicians and journalists to paint a rosy picture or prognosticate doom and gloom as required. Take the following two excerpts from British newspapers:

"George Osborne will acknowledge that his target for a decline in public debt as a percentage of gross domestic product – currently 75 per cent – has been pushed back to the 2017–18 fiscal year. He had originally forecast that the government's debt burden would begin to fall in 2013–14." *The Financial Times Online*, 19 March 2013

"Government borrowing falls £9bn – helped by 4G mobile airwaves sale: Statistics office says public sector net borrowing, excluding bank bailouts, fell to £2.8bn last month from £11.8bn a year ago" *The Guardian Online*, 21 March 2013

Within a matter of a few days, the picture on public sector finances has turned from one of doom and gloom to one that gives reason for optimism. Of course, it is not actually that the public finances turned around within those few days, the *Financial Times* is focusing on the debt – a stock, while the *Guardian* is focusing on the deficit, a flow that captures the rate at which the debt is increasing. As part of any attempt to get finances under control, a period should be expected where the deficit falls but debt continues to rise.

online retailer (say iTunes) and the band who performed the song in question. Within the retailer, their share of that $1 will be split in some way between their programmers and managers in terms of their wages and their shareholders in terms of dividends on their shares.

No matter how complicated the economy is in practice, a fundamental truth of accounting is that every time someone spends $1, someone else's income increases by $1. So it doesn't matter whether GDP is defined by measuring people's incomes or measuring people's expenditure; the same flow will be measured.

Problems with GDP comparisons

A naive summation of income or expenditure in one country is a large statistical exercise, but will it be that informative? For starters, it doesn't tell anyone that much unless we also know the GDP of another country or the GDP of the same country at some point in the past – in short, we need something to which to compare it.

However, once comparisons are being made more problems begin to emerge. Does the fact that American GDP is six times larger than British GDP really mean that Americans are six times better off? Does the fact that French GDP in 2011 was approximately twice its level in 1994 mean that French people are twice as well off as they were in 1994? Naturally the answer to both of these questions is no, because of issues to do with population levels, exchange rates, and inflation.

It is actually fairly easy to construct, from GDP, statistics that control for these problems, and some of those techniques will be shown below. Just as with stocks and flows, some less scrupulous people might deliberately compare countries without making the requisite adjustments to GDP, because doing so would get in the way of the point they want to make. This is an illustration of the adage that there are "lies, damned lies, and statistics". This is why an understanding of what is the correct comparison to make is important.

Population

In the USA, predicting when China's economy will become bigger than the American one has almost become a national pastime.

> By 2030 China will blow past America as the world's largest economy and global power will shift decidedly in favor of Asia, a new report from the U.S. intelligence community forecasted [sic] on Monday.
>
> Foxbusiness.com, 10 December, 2012.

> By 2017, the International Monetary Fund predicts, the GDP of China will overtake that of the United States.
>
> Professor Niall Ferguson in *Newsweek Magazine*, 19 August, 2012.

These headlines illustrate one of the dangers of using GDP to make international comparisons. Apparently, China will soon have a higher income than the United States. But is this plausible? If anyone had a choice as to where they would live after 2030 or 2017, China or the USA, where would they actually choose? If Niall Ferguson had the choice, on purely financial grounds, would he really choose China? Probably not.

Table 11.1 (below) includes not only the GDP, but also the population of each country. While China's GDP is only slightly below that of the United States, China's population is more than a billion people larger than that

Country	GDP	Population	GDP per capita
United States	$15.65tn	316,668,567	$49,421
China	$12.38tn	1,349,585,838	$9,173

Table 11.1: GDP and population (according to *CIA World Fact Book*).

of the United States. So, there is a clear need to take account of population when making income comparisons across borders.

There are two important implications of this, with the first being that the GDP in China needs to be shared out among many more people than the GDP in the United States. Dividing between all the people, GDP in the United States provides nearly $50,000 for each person, but less than $10,000 for each person in China. The other way of looking at this is to consider the efficiency of each economy. The economy of the United States is able to convert the labour effort of just over 300m people into more than $15tn whereas the Chinese economy is only able to generate $12tn from the labour effort of more than 1.3bn people.

While this is a problem with using GDP as a means of comparing how well off people are in different countries, it is one that is relatively easily resolved. The key is to look at GDP per capita to make comparisons; this will take account of the number of people that income must be shared among.

If the goal is to assess the relative efficiency of the two economies, then it might also be wise to take account of sociological differences in terms of how many people are actually working to produce this GDP. It is entirely possible that a greater proportion of the population in the United States are not working than in China. This could be because they are retired, or because they are still in education in school or college. So GDP per worker might be a more relevant statistic for those purposes.

Units of account

Suppose we want to compare how well off people in the USA are as opposed to people in Japan? Population differences can be accounted for by looking at GDP per capita, but there is another problem. The value of goods and services in the USA is measured in dollars; but the value of goods and services produced in Japan is measured in yen. It is impossible to compare the value of the goods and services produced in the two countries without being able to compare the value of dollars and yen. One way of doing this would be simply to use the market exchange rate between the two countries' currencies to convert yen into dollars or vice versa. But does this really represent an accurate measure of the relative worth of a yen and a dollar?

As any international tourist will know, the reality is that the same amount of money, converted into whatever the relevant currency might be at the prevailing market exchange rate, will generally have different **buying power** in different countries. This is one reason why so many Western retirees head for places such as Southeast Asia or the Caribbean: the cost of living is lower and so their retirement income goes further. It isn't just about the sun.

The solution is not to use market exchange rates when converting GDP from one currency to another, but to use exchange rates based on **purchasing power parity (PPP)** reflecting the true cost of living in different countries. One example is the "Big Mac Index" periodically published by *The Economist* magazine. The idea is to take the price of a Big Mac in several countries, and work out the implied exchange rate between the currencies used by those countries on the basis that the price of a Big Mac should be the same everywhere. For example, if the price of a Big Mac in the UK is £2.50 and the price of a Big Mac in the USA is $3.80, then that would imply a dollar to sterling exchange rate of $1.52 to £1. Anyone who has read the international edition of *The Economist* might be a bit confused as to why the

The Big Mac Index is one of the best known measures of buying power or purchasing power parity (PPP) in different countries.

The law of many prices

Why do market exchange rates differ from purchasing power parity exchange rates? Put another way, how can price differences persist? If wine costs $10 a bottle in France (after converting euro prices to dollar prices at the market rate) and $15 a bottle in the USA, why don't people buy large numbers of bottles in France, ship them to the USA in bulk, and sell them at the higher price? This process is known as **arbitrage** and over all goods it should result in only one price for each good.

In reality of course, there are numerous barriers to engaging in such trades. The USA may well have tariffs on importing wine into the country, and the sale of wine may be subject to taxation in the USA at a higher rate than in France, explaining some of the price difference. However, even once these barriers to trade are taken into account, price differences on many goods are excessive when compared to what the law of one price would predict.

Part of the problem can be explained by goods that simply cannot be picked up and shipped from one country to another. The price of a haircut or a taxi journey for example will vary markedly from one country to another. That is, in part, because it is impossible to buy a haircut or a taxi journey in France and sell it in the USA. These are services that cannot be easily shipped and so are not susceptible to arbitrage.

magazine bothers researching the price of the Big Mac in so many countries in order to perform this comparison: the price of *The Economist* in a large number of currencies is already printed on the front page!

The relevance of purchasing power parity exchange rates will depend on the goods used for calculating the exchange rate. This should ideally be a representative sample of goods that people would actually buy in each country – man cannot live on Big Macs alone! Statisticians calculate purchasing power parity exchange rates based on a much more sophisticated basket of goods than simply the Big Mac, but the principle is the same. Exchange rates based on purchasing power parity are the best ones to use when making cross-country comparisons of GDP.

Comparisons in the same country, but over time, are vulnerable to a similar problem. Although, in principle, the same currency is being used when making comparisons of GDP in the USA in the 1970s and today, economists need to remember that a dollar in the 1970s would buy more than a dollar would today. Even the relatively moderate inflation since the beginning of the twenty-first century has an effect on buying power when accumulated over ten years or so. For example, if inflation remained at a moderate two percent per annum for 35 years, then prices would double over that 35-year period.

In order to make comparisons of GDP per capita between different time periods, economists account for inflation by calculating today's GDP in prices at a single point in time, for example in 2005 dollars. For the purposes of GDP comparisons, the past is indeed another country.

Imputed services

Not all services are bought and sold in a market and so not all services have a price attached to them. Take the example of two apartments, 15a and 15b Fake Street. The people who live in 15a also own 15a, they are owner-occupiers. The people who live in 15b are renting it from someone else. The rent paid for 15b is part of that someone else's income, and so is included in GDP. However, the flat 15a is in many respects identical to 15b, but if GDP is calculated as a naive summation of everyone's income, the owners of 15a receive no income from this asset.

The definition of GDP is that it represents the value of all goods and services produced in the economy. Housing services should be included among all these goods and services, but not all of the housing services produced will show up in a simple addition of everyone's income if people own the property in which they live. Owner occupiers are effectively their own landlord and so pay rent to themselves – a transaction which does not show up on anyone's books. For this reason, when calculating GDP, a figure known as **imputed rent** is included. This is the notional payment that an owner-occupier pays to themselves as their own landlord, and it is calculated through various statistical techniques. In the UK in 2009, imputed rent was more than £95bn of GDP – this is more than double the £41bn of GDP that came from actual rent.

Figures like imputed rent sometimes seem fanciful, but to try and calculate GDP as a naive summation of everyone's income making no allowance for imputed services would be fraught with difficulty. Taking the example above, suppose the owners of 15a move somewhere else in the country, but continue to own their apartment and rent it out. If no account was taken of imputed rent, that would imply GDP has increased:; but has it? Has the value of housing services produced each year actually increased because an apartment that was once owner occupied is now rented? Similarly, what if the tenants in 15b buy their apartment– and so there are no longer any rental payments associated with it: would GDP have fallen?

Clearly the answer to these questions is "no" and changes in who consumes the housing services should not lead to changes in whether the housing services are included in GDP or not. For this reason alone, imputed rent should be included in GDP statistics.

Second-hand goods

While economists generally try and measure GDP by looking at expenditures and incomes, there are some expenditures and incomes, which need to be excluded from consideration. Recall that the goal is to get a true picture of the quantity of goods and services produced in an economy in a given year. Suppose John bought a new car four years ago and now he sells it to Jane in order to go and buy another new one. He sells his old car to Jane for £4,000 and buys a brand-new car for £10,000.

If GDP were based indiscriminately on expenditures and incomes with no eye for what the money is spent on or received for, then these transactions might be thought to contribute £14,000 to GDP. In reality, they should only contribute £10,000 to GDP and in fact this is what would be recorded. Recall that GDP is an attempt to measure the value of goods and services *produced* in an economy over a given time period. When John sells his used car four years after he bought it, he has not produced any good or service; he is merely transferring an asset that was actually produced some time ago. So the only purchase that should contribute to GDP is the purchase of the brand-new car for £10,000.

In many ways this is a blessing for the statisticians who have to compile GDP statistics. If GDP did aim to capture the revenues gained from transferring assets in this way, they would have to spend a lot of time monitoring websites that specialize in the trading of second-hand goods such as eBay, GumTree, and Craigslist.

Revisions

With so many factors complicating the calculation of GDP, it is little wonder that, even once GDP figures have been published, they may well be revised later. Sometimes the revisions can be surprisingly large, but even small revisions can be significant. For example, in early 2013, the US Bureau of Economic Analysis (BEA), the agency charged with estimating GDP, revised their estimate of growth in the American economy upwards by 0.2 percentage points. This is only a small revision, but the initial estimate had been a 0.1 percent contraction in the American economy over that quarter. So it made the difference between whether the economy had shrunk or grown.

An example of a larger revision is that in August 2011, the BEA revised their estimate of the change in GDP over 2009 from a contraction of 2.6 percent to a contraction of 3.5 percent. Changes like this only go to show that early estimates of GDP growth should be treated with some scepticism. Indeed, many people say the only reason for economists to estimate or even forecast GDP growth to one decimal place is to demonstrate that they have a sense of humour.

The UK's statistical authorities have been undertaking similar revisions to GDP estimates over the financial crisis. What was once thought to have been a "double dip" – two recessions in quick succession, is now thought to have been one recession much sharper than thought followed by a recovery.

The shortcomings of GDP

There are several problems with *measuring* GDP that have been discussed above, but the question remains as to whether GDP is the right thing to measure. Some of these issues were highlighted most eloquently by Bobby Kennedy in 1968 when running for president.

> Our gross national product ... if we should judge America by that – counts air pollution and cigarette advertising, and ambulances to clear our highways of carnage. It counts special locks for our doors and the jails for those who break them. It counts the destruction of our redwoods and the loss of our natural wonder in chaotic sprawl. It counts napalm and the cost

GDP in focus: Robert Kennedy addressing Kansas university students, March 1968.

of a nuclear warhead, and armored cars for police who fight riots in our streets. It counts Whitman's rifle and Speck's knife, and the television programs which glorify violence in order to sell toys to our children.

Yet the gross national product does not allow for the health of our children, the quality of their education, or the joy of their play. It does not include the beauty of our poetry or the strength of our marriages; the intelligence of our public debate or the integrity of our public officials. It measures neither our wit nor our courage; neither our wisdom nor our learning; neither our compassion nor our devotion to our country; it measures everything, in short, except that which makes life worthwhile. And it tells us everything about America except why we are proud that we are Americans.

> Robert F. Kennedy address, University of Kansas,
> Lawrence, Kansas, 18 March, 1968

Defensive expenditures

Defensive expenditures are expenditures with the goal not of improving the quality of life, but of keeping it where it is. As Bobby Kennedy pointed out, GDP is the sum of the value of all the goods and services that are being made within the economy, and to the extent that a higher GDP is a result of making fun stuff that people enjoy, a society with a higher GDP is probably one that is better off. But not all GDP is a result of making fun stuff. A large chunk of GDP is a result of spending either to undo the damage of crime and other social problems, or to prevent it happening (to you) in the first place. These kind of expenditures are called **defensive expenditures** because they do not actually raise anyone's standard of living, but rather just keep it where it is.

In their simplest form, defensive expenditures divert society's resources from fun stuff that people can enjoy to less fun stuff like locks and security lights that are designed to protect what people already have. If a society has a high GDP because it is producing lots of fun things, all well and good. However, if a society has a high GDP because it is very efficient at producing lots of goods associated with defensive expenditures, then that probably tells you something about that society.

Bias towards traded services

GDP counts goods and services that are traded and will ignore those goods and services that are not traded. In some senses, this is strange because some of the "goods" which are highly valued are goods that cannot be traded. For example, many people value living in a free society where leaders are decided by some kind of collective choice rather than by force. There is no accounting for this in GDP. Similarly, a lot of people value freedom of speech, and being able to criticize leaders – again something which has no place in GDP estimates. Although one may have good reasons to expect a correlation between GDP and various kinds of freedom, there is no accounting for freedom in GDP statistics, largely because there is no market in which it is traded.

The bias towards traded services might be a factor which exaggerates the economic performance of many countries over the latter half of the twentieth century

Of course, the bias towards traded goods affects other goods too. For example, if a new coal fired power station opens up, then the electricity the power station produces and sells counts as an increase in GDP. But the smoke the power station puts out which will harm the local community doesn't get traded – or, more properly speaking, the clean air which was there before the smoke is not traded. It is an externality. As a result, it is impossible to put a price on the clean air that has been lost.

The bias towards traded services might be a factor which exaggerates the economic performance of many countries over the latter half of the twentieth century. Part of economic growth over this period comes from a social change. In the 1950s, a large number of households operated with a single breadwinner – usually the father, while the mother would stay at home, do the housework, and raise children. By the end of the twentieth century, this model of the household was much rarer. Women would typically have their own careers, and households would have two breadwinners. Thus GDP increased as the labour force had almost doubled in size.

However, the work now done in the market by women is not the only increase in GDP as a result of this social change. Parents did not stop needing to take care of their children or clean their houses, and while these responsibilities are now more equally shared within the family unit, two people with full-time jobs and careers simply do not have enough hours in the day. So they send their children to nurseries and after-school clubs more often; maybe they hire a nanny and a cleaner. The work that was done by housewives in the 1950s is now done (if it is done at all) by cleaners and nannies who are paid for their services. This is not new output; it is simply new that it is measured in GDP.

Technically speaking, past GDP figures from the period before women entered the paid workforce en masse should be revised upwards with the imputed expenditure on the work that they did as housewives cleaning the home and looking after their children. However, the source of data for any such estimates would be contentious.

Alternatives to GDP

So if GDP is so bad and prone to so many different kinds of measurement error, why is it still used? There are alternatives. For example, the **index of sustainable economic welfare** (ISEW) starts by measuring consumption expenditure, as it is felt to be consumption from which people derive economic utility, and then subtracts from that things like defensive expenditures and adds to it things like the services received from domestic labour. (This isn't as *Downton Abbey*esque as it sounds; it is just accounting for the housekeeping activities that people will undertake themselves within the family rather than hire someone to do for them.) Some of these measures may well produce a better picture of how well off people are, but they will only ever be as good as the data on which they are built.

Data quality is a serious problem faced by any new measure if it is going to be successful at replacing GDP. One of the main uses of GDP is in making historical and international comparisons as to how well off people are. Whilst, in the developed world, undertaking these surveys to find how much money people are spending on what we should classify as defensive expenditures is not a difficult task, it might be much more difficult in developing countries. For one thing, in the developed world a telephone survey would be a reasonable way of cutting the costs of a survey. But in the developing world it could introduce a **selection bias,** as it would only include those with access to a phone.

The problems of reliably gathering the data in the developing world are nothing however, compared to the costs of gathering the data for historical comparisons. In many cases, if the data was not recorded in the past, it is simply unavailable.

The good thing about GDP is that it can be assessed by measuring people's income. Whatever else one might say about any particular government, or any form of government – past, present, or future – the best records they keep are tax records. So the data from which a good estimate of GDP can be made is very likely to exist in one form or another in almost all times and places. So this may be a case of economists suffering from **path dependence**. Economists will continue to use GDP, because that is what they have used in the past. However, this is not the stale conservatism that it sounds like when one bears in mind that part of what economists are trying to measure is progress over time.

Happiness economics

The statement that "gross national happiness matters more than gross national product" is normally attributed to the king of Bhutan. There is certainly a point to this: that money does not buy happiness is a theme that runs right through most good literature. With that in mind there has been a great deal of effort in recent years to come up with ways of measuring happiness, and finding out what determines it – a literature known as **happiness economics**. The British economist (and life member of the House of Lords) Richard Layard has worked in this area. Happiness economics is beginning to have a policy effect: for example, the UK has added questions about happiness to its existing household surveys.

The basis for this critique is that surveys aimed at measuring the causes of happiness tend to conclude, with apologies to Jane Austen, that a large income is not the best recipe for happiness, and that in fact income is a pretty poor predictor of happiness. This is not to say that income is unimportant, but once income reaches a sufficient level, such that basic needs are securely met, its importance in determining happiness decreases. Once that level is reached, other things start to become more important, such as health, the quality of family relationships and the amount of leisure time to enjoy pursuits other than work (although being employed is still something that makes people happier). Relative income also becomes important, as people try to keep up with the Joneses; doing so makes people happy, and failing to do so makes them unhappy.

The policy implication is that in order to make people happy, once a basic threshold level of income has been reached, governments should switch their focus from GDP to the other factors that influence happiness. One notable insight from Layard's work concerns the relationship between income taxes and the incentives people have to work. Layard argues that producing more will not increase happiness in society and may indeed decrease it. Although an individual worker might raise their relative income by working more hours, in doing so they reduce everyone else's relative income and make them less happy. Progressive taxation is therefore akin to taxing this externality.

In 2007, through the Institute of Economic Affairs, the economists Helen Johns and Paul Ormerod published a critique of happiness economics and attempts to apply it to public policy called "Happiness, Economics and Public Policy". The authors draw a distinction between the aggregate happiness data which produces an index in a specific country of responses to the question "how happy are you?" and longitudinal studies following specific individuals over time. They point out that most of what we know about the causes of happiness comes from the latter kind of data but the most commonly used data to formulate indices for 'Gross National Happiness' are based on the former kind of data.

Aggregate happiness data based on surveys is stubbornly invariant, not just to income, but to almost everything! Part of the reason for this is the way that human benchmarks adapt quickly to changing circumstances, and another part is in the nature of comparing a scale with a theoretical maximum (where everyone reports feeling very happy) to something like income or government expenditure, which can theoretically increase without limit.

There is also a tension between some policy prescriptions based on the logic of happiness economics and individual freedom. For example, one conclusion from happiness research is that increased income brings no permanent increase in happiness and people should therefore (in their own interests as well as the interests of others whose relative income would decrease as a result) be prevented from working too much or too long. This conclusion seems uncomfortably paternalistic in the way that the happiness expert's research is used to override the individual's judgement about what will make them happier. While economists accept that individuals may not always succeed in maximizing their own happiness, they are sceptical of the idea that a remote policymaker will do a better job!

Chapter 12

Economic growth

Increases in per capita GDP – otherwise known as **economic growth** – can be a panacea for all manner of social ills. Education, conservation, space exploration, novelty kitchenware – economic growth can mean more of everything. And though **Chapter 11** highlighted the pitfalls of using per capita GDP as a proxy for national welfare, few would doubt that, all other things being equal, it's better to have more growth than less.

What's more, when it comes to growth, seemingly slight differences in performance can compound over time into gulfs in prosperity. According to the World Bank, real GDP per head has grown by around 1.7% per annum in Argentina over the last fifty years and 2.7% in Israel. A single percentage point doesn't sound like much of an advantage, but growing at 1.7% it will take about forty-one years for income to double, compared to twenty-six years at 2.6%. And growing at China's fifty-year average of 6.8% means doubling occurs in just over ten years. These sorts of numbers have profound ramifications for living standards – by way of comparison, the UK's real GDP per capita was only around five times larger in 2013 than it was at the end of World War I. The question of how growth comes about and what – if anything – the government should do to promote it, is therefore one of the most pressing in macroeconomic analysis. It is the question to which this chapter is addressed.

Up until the eighteenth century, economic growth was fitful and decidedly modest in scale and scope. A number of civilizations, including the Greeks, Romans, Maya, and Chinese managed to raise living standards above subsistence levels, but none ever kindled sustained economic progress, and most wealth that was created accrued to a narrow elite. The economist Angus Maddison (1924–2010) estimated that by 1700 real GDP per capita had reached around $1,000 (at 1990 prices) in Western Europe – compared to roughly $800 in Roman Italy and a subsistence level of $400. This is slow progress even by Western Europe's current standards.

But starting from around 1800, this suddenly changed. Developments in technology and institutions (on which more to follow) culminated in a takeoff in economic performance. Led by a vanguard of the UK and the Netherlands, real GDP per capita in Western Europe trebled during the nineteenth century, then accelerated further in the twentieth century. GDP per head in the US, which by this time had become the economic frontrunner, grew by more than two percent per year in the twentieth century. Average incomes, expressed in today's prices, shot up from roughly $6,000 to $45,000 in the space of a hundred years. If its economy manages to grow at two percent for the next century, American GDP per head will top $300,000 – an unfathomable level of prosperity.

This chapter attempts to explain this historical experience and offer a prognosis of what may happen in the future – and what governments can do to affect it. It begins with a first macroeconomic model of the economy which will serve as a foundation for the next few chapters, before showing how economic growth can arise due to **capital accumulation** and **technological progress**. It then goes on to embellish this story, looking at the roles of learning, human capital, knowledge, and institutions in the process of growth.

The essentials of economic growth

Chapters 3 to **10** starred a large and varied cast, ranging from consumers and workers to firms and investors, with the government always looming large. An economy's GDP per capita will result from the rich and dauntingly complex interplay between these characters. But as always, the best way to get a handle on such a complicated process is to strip it down to its most important components: to build a **model** of it. The next few paragraphs zoom out as far as it is useful to go, setting out a very simple model of the economy – in fact, *too* simple a model – that shows how GDP per capita is determined. The remainder of this chapter – indeed much of the rest of this part of the book – is given over to elaborating upon it in various ways.

A model of the economy

In some senses an economy is just like a very large firm. Both take inputs – factors of production such as labour, capital, and natural resources – and turn them into output, known, in the economy's case, as GDP. There are, of course, many different ways an economy could transform the resources at its disposal into GDP – it may use markets or some form of state-led production – but at this stage it doesn't really matter how this happens. For now, it will be enough to suppose that the economy has a **production technology** that transforms inputs into GDP.

Just as with the account of firms in **Chapter 4**, to keep things simple economists start by assuming there are only two inputs in the economy: labour and capital. And – again analogously to a firm – then assume that each factor of production has **positive but diminishing marginal returns**. That is, the more of each input there is, the more GDP the economy will churn out (positive marginal returns); but, holding the other input constant, each factor gets progressively less useful the more of it is added (diminishing marginal returns). A particularly important consequence of this is that the more capital each worker has to use, the less difference an additional unit of it will make to her output. Less formally, you could say the first few tools you give a worker have a big impact on her productivity, but she eventually gets overwhelmed by kit. This means there will be a relationship between output per worker and capital per worker as in figure 12.1 below.

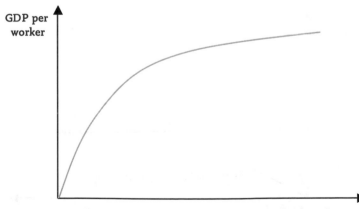

Figure 12.1: Positive but diminishing marginal returns to capital.

The steady state

Still keeping things simple, assume that the size of the labour force always stays the same (for more on this, see the box on p.214). So any addition of capital to the economy means more capital per worker and thus higher GDP per worker, while any loss of capital translates into lower GDP per worker. In this context, explaining GDP per worker simply boils down to explaining capital per worker. So what determines how much capital there is in the economy?

On the one hand, the way to *add* capital to an economy is via **investment**. This involves devoting some portion of the country's output to capital goods such as machinery or buildings, which are added to the economy's capital stock. Usually the way this happens is through individuals **saving** a chunk of their income so firms can use the money to purchase equipment (see **Chapter 13**), but the details aren't important yet. Assume for now that the economy invests some fixed percentage of its GDP.

However, on the other hand capital goods don't last forever. Ageing machines clap out, delivery vans break down, and computers start to get temperamental. Like students frantically trying to work all night on an assignment, capital goods get gradually less productive until they become entirely useless. As a result of this process of wear and tear – known as **depreciation** – the effective amount of capital in the economy *goes down*. It is reasonable to assume that a fixed percentage of the economy's capital stock depreciates every year.

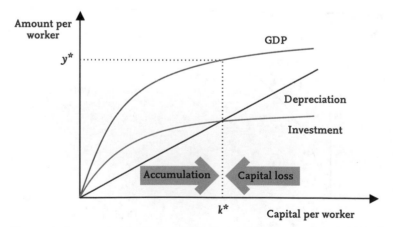

Figure 12.2: A constant proportion of GDP is invested and a constant proportion of capital depreciates.

Figure 12.2 opposite illustrates both of these processes. Because the economy invests a fixed proportion of its GDP, investment per worker is just a scaled down version of the line in figure 12.1. And since a given percentage of the economy's capital depreciates each year, depreciation per worker increases in proportion to the amount of capital per worker.

At levels of capital per worker below **k*** on the figure, investment per worker is greater than depreciation per worker. This implies that more capital is being added than lost, so capital per worker goes up. By contrast, when capital per worker exceeds **k***, depreciation exceeds investment, so capital per worker falls. Thus, no matter where the economy starts out, capital per worker will tend towards **k*** – known as its **steady-state** level. GDP per worker will correspondingly go to **y***, the steady-state level of income per worker.

Post-war Europe and America: swinging versus going steady?

World War II devastated the economies of continental Europe, with the fighting destroying much of the region's capital stock. In 1945, the GDP levels for France, Germany, and Italy were lower than they had been before World War I. The US, by contrast, emerged more or less unscathed, with military spending causing GDP to increase sharply over the war years.

In the following decades these relative performances reversed. The US economy grew at a respectable pace, with real GDP per head rising by around 50% between 1950 and 1970. But if the US economy went uphill, its continental counterparts put in a truly Alpine performance: French, West German, and Italian real GDP per head all more than doubled over the same period. Leaders of these countries hailed an "economic miracle".

Impressive though this was, the analysis given here suggests there was nothing miraculous about it. All of these economies were organized in similar ways and invested similar proportions of their income to the US; so the model says they should all have similar steady states to America's. The fact that the continental economies had significantly less capital per worker than the US in 1945 means that they were *further away* from their steady state than America was – and should therefore be expected to grow more quickly. In technical terms, the model predicts **convergence** between the economies, where rich countries trundle along at their steady states and poor countries catch up.

However, the post-war period didn't witness convergence across the world. Generally speaking, African and Latin American countries were poorer than the US in 1950 but grew more slowly than it over the next two decades. One explanation for this, explored in more depth in **Chapter 18**, is that for some reason these economies have lower steady states than their Western counterparts. In other words, there is **conditional convergence** where similar economies converge, but not **absolute convergence** where all economies converge.

This gives a first account of the growth process. Each unit of capital helps to make GDP, some of which goes towards investment, *increasing* the amount of capital in the economy. But the same unit of capital also depreciates at a certain rate, which *depletes* the capital stock. So if, as was the case in postwar Western Europe, the economy starts out with little capital per worker, the marginal product of capital is high, so the investment it generates more than offsets its depreciation. The economy's capital stock therefore multiplies – fuelling growth in GDP per worker. But as the capital piles up, its marginal product falls, meaning each unit leads to less investment, while depreciating at the same rate. So growth in the capital stock – and therefore GDP per worker – slows down, eventually grinding to a halt at the steady state.

Some aspects of this story ring true (see the box on p.209), but others are hard to square with experience. In particular, two things stand out.

First, the model implies that economic growth gradually runs out of steam, something that – recent travails aside – has not been witnessed over the last two centuries, when growth has mostly accelerated. Something else is needed to generate **long-run growth** in the model.

A very iconic example of the West German *Wirtschaftswunder* (economic miracle): the millionth Volkswagen Beetle off the assembly line in 1955. During this period the West German economy was not yet at a steady state.

Second, it explains growth *entirely* in terms of the accumulation of capital. In fact, the data suggest that purchases of capital can't be the only factor behind growth in the real world. These econometric exercises in **growth accounting** find that, as well as growing stocks of labour and capital, something else must be changing. This mystery x-factor goes by the suitably enigmatic name of **total factor productivity (TFP)**.

Technological progress

So what is missing from the picture? The basic answer was given in papers published independently by Robert Solow (1924–) and Trevor Swan (1918–89) in 1956 – and the framework they used has come to be known as the **Solow-Swan model** of economic growth.

Solow and Swan pointed out that, as well as collecting capital, economies also experience improvements in **technology**. Technology reflects *how good* the economy is at turning its inputs into GDP. As you would expect, the better the state of technology in an economy, the more productive workers are in using capital to make GDP. It's worth emphasizing that the word technology is used in a very broad sense here, encompassing *everything* in the process of turning inputs into outputs. It therefore includes high tech processes involving blinking computer banks and shiny iPads, but also management techniques and nutritional regimens.

What, then, does the technologically enhanced version of the model say about growth? Just as before, there is a tendency for economies to converge to their steady-state levels of capital and income per head. But as the state of technology improves, workers become more adept at using capital, so its marginal return increases. All of a sudden, the investment generated by any amount of capital goes up, while the rate of depreciation stays the same. So the steady-state level of capital per worker increases with technological progress. This means that even if the economy reaches its steady state, technological progress will push this state up to ever higher levels of capital per worker, driving capital accumulation and growth in GDP per worker. Figure 12.3 below illustrates.

This account of the process of growth is more amenable to the data. Taking the two points at the end of the previous section in turn:

▶ Provided technology keeps on improving, the steady-state level of GDP per worker will increase perpetually, meaning economic growth *can* continue in the long run and need not slow down. It's a case of *Vorsprung durch Technik*.

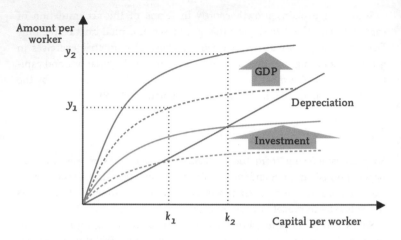

Figure 12.3: Technological progress shifts out the relationship between capital per worker and GDP per worker. This raises investment and shifts out the steady-state GDP per worker from y_1 to y_2.

► What's more, at first blush the state of technology seems a reasonable candidate for the mysterious "total factor productivity" in growth accounting studies. Testing this is difficult without a clearer picture of how technology is meant to be measured, but the story is at least an intuitive one.

Endogenous growth theory

The story developed so far is sensible enough in itself, but in some ways it is quite unsatisfactory. Technological advances such as Apple's iPad or Google's Streetview do not take place in a vacuum – yet in the description of growth above, this is precisely what happens. "Technology" rains down on the economy like manna from heaven, with no indication given as to precisely what it is or where it comes from. In the jargon, technological progress, and hence long-run growth in GDP per worker, is **exogenous** – it happens "outside" the model. Anyone interested in understanding the true causes of growth could thus be forgiven for being left a little cold by what's been set out so far.

The next couple of sections attempt to delve deeper into the process of technological progress. Economists bracket these ideas under the ungainly title of **endogenous growth theory**, so called because, by explain-

Growing apart

"A rising tide lifts all boats" is the favourite analogy of reform-touting politicians: since economic growth means there is more to go round, everyone in the economy can benefit from it. But the experience of Western economies in recent decades has torpedoed such notions of plain-sailing progress. Though GDP per capita has increased markedly, the chief beneficiaries have been the rich while the poor have been left behind. According to the OECD, real household incomes of the top 10% of US earners grew by 1.5% per annum from 1985 to 2008, while the corresponding figure for the bottom 10% is only 0.1%.

One possible explanation for this is based on the nature of the technological progress seen over this time. Many of the most important advances were of the kind that make skilled workers more productive – think accountants plugging numbers into spreadsheets and lawyers firing off correspondence by email – but made little difference to the likes of waiters or shop assistants. According to this story, highly skilled workers have been made even more valuable by technological progress – hence their ever-expanding wage packets – while poorer workers remain as they were.

Technology may seem like a plausible culprit for rising income disparities in the West, but it's not the only one. As **Chapter 17** will argue, globalization may also be a reason.

ing the processes that drive it, they determine economic growth "inside the model" or **endogenously**.

Learning-by-doing and investing in human capital

One way in which technology may advance is via the **learning effects** of investment. It's possible that, as workers gain experience of making things using capital, they become better at doing it, and the more capital they have to play with the stronger this effect is. In other words, a process of **learning-by-doing** makes the economy more productive. Investment induces learning, which raises the return on capital and thus supports even more investment, potentially resulting in long-run economic growth, just as in figure 12.3. Learning-by-doing might explain, for instance, why a mobile phone that cost hundreds of dollars to make a decade ago can be produced for a fraction of the cost today – significant investment in the sector has yielded large learning effects.

> Investment induces learning, which raises the return on capital and thus supports even more investment.

Malthus: an erogenous growth theory

An early contributor to the economic theory of growth was the English cleric and demographer Thomas Malthus (1766–1834). In his *Essay on the Principle of Population*, Malthus claims that any increase in living standards above subsistence levels leads to population growth, and that this extra burden of people will tend to draw living standards back down to the breadline. According to Malthus, humanity's insatiable appetite for breeding condemns us all to eventual poverty: only "moral restraint" can possibly save us.

If this all sounds very much like repressed nineteenth-century sermonizing, then the Solow-Swan model is, by comparison, a study in post-war permissiveness. Consider figure 12.2 again. If, starting at an economy's steady state, the population were to increase, this would cause the amount of capital per worker to fall, depressing living standards as Malthus envisaged. But as capital per worker falls, the return on investment goes up, leading to capital accumulation until the economy is back at its steady-state level of capital per worker. GDP per worker is therefore unaffected by population growth, as the economy just adds more capital to accommodate the extra workers. It's a formal version of the old adage that each extra mouth to feed also comes with a pair of hands to feed itself – hands that can be equipped with capital, in this case.

Nonetheless, more complicated models of the economy can generate predictions closer to Malthus's grim theory. If the economy relies on some inputs that are always fixed – such as the supply of arable land – or natural resources that will eventually run out, then it's impossible to give each new worker the same inputs as everyone else already has. So a growing population will tend to reduce GDP per worker.

This isn't to say that living standards are set to be rendered barren by the force of human reproduction. For one thing, improvements in technology may serve as a countervailing force to the effect of any natural resource constraints an economy faces. And for another, there is a striking negative correlation between GDP per capita and fertility. As the former Indian minister Karan Singh put it: "Development is the best contraceptive."

In a similar vein, workers' productivity may also be boosted by investment in **human capital**. This is investment in workers' skills through purchases of things like degrees, residential courses, or on-the-job training. There may be ulterior motives at play in these investments – signalling (see **Chapter 9**), networking, or even a buffet lunch and a day away from the boss. But it seems fair to suppose that some of this spending does succeed in making workers more effective at using **physical capital**.

By adding some colour to the account of investment in the Solow-Swan model, it's possible to show how human capital investment can lead to long-run growth. Suppose that – as is true of most economies

– investment is funded by the population's savings, and that people will always choose to invest wherever they earn the highest **return** (see **Chapter 10**). They have the choice of investing in two *types* of capital, human and physical.

As noted earlier, investment in human capital makes workers use physical capital more effectively, which raises the return on investment in physical capital. And the more physical capital there is, the more worthwhile it is to train workers to use it better – so investment in physical capital pushes up the return on investment in human capital. It is possible, therefore, that the two forms of investment mutually reinforce each other, ensuring the return never falls on either. Long-run growth could thus be sustained by the **complementary** nature of investment in human and physical capital.

However, these are just stories. And though learning-by-doing and human capital investment seem to be important to the process of capital accumulation, empirical studies suggest something else is needed to generate long-run growth. The next section offers the most promising explanation.

Knowledge and R&D

An important feature of technological progress is that it involves the accumulation of **knowledge** in the economy. This can range from abstract truths, such as the laws of thermodynamics, to practical techniques, such as how to make a new flavour of ice cream. Directly or indirectly, all of this knowledge makes it possible for workers to make whatever resources they have at their disposal go further. The discovery of more knowledge thus makes workers more productive, shifting out the economy's steady state and driving growth forward, just as technological progress causes growth in the Solow-Swan model.

A critical feature of knowledge is that one worker's "use" of it in no way encumbers another's: Marlon's deployment of the laws of physics to design a bridge is completely unaffected by whether or not Ravindra uses them simultaneously to construct a power station, for instance. Knowledge is thus **non-rival**, meaning it is a **public good** (see **Chapter 6**) that will be produced in inefficiently low quantities in a free market. If this is correct then government support for a knowledge-making **R&D sector** can be justified in order to correct this market failure (though see p.216). **Patents** exist as a way of making the public good of knowledge excludable (see **Chapter 6**) and thereby increasing private incentives to produce it.

The Schumpeterian gale

Much as innovation makes the economy more productive, it also has the effect of rendering existing products obsolete. Growth-fostering technological progress thus uproots the established economic order – a process known to growth economists as **creative destruction** and associated with the work of Joseph Schumpeter (1883–1950).

An intriguing implication of creative destruction is that R&D in some areas can be inefficiently *high* in the free market. Provided that their ideas won't be ripped off immediately (perhaps thanks to patent protection), private entrepreneurs have an incentive to expend resources on dreaming up innovations. Part of this incentive derives from the fact that innovations create more surplus (see **Chapter 5**) than whatever they replace, and some of this extra surplus will accrue to the entrepreneur. For example, the next generation of smartphones will have additional features that consumers will be willing to pay more for – this additional premium represents the social value of the innovation.

But part of the incentive reflects the fact that novelties *displace* products offered by competitors – who uses a Nokia 3330 these days? So the entrepreneur also has a **business-stealing incentive** to innovate. From a social point of view, expending resources merely to capture one's rivals' surplus is of no benefit: all it does is move existing surplus around, rather than increasing the amount generated by the economy. So business-stealing incentives can induce firms to innovate more than is socially optimal. Suddenly phone technology doesn't look so smart after all.

So how does knowledge "production" work in the R&D sector? For most industries, economists' default assumption is that there are **constant returns to scale** in production (see **Chapter 4**) – doubling the inputs results in a doubling of output. The argument for this is based on replication: for instance, in the cake sector, it's always possible to duplicate whatever productive arrangement bakes the economy's cakes, so doubling the inputs devoted to it will result in twice as many cakes produced.

However, coming up with a new idea isn't as straightforward as whipping together a Victoria sponge. By its nature, each new nugget of knowledge can only be "produced" – that is *discovered* – once, so it would be pointless to replicate production in the R&D sector. Instead, each new idea must build upon what has come before. This raises two issues:

▶ It's not obvious whether to expect constant, increasing, or decreasing returns to scale in the R&D sector. Recent experience, where the proportion of economic activity devoted to research has increased while economic growth has remained roughly constant, suggests decreasing returns.

▶ Productivity in the R&D sector depends on what is already known. It may be that a fundamental advance, such as the development of the internet, spurs a sudden glut of innovations exploiting it: in the words of Isaac Newton, researchers are able to "stand on the shoulders of giants" and come up with new ideas more easily. Or it could be that all the easy discoveries are made first, so the more extensive the existing body of knowledge is, the harder it is to add to it (see the box below).

The white heat of technology or the dying embers of progress?

In a 2012 paper, Robert Gordon of Northwestern University examines the history of R&D and economic growth and considers the prospects for the next century.

Gordon identifies three periods of "revolutionary" progress in the modern era: a first from around 1750 to 1830, which gave the world steam engines, cotton mills, and railways; a second, from 1870 to 1900, which brought electricity, plumbing, and the internal combustion engine; and a third, roughly from 1960–2000, responsible for information and communication technology. Each wave of revolutionary innovations paved the way for decades of more incremental progress that sustained economic growth. For example, Gordon reckons the second revolution fuelled growth until the 1970s, with expanding motorway networks and new household electrical appliances continuing to build on fundamental advances made in the Victorian era.

However, many of the big improvements in labour productivity and the quality of life seen in the last two centuries are, by their nature, one-offs. For example, before the industrial revolution, homes were dark, cold, and smoky places; the transition to the light, warm, clean dwellings of today can only happen once. And other improvements seem to have run their useful course: cars and aeroplanes today are no faster than they were in 1970. Gordon argues that the fact that these basic advances had already been made explains the relatively modest and short-lived effect of the third revolution on growth – he detects only a one-percentage point uptick between 1995 and 2005.

If there really are fewer growth opportunities left to exploit, then a future slowing is inevitable. Gordon provocatively suggests 0.2% per annum by 2100 – roughly the same as the pre-industrial rate. If this is true, you should learn to live with this world of cars, laptops, and shirts that take ten minutes to iron. But set against all this pessimism, it's worth remembering that even the most technologically savvy minds can struggle to imagine what unexplored improvements might be out there. Speaking on the subject of computer memory, Bill Gates famously mused that "640 kilobytes ought to be enough for anyone". A modern laptop can have as much as ten thousand times as much RAM.

Institutions

The discussion so far has stressed the importance of **investment** – in R&D, human, and physical capital – in determining growth. But the returns generated by investment will depend not just on how much of it there is, but how effectively it is organized. And this will hinge on whether the people who make the investments have the right **incentives** both to invest and to invest in the right projects. Broadly speaking, the political, legal, and social structures that govern incentives in an economy are known as its **institutions**. These are fundamental to the process of economic growth.

One type of institution discussed at length in **Parts Two**, **Three**, and **Four** of this book is that of the **market**. As argued in **Chapters 5** and **10**, if investment is channelled from private savers to firms through financial markets, then investors will have a strong incentive to maximize their risk-adjusted returns. And this will tend to ensure that the right amount of investment is made in the right places. But, as witnessed in **Parts Three** and **Four**, markets do fail and the government may wish to attempt a remedy, though the likelihood of government failure limits the appeal of this. The market for R&D – a crucial determinant of growth – seems particularly apt to fail.

In any market economy, an important feature of almost any type of investment is the pattern of cashflows involved. Usually, the investor stumps up a large upfront expenditure – perhaps on equipment, tuition fees, or assembling a research lab for which she receives payments later on through selling more output, receiving higher wages, or exploiting a new idea. Anything that makes investors doubt they'll attain these later rewards will make them more reluctant to sink in the initial outlay. In short, **confidence** is crucial to investment. And broader institutions can shape confidence in at least two ways:

▶ A lot of investment is predicated on **contracts** between agents. For instance, building a cigarette factory only makes sense if employees subsequently turn up for work, suppliers honour delivery agreements, and buyers pay their bills. Unless there is some sort of institution to enforce contracts in a predictable fashion – possibly a legal system, maybe something less formal based on social norms and reputations – then investors will have little faith in the other party keeping their side of the bargain. This will stifle investment.

▶ Even where no contracts are signed, confidence still depends on a stable regime of **property rights**. If investors believe that any successful venture will be appropriated or any decent new idea ripped off by a rival, they simply won't bother. Once again, legal or social institutions can build confidence in property rights – including **intellectual property rights** over innovations. An important part of this involves constraints on the use of power: the fear of over-mighty sovereigns arbitrarily relieving their subjects of their wealth has been a particularly potent confidence-sapper over history.

Sustaining confidence thus seems to require some sort of even-handed regime for upholding contracts and protecting property rights that all, including the most powerful, respect. Most market economies in the world today have institutions of this sort – usually in the form of independent judiciaries and constitutional limits on executive power – though some are more effective than others (see **Chapter 18**).

What about political systems? Is there anything about, say, **democracy** that promotes growth? Some researchers think there is. As explained earlier, technological progress is a force of creative destruction – by changing the way the economy works, it upends the established order. Political systems dominated by entrenched elites, who by definition benefit from the status quo, are thus likely to be hostile to technological change. Democracies, where everyone who benefits from technological improvement has a voice, are likely to be more receptive.

Institutions go some way to explaining why the first period of sustained growth in history took place in Western Europe at the turn of the nineteenth century. By 1800, Britain had strong legal enforcement of contracts and property rights and a monarchy circumscribed by a democratic parliament (albeit one with a limited franchise). Institutions were thus in place to fuel continuous innovation and investment. These were absent in earlier leading civilizations – such as the Aztecs, Mughals, and Maya – all of which were essentially authoritarian.

Chapter 13
The classical model

Most macroeconomists thought of the economy in terms of "the classical model" in the days before the Great Depression and Keynes's "*General Theory*". No single classical economist's work encapsulated the classical school, although Adam Smith (1723–90), David Ricardo (1772–1823), and even John Stuart Mill (1806–73) could all be thought of as classical economists. The version of the model set out here is the one typically presented in university-level courses.

Scottish thinker Adam Smith. His work *The Wealth of Nations* (1776) contributed to the body of theory that became known as the classical model.

The classical model is perhaps best thought of as the pre-Keynesian consensus, to the extent that any such thing existed. In his preface to the *General Theory of Employment, Interest and Money* (1936), Keynes referred to the orthodoxy he was writing to contradict as "the classical model". While Keynes doubtless was not the first to use the term, it was probably his use of it that made it stick.

The model elaborates on the description of the economy in **Chapter 12**, by assuming that investment, production, and consumption are allocated using markets. In other words, it breaks down the entire economy into:

- the **product market** – the things households want to consume;
- the markets for the factors of production, called **factor markets** – the inputs of the production process usually simplified to labour and capital; and
- the **market for loanable funds** – this is the financial sector of the economy.

In each of these markets, it is assumed that prices move to clear the market so that in equilibrium there is neither excess demand nor excess supply of any good. To keep things as simple as possible, the description in this chapter will assume that the economy is a **closed economy**, meaning that there are no exports and no imports. (**Chapter 16** introduces international trade.)

The result is a model that sometimes seems to assume and conclude that we live in the best of all possible worlds: the economy will always operate at full capacity and there will be no involuntary unemployment. Government intervention through fiscal and monetary policy is therefore useless. With markets in everything, the first fundamental theorem of welfare economics applies and the outcomes are Pareto efficient (see **Chapter 5**).

The classical model effectively takes the simplifying assumptions that form the basis of the simpler models of microeconomics and applies them to the whole economy. The conclusions reached about the ineffectiveness of fiscal and monetary policy and the absence of involuntary unemployment seem strange and counterintuitive. Nevertheless, there is something to the central observation that an economy cannot produce more than the available technology allows, from the capital and labour that are available.

The markets and prices

In the classical model, prices move to clear all markets, but which prices? Since firms and consumers both fund whatever they purchase (inputs, consumer goods) by *selling* things (output, labour or capital), if a couple of noughts were added both to the price of what they sell and the price of what they buy, it would not change what they can afford. So what matters to them is not the **absolute** level of prices, rather they are interested in the **relative prices** of different goods. To calculate these, one of the goods must be used as a *numeraire* – the units in which everything else will be measured. In macroeconomics, this is usually the economy's output, which has a price of p per unit. So **nominal prices** (expressed in money terms) for everything else can be converted into **real prices** (how much output they are equivalent to) simply by dividing the nominal price by p.

Workers will base their labour supply decisions not on the **nominal wage** (w), but rather on the **real wage** (w/p). Firms will similarly base their demand for labour on the real wage and their decision on how much capital to hire on the **real rental price of capital** rather than the **nominal rental price**, and so on.

The one price that is slightly different is the **interest rate**. The **nominal interest rate** (i) records the return money would earn if it were left in the bank for a year, and reflects the opportunity cost of holding wealth as cash rather than putting it into some interest bearing investment. However, over that year, the price of output will change as well as a result of **inflation** (π). The **real interest rate** is less than the nominal interest rate to take account of how inflation will have reduced the purchasing power of the money and interest repaid while it was in the bank, $r = i - \pi$.

It is worth emphasizing that the interest rate used in all of the major macroeconomic models covered in this book is not the same as the policy variable announced by central banks such as the Federal Reserve or the Bank of England. The interest rate discussed here is a price paid by borrowers to lenders, which is determined in a market. The policy instrument normally set by central banks (and which journalists pay particular attention to) is the interest rate at which the central bank will be willing to lend to commercial banks. This policy instrument will often feed through to affect the interest rate as the price paid by borrowers to lenders, by changing the money supply. These issues will be discussed in more depth in the following two chapters.

The product market

While there are many different kinds of goods and services in a modern economy, this model will continue with the simplification used in **Chapter 12** and imagine that the economy only produces one good, called **output**. This represents the real value of goods and services produced by the economy, otherwise known as GDP.

It is best to think of the demand for output by breaking it down into three sources:

▶ some of the output is demanded by households for consumption,
▶ some is demanded by the government as the goods and services they buy on behalf of the public, and

▶ the rest is demanded by firms for the purposes of investment.

The level of investment expenditure by firms depends on the real interest rate.

The amount of consumption by households depends on the level of real income, which, as **Chapter 11** explained, is also the level of output. The amount of government expenditure depends on various obscure political processes, that most economists do their best to steer clear of, and so for the purposes of this model, it is simply assumed that there is a certain level of government expenditure (this does not stop economists from asking what happens if this level changes). Finally, the level of investment expenditure by firms depends on the real interest rate. For reasons set out later, investment generally increases if the real interest rate falls.

So much for demand, but what about supply? In answering this, the classical model follows the same path as in **Chapter 12**, treating the economy as one firm with a production function. So supply is determined by the level of output that the economy can actually produce given:

▶ the stock of **capital** the economy has at its disposal;
▶ the number of workers employed (**labour**) ; and
▶ the efficiency of the method used to turn these inputs into outputs, sometimes referred to as the **technology** of the firm or economy.

While technology is fixed, the quantity of labour and capital available to the economy are determined in the markets for the factors of production.

The markets for factors of production

First consider the demand for factors of production. Since slavery is illegal, firms can only "rent" their workers – paying them a wage per hour they work. And likewise, economists usually think of firms as "renting" capital – even if in reality most firms own their buildings and machinery. This reflects the fact that regardless of whether they own it, firms always pay an opportunity cost of *not* hiring out their capital to another firm. Firms, then, will want to rent an extra unit of a factor of production if doing so would be profitable.

The revenue they make from renting more factors depends partly on how much extra output they will make. These outputs are indicated by the **marginal product of capital** and the **marginal product of labour**, which represent the additional output from using an extra unit of capital or labour respectively (see **Chapter 4**). As in **Chapter 12**, the marginal products of capital and labour are assumed to be positive, but decreasing. Naturally, the revenue from using more factors of production will also depend on how much this output sells for – the price. So in monetary terms, the extra revenue firms receive from employing an extra unit of labour is the **marginal revenue product of labour** – the marginal product of labour multiplied by the price of output – while that from renting another unit of capital is similarly the **marginal revenue product of capital**.

The cost of taking on another employee is simply the wage the firm has to pay him or her, while that of renting another unit of capital is the rental price of capital. As always, firms choose optimally where the marginal cost equals the marginal benefit. So they will employ labour until the marginal revenue product of labour is equal to the wage ($p \times MPL = w$). This means that they employ labour until the marginal product of labour is equal to the real wage (similar reasoning, other factors holding constant, applies for capital).

This means that if the price of labour is measured by the real wage, the marginal product of labour will describe the demand curve for labour (because we know $w/p = MPL$). And for parallel reasons, the marginal product of capital would represent the demand for capital. So these are the demand curves for the factors of production used in the model.

What, then, about the supply of factors? Households generally derive no utility from just holding on to capital, so they have no incentive not to rent it out to the firms. As such, economists usually see the supply of capital as fixed and something that doesn't depend on the real rental price of capital. The supply of capital is simply given by the level of the capital stock that happens to be available in the economy. (For more on the determination of that capital stock, see **Chapter 12**.)

The supply of labour has the potential to be something different. Economists assume that, to households, leisure is a good, but labour is a bad (this does not imply good things about the job satisfaction of those who study the "dismal science"). The benefit of labour is that the wages

The classical model assumes that the payments to the factors of production adjust quickly to eliminate any excess demand or excess supply.

earned can be used to purchase consumption goods, which are a definite benefit to households. So the higher the real wage, the more output households can buy with their labour power and the more labour they will be willing to supply. For this reason, the supply of labour is modelled as increasing as the real wage increases.

To summarise the markets for the factors of production:

▶ Demand is determined by the marginal product of a particular factor of production, which falls as more of it is used.
▶ Supply in the market for capital is fixed.
▶ Supply in the market for labour is increasing with the real wage.

In both markets, the real payment to each factor of production will adjust until the markets have cleared: that is, until there is no excess supply or excess demand in either market. This is shown in figure 13.1.

The equilibrium in the markets for the factors of production determines the amount of labour and capital that is at the disposal of firms to turn those factors into output. So these quantities, along with the technology that is available to the economy, determine how much output the firms in the economy will be able to produce.

The classical model assumes that the payments to the factors of production adjust quickly to eliminate any excess demand or excess supply. Such an assumption necessarily means that there can be *no involuntary unemployment*. **Involuntary unemployment** occurs when there are people willing to work at the prevailing wage, but unable to find a job. In other words, given the wage rate, more workers are willing to work than firms are willing to hire, or, as economists would say, there is an excess supply of labour. The classical assumption of equilibrium in the labour market means that the wage would quickly reduce to clear the excess supply; this would happen naturally as workers unable to work would begin to offer their services at a lower wage.

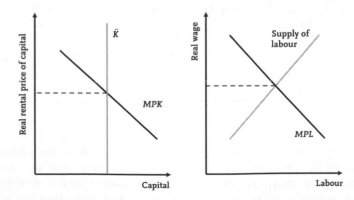

Figure 13.1: The supply and demand for factors of production.

Callous economists?

Almost every developed country has a minimum wage, normally expressed as an amount that must be paid per hour. In the USA, the federal minimum wage is $7.25 per hour, while in the UK, there are four minimum levels, ranging from $9.52 for workers over 21 to $4.04 to young apprentices (at current market exchange rates).

Some economists oppose minimum wage legislation. This is not (normally) because they are on the side of businesses against workers trying to help bosses get as much profit as possible. They see minimum wages as a cause of unemployment and believe that low pay is better than no pay. To an economist, assuming the labour market is operating as above, if a minimum wage is set then there are two possibilities:

▶ The minimum wage is set below the market clearing real wage rate, in which case it has achieved nothing.

▶ The minimum wage is set above the market clearing real wage rate, in which case the amount of labour firms will want to purchase at that price will be less than the amount of labour households are willing to supply, so there will be involuntary unemployment.

So minimum wages might be very good for those workers who still have a job after they are implemented, but for all those who end up unemployed as a result, it is little solace that work has become even more rewarding! Of course not all economists oppose minimum wages, and that is because not all economists agree that a properly functioning market where wages adjust quickly is the best way of analysing the labour market.

Interestingly, whenever government ministers are challenged about the lower minimum wage for young people in the UK, their response often justifies the lower pay for young people with reference to concern about youth unemployment. For example, justifying the decision to freeze the minimum wage for young people while increasing it for older workers, the UK business secretary, Vince Cable said:

> In these tough times freezing the youth rates has been a very hard decision – but raising the youth rates would have been of little value to young people if it meant it was harder for them to get a job in the long run.

> *The Guardian Online* 19 March 2012.

So among policymakers there is some acknowledgement of a trade-off between higher minimum wages and the danger of creating unemployment.

So one of the major concerns people have about the economy is effectively assumed away by the classical model! If there really isn't any such thing as involuntary unemployment, the news doesn't seem to have filtered through to politicians, the media, or the dole queue. And indeed, everyday experience shows that involuntary unemployment does exist and is a large social problem. The usefulness of a model that blithely assumes it away is distinctly questionable.

The market for loanable funds

So to recap: the supply of output depends on the amount of labour and capital employed in the factor markets, and the demand for output can be broken down into purchases by consumers, the government, and firms. Equilibrium GDP is where demand and supply intersect. But what exactly determines demand? As described earlier, consumer spending is just some proportion of their income while government spending is treated as some fixed amount (that the model doesn't attempt to explain). This just leaves investment spending by firms, which is set in the **market for loanable funds**.

What, then, shapes firms' demands for investment funds? Think about a firm with a set of investment projects and suppose that the firm has zero cash reserves, and so must borrow in order to pursue any of the investment projects. The net return on any one of the firm's projects is simply the profit that the individual project will yield less the cost of borrowing the money to finance the investment. The lower the real interest rate, the lower this cost is and the more investment projects will have a positive net return. So more investment projects would be pursued.

Now suppose that the firm has plenty of cash reserves, enough to finance all of their investment projects should they choose to pursue them. Will that change the way in which their investment decisions depend on the interest rate and the cost of borrowing? Perhaps surprisingly, the answer is no. The real interest rate represents the **opportunity cost** of using that money for the firm's own investments rather than lending it to someone else. This opportunity cost of investing when the firm has cash reserves is the same as the financial cost of investing when the firm must borrow in order to invest. Thus, the key result that the demand for investment decreases as the interest rate rises still holds whether the firm has cash reserves or not.

In macroeconomic jargon, the demand for investment is just the same thing as the demand for the use of loanable funds. Because investment demand increases as the interest rate decreases, so does the demand for loanable funds. But where does the *supply* of loanable funds come from?

Once again, it's best to break this down into the three main groups of agents in the economy:

- ► **Households:** All of the income generated in the economy comes back to households eventually as payment for the use of their labour or capital. Some of this will be taxed, leaving households with a **disposable income**. And of this, some will be spent and the rest saved. This saving is known as **private saving**.
- ► **Firms:** The classical model assumes that competitive firms make no economic profits, meaning all of their revenue ends up being paid to workers and the owners of capital. As a result, firms never have any of their own money to spend on investment.
- ► **The government:** The government gets an income from taxation, the difference between households' income and disposable income, while it also spends a certain amount of money. There is no rule saying that the amount they spend must be the same as the amount they tax, and the difference between the two is known as **public saving** (which can be negative if the government spends more than it taxes).

The sum of private and public saving is **national saving** and is always equal to the total amount of output less what consumers and the government spend. This national saving constitutes the supply of loanable funds.

National saving *must* be equal to investment. Recall the division of output according to who's spending the money? Output must be equal to the sum of consumption by households, investment by firms, and government expenditure. National saving has been defined above as the amount of output left over after consumption by households and spending by government. So by definition, this must be the amount invested by firms. What economic

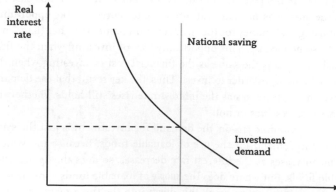

Figure 13.2: The market for loanable funds.

process ensures that investment always comes into line with national saving? It is the movement of the real interest rate in the market for loanable funds.

The demand for investment decreases as the interest rate rises. Meanwhile the overall level of income, household consumption, and government expenditure are all independent of the interest rate. So, the supply of loanable funds is fixed at a level which is not affected by the interest rate.

The real interest rate will move to clear the market for loanable funds and bring the amount of investment in line with the amount of savings that can be lent out to firms looking to invest.

► Where national savings exceed the amount of investment, the interest rate will fall, as savers will accept lower interest rates in order to make sure they receive some return on their savings.

► Where investment exceeds the amount of loanable funds available, there will be upwards pressure on the interest rate as firms will bid up the reward they would be willing to give a lender who helped them to fund their investment project.

How low can you go?

While the classical model, for the most part, rejects the idea that an economy might suffer from a problem of insufficient demand, there is one important exception, where there is insufficient demand for investment. A situation like this will occur when, even at an interest rate of zero, the demand for investment by firms would be less than the amount of national savings. In such a situation, there will be insufficient demand for the amount of output that the economy produces. This is sometimes known as the **zero lower bound problem**, which captures the idea that if the interest rate could become negative, then investment demand could increase sufficiently to use all the savings in the economy.

The way in which the market for loanable funds equates investment and savings is the mechanism in the classical model that ensures that there is demand for all of the economy's output. If there was not demand for all the economy's output, then recessions could occur as a result of deficient demand, and this is what will happen if the interest rate is unable to ensure that all savings are used as investment.

Where there is a zero lower bound problem in an economy, there may well be room for productive government intervention in the economy to avoid a recession as a result of deficient demand. The solution is for the government to spend more money (or reduce their taxation so that consumers will spend more money). Such a policy will reduce the level of national savings and ensure that investment is equal to national savings at some positive interest rate. In effect, the government becomes the borrower of last resort.

An equilibrium in the market for loanable funds is shown in figure 13.2. Once again, the classical model has implications for policies, notably for any attempt to "stimulate" the economy through government spending – what's known as **fiscal policy**. In the model, an increase in government spending will do nothing to increase the amount of income in the economy. Instead, increased government expenditure will simply reduce public savings – and hence the supply of loanable funds – by exactly the same amount as government expenditure was increased.

So in the market for loanable funds, supply falls and interest rates will rise until investment has fallen by exactly this amount. Every dollar increase in government expenditure will **crowd out** a dollar of investment expenditure. Unsurprisingly then, classical economists do not sympathize with suggestions that a solution to an economic recession is for governments to spend money. The increased output as a result of increased demand from the government is exactly cancelled out by reduced demand from the private sector.

Putting it all together

The heart of the classical model of the economy lies in the labour market. The amount of capital at the economy's disposal is treated as fixed, as is the technology that turns inputs into output. So the only variable in the classical model which can change and which will alter the output of the economy is the amount of labour.

The only variable in the classical model which can change and which will alter the output of the economy is the amount of labour.

Output increases as labour increases, but the rate at which it increases slows down as more labour becomes available owing to diminishing marginal returns. This relationship is encapsulated in the production function. The real wage adjusts until labour supply is equal to labour demand, determining an equilibrium supply of labour. Via the production function, the labour supply determines the level of output.

Households' preferences then determine the amount of output households consume and government policy determines the amount of government spending. The remainder of output is used by firms for investment purposes via the market for loanable funds.

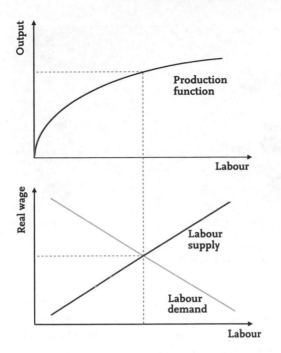

Figure 13.3: The determination of output in the classical model.

The role of money

So far there has been no role for money in the story of how the classical model of the economy works. Before discussing the precise role of money in the classical model of the economy, it is worth pausing to reflect on what money actually *is*.

The most important function of money is that it acts as **a medium of exchange**. The use of money as a medium of exchange eliminates the need for what economists refer to as a **double coincidence of wants** which would exist in a **barter economy**. In order for Anne to trade with the next person she meets, call him Bob, a barter economy would require two "coincidences":

▶ Bob must have something Anne wants; and
▶ for Bob to be willing to trade with Anne, Anne must have something Bob wants.

Cigarettes were used in prisoner of war camps during the World War II as a commodity money. Would they work as well in today's health-conscious environment?

Using money as a medium of exchange increases efficiency because only one coincidence is needed between two people who meet in order for trade to occur. If Anne and Bob meet and Bob has something Anne wants, Anne does not need to have something that Bob wants in order to trade with Bob. He will accept money from Anne, confident that when he does meet someone with something he wants, they will also accept money from him in return for whatever it is.

To an economist, the expression that money "greases the wheels" is not a sleazy indication of corrupt payments, but an appropriate simile between the economy and an engine. Money reduces the frictions involved in transactions and so allows the different moving parts of the economy to interact with each other more easily in much the same way as grease reduces the friction between the different moving parts of an engine.

The money supply and the price level

It doesn't take a genius to see that the more money people have, the more they consume. This observation has not escaped even classical economists. So it might be tempting to think that an increase in the amount of money in the economy might lead to an increase in the amount of spending and the amount of output. Sadly, in the classical model this use of **monetary policy** to affect output simply doesn't work.

Monetary evolution

Money turns up in some of the most unlikely places. In prisoner of war camps in World War II, for example, cigarettes were used as a medium of exchange, fulfilling the function of money. Even non-smoking POWs would accept cigarettes in return for other items, because they were confident other people would accept cigarettes as well. When a commodity with its own intrinsic value fulfils the functions of money in this way it is referred to as a **commodity money**.

The currencies used in most of the world today started as a commodity money. Precious metals such as gold and silver were widely valued, which meant that everyone could be pretty sure they would be accepted in exchange for other goods and services. This actually made people willing to accept gold and silver even if they did not value it themselves.

Coins began to appear when, to save time weighing and assaying precious metals offered in transactions, governments forged them into coins. The idea was that each coin was a specified weight and purity and would not need to be tediously "assayed" (assessed and measured) every time the metal was used in an exchange.

Naturally, as the amount of gold and silver in circulation increased and people started spending it on more and more valuable items, prices went up until the point was reached where actually exchanging the physical metal in each and every transaction became impractical. At this point people began to pay their debts with promissory notes, asking their banker to pay the bearer of a note a certain amount of money. Recipients of promissory notes did not need to go to the bank and claim their gold: they could simply pass on the note in order to pay their own debts. Eventually the government's promissory notes became the only ones that circulated: it was easier to keep track of the creditworthiness of the government rather than every individual who might try and pay with their own promissory note.

Bank notes were still technically linked to a certain quantity of gold until quite recently, meaning most currencies were commodity monies. From the end of World War II until 1971, most countries had agreed to fix their currency exchange rates to the US dollar at pre-agreed rates under the **Bretton Woods system**. The US itself kept the dollar convertible into gold at a pre-agreed price, effectively linking all currencies to gold. But with mounting public debts, the US allowed the dollar price of gold to float in 1971, and most countries have since then allowed their own currencies to float against the US dollar.

As a result, these currencies have been **fiat money** (from the Latin *fiat* – "let it be done"), so called because they are not linked to anything that it valued for its own sake by anyone. Rather they perform the role of money because the government has decreed that they will perform the role of money. Their success or failure in this regard depends on how many people accept these currencies in payment of debts. Ultimately most people accept these currencies because most people believe that they will be accepted.

The classical dichotomy

Economists refer to a variable that takes no account of the price level as a **nominal variable**. Examples include the wage, the interest rate, and the money supply. By contrast, variables that do take prices into account are known as **real variables**, with examples including the real wage, the real interest rate, and the supply of **real money balances** (money supply divided by the price level). The **classical dichotomy** effectively states that there are real variables and nominal variables, and never the twain shall meet. Changes in nominal variables can induce changes in other nominal variables, but cannot affect real variables.

The reason is that there is an identity that must hold true in any economy. The price paid per transaction multiplied by the number of transactions – that is the total amount of spending – must be equal to the number of dollars in circulation multiplied by the number of times the average dollar changes hands, called the **velocity of circulation of money**. Since each transaction corresponds to a unit of output changing hands, the number of transactions, broadly speaking, corresponds to the output of the economy, which can be denoted with a Y, while the price level is given by a p. The velocity of circulation of money can be written as V and the number of dollars in circulation as M. So, expressed as an equation, the identity is as follows:

$$M \times V = p \times Y$$

Now, as shown earlier, Y is set in the labour market. And V depends on what might be termed the monetary technology: for instance, when an economy switches from using gold coins to using notes, each unit of money can circulate faster. But over the sorts of time periods that concern the classical model, the velocity of circulation can be considered fixed.

So on one side of the equation, the only variable free to move is the price level, p. On the other side of the equation, the only variable that the government can affect is the money supply. As a result, if the government were to fire up its printing presses and make more money, all that would happen is that the price level would increase. It's a situation familiar to students of history from Weimar Germany. More recently Zimbabwe has experienced a similar episode of **hyperinflation**.

Another way of thinking about this is that having more money may well increase the *demand* for the economy's output, but the *supply* of the economy's output is fixed in the labour market. So the price level will adjust in order to ensure these are equal.

Increases in the money supply therefore simply lead to rising prices – **inflation**, while decreases in the money supply will lead to falling prices – **deflation**. The irrelevance of the money supply to output is known as the **neutrality of money**: an example of the more general **classical dichotomy** (see box opposite).

Summary

While the classical model makes several unrealistic assumptions, especially as regards the labour market, there is one fundamental truth at its heart, which explains why it is still taught today. There are only three ways to increase output in an economy:

▶ Increase the amount of capital available (see **Chapter 12**).
▶ Increase the amount of labour available.
▶ Become more efficient at turning labour and capital into output.

While there might be departures from this in the short run owing to disequilibrium in one sector or another, if the economy contains well functioning markets, then prices will eventually adjust to clear those markets and bring them back into equilibrium. Attempting to alter the level of output through monetary policy is pointless: all it will do is change prices. Attempting to alter the level of output through fiscal policy will merely change the composition of output, with more output being spent by the government (in the case of increased government expenditure) and less money being invested by the private sector. Once the government has stepped in to provide public goods, it's likely that investment is more efficiently carried out by the private sector. So you would not want to increase public sector expenditure at the expense of private sector investment beyond a certain point.

The ideal public policy from the perspective of a classical economist would thus be to stay out of the economy as much as possible – what some socialists have described derisively as the night-watchman state. The next chapter presents a counter-argument.

Chapter 14

The Great Depression and Keynes

On Monday 28 October 1929, the Dow Jones Industrial Average lost 13% of its value – an event so calamitous it earned it the name "Black Monday". But as if this wasn't dark enough, the very next day, "Black Tuesday", the stock market lost a further 12%. Individuals who put their savings into the stock market lost, on average, nearly a quarter of those savings in a mere two days. This was the Wall Street Crash, a sudden collapse in the stock market that brought an abrupt end to the Roaring Twenties, and heralded in the Great Depression.

Whether the stock market crash *caused* the ensuing Great Depression is a topic that is debated among economic historians, but the crash was followed by a huge slump in GDP and increase in unemployment. In 1929 unemployment stood at 3.14% of the workforce; in 1930 that had more than doubled to 8.67%. In 1931 unemployment stood at 15.82%, and in 1932 unemployment was 23.53%. By 1933, nearly one in every four people who wanted a job did not have one. What is more, high unemployment was persistent: it did not start to fall until the USA began to mobilize to fight the World War II.

Given that macroeconomic theories of the day made no allowance for sustained unemployment, economists were not in an excellent position to offer advice as to how to end the depression. The orthodoxy was ripe for a challenge, and in 1936, the challenge came. John Maynard Keynes (see p.238) published *The General Theory of Employment, Interest and Money*, in which he proposed an economic model where:

► Involuntary unemployment could persist for considerable periods of time; and

► It was possible for the government to tackle this using fiscal and monetary policy – what came to be known as **demand management**.

The main difference between the Keynesian model of the economy and the classical model of the economy was that Keynes held that prices did not adjust quickly to clear all markets in the way that the classical model implied. They could in fact be quite sluggish and adjust quite slowly. In particular Keynes felt that nominal wages (or **money wages** as he called them in the *General Theory*) were **sticky downwards**, which means that while nominal wages are quick to rise, workers resist reductions. So the only way for the real wage to fall is to wait for prices to rise.

The ideas Keynes espoused in this book had a huge effect on policymakers across the world. For much of the post-war era, securing full employment by actively managing the level of demand in the economy was seen not only as a legitimate objective for government policy, but as a duty.

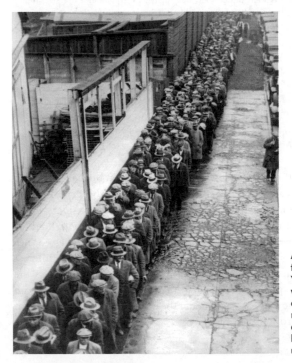

A breadline (queue for food) in New York City in 1931, visible proof that classical economic models could not explain sustained high levels of unemployment.

John Maynard Keynes (1883–1946)

Keynes was born in Cambridge where his father was an academic economist. His early academic promise was rewarded with scholarships to study at Eton and then King's College, Cambridge. After completing his undergraduate degree, Keynes went to work for the civil service, but after two years had become bored and returned to Cambridge. However, he failed to get the fellowship he had wanted to study the principles of probability. It was Alfred Marshall (1843-1924) who offered Keynes a lectureship in Economics, and the rest, as they say, is history.

At the outbreak of the World War I, Keynes took up a position in the British Treasury to help with the war effort. It was immediately after the war when Keynes first became a controversial figure in public policy debates. He had been appointed to the British delegation to the Versailles Peace Conference at the end of the war, but was opposed to the harsh terms imposed on Germany, particularly the high reparations payments. Keynes resigned from the Treasury and wrote a book highly critical of the treaty entitled *The Economic Consequences of the Peace* (1919). The book was a bestseller and only improved Keynes's reputation.

However, *The Economic Consequences of the Peace* is only Keynes's second most famous and influential work. After the advent of the Great Depression, Keynes felt that economic theory as then understood was unable to explain the massive and persistent unemployment that had followed the Wall Street Crash. So in 1936, Keynes published his magnum opus, *The General Theory of Employment, Interest and Money*.

This book was a challenge to the economic orthodoxy of the day (see **Chapter 13**) in that it did not assume that real wages moved quickly to clear the labour market. In so doing, Keynes's model could allow for persistent unemployment. In a further challenge to the economic orthodoxy of the day, Keynes showed how government action, through monetary or fiscal policy, could alleviate the problems of unemployment.

This chapter will closely follow the way Keynes's model is taught in many universities today, which actually owes a lot to the exposition of British economist John Hicks (1904–89). The chapter first considers which combinations of output and the interest rate are consistent with equilibrium in the goods and money markets when prices are sticky as Keynes suggests. As will be shown, there is only one combination of the interest rate and output that will produce an equilibrium in both markets at the same time. The chapter then considers the long run, where prices can adjust, and shows how in Keynes's model the economy can get stuck in an equilibrium away from full employment.

As in **Chapter 13,** the analysis is restricted to the closed economy. The differences when the economy is one that is open to international trade are handled in **Chapter 16.**

The product market

As in **Chapter 13,** the Keynesian model divides demand in an economy into its three sources: households, firms, and the government. And as before, the combined expenditure in these three sectors is equal to both the value of the economy's output and the income of everyone in it. Households and the government spend whatever they plan to, so there's no difference between *planned* and *actual* expenditure in these two parts of the economy. However, for firms, which face uncertain levels of demand, there can be a divergence between planned and actual investment.

Some investment projects are planned and budgeted for well in advance, such as upgrading the word processors used at a publisher to boost productivity. However, other spending by firms can be unplanned, just resulting from fluctuations in demand. When a publisher sells fewer books than they had planned to, the unsold books have been produced so need to be counted in GDP, but they have not changed hands. As a result, they show up in the national income accounts as an "investment" by the publisher in its own books – that is, **investment in inventories.** Similarly, when firms underestimate demand, they draw down their inventories – they carry out unplanned **disinvestment**, i.e. a negative investment. Firms generally aim to hold a level of inventories to allow them to avoid disappointing customers if demand turns out to be higher than expected. These **unplanned investments** and **disinvestments** in inventories are the difference between the level of **planned expenditure** and **income** across the economy.

What, then, determines planned expenditures? In this respect, the Keynesian model is quite similar to the classical model:

▶ Consumption by households is determined on the basis of their incomes. However, Keynes was quite specific about the way in which consumption would increase as income rose: not by as much as the increase in income. Economists call the proportion of any increase in income that is consumed the **marginal propensity to consume.**

"The fundamental psychological law ... is that men are disposed, as a rule and on average, to increase their consumption as their

income increases, but not by as much as the increase in their income."
The General Theory of Employment, Interest and Money, Chapter 8.

► Planned investment decreases as the interest rate increases for the
same reasons as discussed in the classical model in **Chapter 13**.

► Government expenditure is treated as exogenous to the model just
as in the classical model. However, the consequences for income of
changes in the level of government expenditure will be important.

The fact that consumption increases as income increases means that
planned expenditure will increase as income goes up, as shown in the
graph in figure 14.1.

The way the line in figure 14.1 is drawn incorporates all of the features of
the Keynesian model described so far. Even when income is zero, planned
expenditure is positive because there will be some positive amounts of:

► planned investment (given the interest rate);
► government spending (which is determined politically); and even
potentially
► consumption based on subsistence requirements.

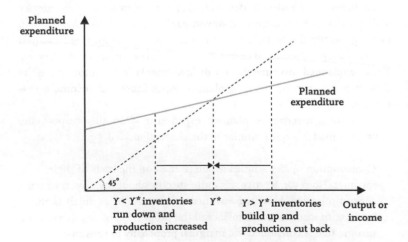

Figure 14.1: The determination of equilibrium output. This diagram is sometimes
referred to as the Keynesian Cross.

The slope of the planned expenditure function is positive but less than one because of the way that consumers raise their spending as their incomes increase, but not by as much as their incomes go up.

If output is less than planned expenditure, that means that firms must have unplanned inventory disinvestment. In other words, they underestimated demand, did not produce enough output, and are running down their inventories to make up the difference. In response, firms should increase their output, and so income will tend to increase.

By the same token, if output is greater than planned expenditure, firms will find that they are making unplanned inventory investments. This just means they overestimated demand, produced too much output, and are now having to "buy" that output from themselves and stash it in a warehouse in the hope that they can sell it later. In a situation like this, it makes sense for firms to cut back on production and so output will tend to fall.

The only level of output where there will be no pressure on output either to fall or increase will be where output is equal to planned expenditure – where the planned expenditure line intersects the 45 degree line on figure 14.1. So this is the equilibrium level of output.

Income and the interest rate

For now, suppose that there will be no changes in the level of government expenditure. (See the box on p.242 and next section for more on this). The total level of planned expenditure, and thus equilibrium output, depends only on investment and consumption. It's already been shown how consumption depends on income, so this just leaves investment, which, as before, depends on the interest rate.

At lower interest rates, there will be more planned investment. When planned investment is higher, that means that the level of the planned expenditure function is higher, which leads to a higher level of income. In essence, keeping all other factors constant, the interest rate determines the level of planned investment, which determines the height of the planned expenditure function, which determines the equilibrium level of output.

This set of relationships is shown in figure 14.3.

If all other factors stay constant, the interest rate determines the level of planned investment, which determines the height of the planned expenditure function, which determines the equilibrium level of output.

A magic money tree?

Suppose the government decided to spend more money. In the classical model, this had no effect on GDP, since it caused investment to fall by exactly the same amount. But in the Keynesian model of the product market, the increase in government expenditure shifts the planned expenditure function upwards. The resulting increase in output is *greater* than the increase in government expenditure.

What causes this? The reason is that whenever the government spends more money buying goods and services, the money becomes someone's income, some of which they go on to spend.

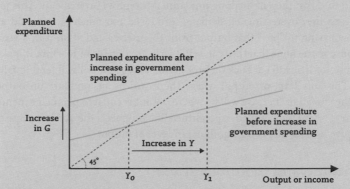

Figure 14.2: An increase in government expenditure leads to an even larger increase in output.

To illustrate, consider the following example:

The government buys apples from Anne;

▶ Anne saves some of the money and spends the rest on bananas she buys from Bob;

▶ Bob saves some of this extra income and spends the rest on cherries he buys from Charlie;

▶ Charlie saves some of this extra income and spends the rest on dates he buys from Dave;

▶ Dave saves some of this extra income and spends the rest;

and so on and so on and so on...

So the overall increase in income ends up being far larger than the increase in government expenditure, as the government's spending becomes someone's income, leading them to spend more; and so on... This effect is known as the **Keynesian multiplier effect**.

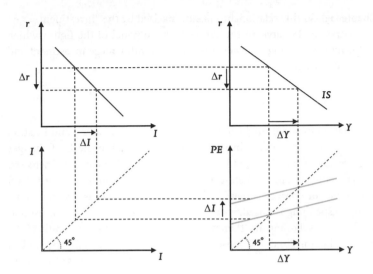

Figure 14.3: The derivation of the investment = savings (IS) curve. The initial reduction in the interest rate is shown by Δr in the graph in the top left of the figure. The resulting change in investment is denoted by ΔI and is converted onto the vertical scale on the graph in the bottom left of the figure. Thus the planned expenditure line shifts up as shown in the bottom right, leading to an increase in income denoted by ΔY. The graph in the top right records the initial change in the interest rate that started everything off and the increase in income that resulted.

► Start from the top left, where a reduction in the interest rate leads to an increase in investment.

► The size of this increase in investment is then converted onto the vertical scale in the graph on the bottom left.

► This helps to show by how much investment must shift the planned expenditure function upwards in the bottom right of the figure where the increase in investment leads to an even larger increase in output via the Keynesian multiplier (see box opposite).

► The increase in output and the change in interest rate that initially brought it about are shown in the top right of the figure.

All of the foregoing implies a relationship between the interest rate and the level of output that would be consistent with income being equal to planned expenditure in the whole economy. When income is equal to expenditure, it must be the case that investment is equal to savings (see

Chapter 13). So this relationship is summarized by the "investment = savings curve" or **IS curve**, in the top right-hand panel of the figure, which is downwards sloping as lower interest rates imply more investment and so higher output.

Fiscal policy and the IS curve

Although factors that might influence government spending and taxation decisions are not captured by the Keynesian model, the effects of changes in government spending and taxation are very much a concern. Increased government spending will shift up the planned expenditure at every level of income (for every given level of investment). This means that, once government spending is raised, every level of the interest rate will correspond to a higher level of income than it did previously. The IS curve shifts to the right, and thanks to the Keynesian multiplier effect, the rightward shift in the IS curve is greater than the increase in government expenditure.

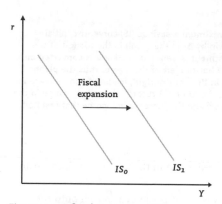

Similarly, a tax cut will shift the IS curve to the right because, for any level of national income, the amount consumers have to spend (their disposable income) is greater, and so their planned consumption will increase. This shifts the planned expenditure function higher for every level of investment and the interest rate, ensuring that each interest rate now corresponds to a greater level of output.

Figure 14.4: A fiscal expansion either by increasing government spending or decreasing taxes shifts the IS curve outwards.

Animal spirits

Keynes did not believe that the interest rate was the only thing that could affect investment. Recall that investment decreases as the interest rate rises because there are a certain number of investment projects open to firms and the interest rate represents the opportunity cost of investment. As the interest rate rises, so does the opportunity cost and fewer investment projects look profitable. However, the expected payoff of an investment project depends on what people will be willing to pay for the output that results. This is based on *subjective* assessments by managers and entrepreneurs as to how much people will be willing to pay for the fruit of the investment, something that will depend on the quality of the output and how much spare cash people will have to spend on it.

This means that if entrepreneurs and managers are more optimistic about their investment projects, or the amount people will be willing to pay in

John Maynard Keynes in 1929, the year of the Wall Street Crash when "animal spirits" certainly took a downturn.

future, then more investment projects will appear to be profitable and will be undertaken at every level of the interest rate. The investment schedule in figure 14.3 will shift outwards, meaning more investment at every level of the interest rate, which will in turn mean a higher equilibrium level of output at every level of the interest rate, so the IS curve would shift out. Keynes referred to these perceptions as to future economic conditions, and so to the profitability of various investment projects, as **animal spirits**.

> Most, probably, of our decisions to do something positive, the full consequences of which will be drawn out over many days to come, can only be taken as a result of animal spirits – of a spontaneous urge to action rather than inaction, and not as the outcome of a weighted average of quantitative benefits multiplied by quantitative probabilities ... Only a little more than an expedition to the South Pole is it based on an exact calculation of benefits to come. Thus if the animal spirits are dimmed and the spontaneous optimism falters, leaving us to depend on nothing but a mathematical expectation, enterprise will fade and die – though fears of loss may have a basis no more reasonable than hopes of profit had before.
>
> *The General Theory of Employment, Interest and Money,* Chapter 12.

A more succinct way of putting the same point would be that success-ful entrepreneurs and managers have an ability to leap before they look. They are more like Captain Kirk than Commander Spock. Animal spirits may be an apt term to describe this pattern. In 2008, Coren L. Apicella and (numerous) colleagues published an article called "Testosterone and Financial Risk Preferences" in *Evolution and Human Behavior*. They found that men with more testosterone had a lower aversion to risk when play-ing an investment game in the lab.

The market for real money balances

The IS curve is only half of the standard Keynesian model. It shows the unique levels of interest rate and output that are consistent with equi-librium in the market for output. The other half of the model concerns the market for **real money balances**. Real money is the amount of money in the economy as measured by the units of output that money would be able to buy. So mathematically it is the total amount of money divided by the general price level. A market for money is somewhat similar to the market for loanable funds that is so crucial to the classical model: the key difference is that the demand for money comes from everyone, all households and all firms, rather than simply firms looking for investment opportunities.

Keynes thought that there were, broadly speaking, three motives for demanding money:

► for transactions
► precautionary; and
► speculative.

The transactions motive for demanding money concerns the money that households and firms need in order to buy and sell things. In this regard the main benefit of money is its **liquidity**. The more goods and ser-vices they buy and sell, i.e. the higher are output and income, the greater the transactions demand for money.

The precautionary demand for money is the money people want in reserve in case of emergency: for example, in case there is a leaking pipe in the bathroom and they have to call a plumber. The demand for money extending from a precautionary motive is relatively static, although the size of one's potential emergencies may increase as income increases. So the amount of money held for transactions or precautionary motives will depend on the level of output in the economy.

Finally the speculative demand for money comes from looking at money as one potential asset in which an individual may hold their wealth. In the Keynesian model, the lower interest rates are, the higher this demand is. Perhaps the simplest way of rationalizing this is just to see the interest rate as the reward that is foregone by holding wealth in money – and thereby enjoying its liquidity – rather than investing it in other assets. When this opportunity cost is lower, there should be more demand for money. The box below describes how Keynes saw this.

To summarize:

► The demand for money increases as income or output increases because there will be more demand for liquidity through the transactions and precautionary motives to hold money; and

► The demand for money also increases as the interest rate decreases, as this encourages more people to hold their wealth in money rather than other assets.

The name's bond...

In the Keynesian model, the alternative to holding money is to invest it in **bonds** (see **Chapter 10**). A bond pays out a fixed quantity every year, called the **coupon**. The ratio of the coupon of a bond to the price of the bond – the rate of return on the bond – is the interest rate in the economy. While the coupon of a bond is fixed, the price of the bond can move, even while the individual owns it. If the price falls over the period that the individual owns the asset, they make a **capital loss**. A movement in the other direction is a **capital gain.**

Keynes's argument as to why the demand for liquidity would increase as the interest rate fell was really about speculation. If an individual believes that the interest rate is low relative to its proper level, they will expect the interest rate to rise. If the interest rate rises, that means the price of bonds will have to fall and bondholders would make a capital loss. Under these circumstances it is better to hold wealth in cash rather than in bonds. So at lower interest rates, there will be more people who believe that the interest rate is too low and will have to rise, so they will want to hold their wealth in cash rather than bonds.

Similarly, at higher interest rates there would be more people who are convinced that the interest rate will fall and anyone holding bonds will make a capital gain. So they will want to hold more of their wealth in bonds and less in cash and demand for liquidity will be lower.

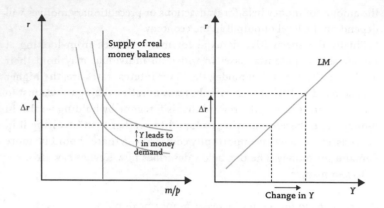

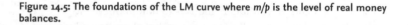

Figure 14.5: The foundations of the LM curve where *m/p* is the level of real money balances.

This negative relationship between interest rates and money demand is illustrated on the left-hand panel of figure 14.5 above.

The other line on the diagram, the supply of real money balances, is simply the overall money supply relative to the general price level. This does not systematically vary either with interest rates or with the level of income, so it is a straight line that is unaffected by a change in income. In fact, it is an instrument of policy insofar as the money supply can be manipulated by the monetary authorities (i.e. the central bank – such as the Fed in the US; the Bank of England in the UK; or the ECB in the euro zone). Equilibrium in the market for money is where the interest rate equates the supply and demand for money.

The relationship between output and the interest rate that will ensure equilibrium in the market for money is captured by the **LM curve**, where LM stands for **liquidity preference money supply** (no prizes for guessing why the abbreviation stuck).

As figure 14.5 shows, a higher level of output leads to increased demand for liquidity at every level of the interest rate as people are engaged in more transactions, meaning their transactions demand for money is higher. With no change in the supply of real money balances, the increased demand for money must lead to higher interest rates. So the LM curve slopes upwards.

Monetary policy and the LM curve

As the name would suggest, monetary policy concerns the broad policy area of the money supply. The effects of monetary policy can be captured in the Keynesian model through the effect that the money supply has on the LM curve. If the money supply were increased, then the line representing it in figure 14.5 would move to the right. Supposing income remained constant, interest rates would then have to fall in order for the speculative demand for money to soak up the extra cash in the economy. This means that there would be lower interest rates at every level of output and so the LM curve would be shifted downwards.

The IS-LM model

The IS curve captures the combinations of the interest rate and output which are consistent with equilibrium in the goods market. The LM curve captures the combinations of the interest rate and output which are consistent with equilibrium in the market for real money balances. The economy will tend towards equilibrium in *both* the market for output *and* the market for liquidity. So the economy *will tend towards* the level of output and the interest rate where the two lines cross (see figure 14.6). Because the LM curve slopes upwards and the IS curve slopes downwards, there will be only one point where the two curves intersect: this will be the equilibrium in the economy.

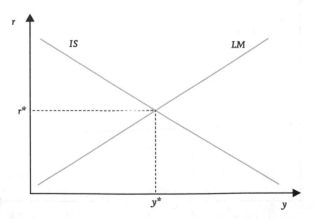

Figure 14.6: The economy in equilibrium at the intersection of the IS curve and the LM curve.

The model of an economy in equilibrium at the intersection of the IS curve and the LM curve can then be used to analyse the effects of various policy options by looking at how those policies will affect the IS curve and the LM curve.

A fiscal stimulus

A fiscal stimulus is where the government uses fiscal policy to expand the amount of demand in the economy. This can be done either through increasing spending or through a tax cut that will stimulate further consumption spending by households. A fiscal expansion has no direct impact on the market for money, but it will (as discussed above) lead to a rightward shift in the IS curve as planned expenditure increases at every level of income, leading to a higher equilibrium level of income at every interest rate.

Take the example of an increase in government spending: the IS curve shifts to the right by an amount that is equal to the increase in government expenditure factored up by the Keynesian multiplier effect. In the case of a tax cut, it is the increase in household consumption as a result of the tax cut multiplied by the Keynesian multiplier effect.

Unfortunately, in equilibrium output does not increase by this whole amount. At higher levels of output there is a greater demand for real money balances to finance the extra transactions, and so the interest rate

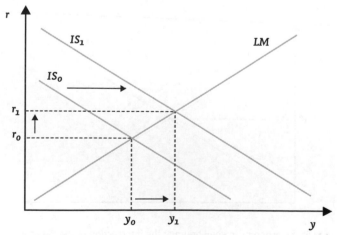

Figure 14.7: A fiscal expansion.

must rise to equilibrate the money market. But if the interest rate rises, there will be less investment, and output would tend to be lower. However, as shown in figure 14.7, the overall effect on output is still positive, and overall income does increase. The increase in the interest rate as a result of increased government spending *does* lead to lower private sector investment (but higher private sector consumption), but private sector investment is only **partially crowded out** and output still increases overall.

So unlike in the classical model (see **Chapter 13**), fiscal policy can have an impact on output.

Monetary expansion

As well as trying to affect the economy through a fiscal stimulus, policymakers might try to affect the economy through changing the money supply. Increasing the money supply will mean that at every level of output, there will be more real money balances available, and so the interest rate will be lower. The LM curve shifts downwards and the interest rate falls. The falling interest rate stimulates investment and leads to a movement along the IS curve. The economy therefore moves to a position with higher output and lower interest rates. This is shown in figure 14.8.

So in the Keynesian model of the economy, there is no **classical dichotomy** and no **monetary neutrality** (see **Chapter 13**). Changes in the money supply can have an impact on the level of income and output.

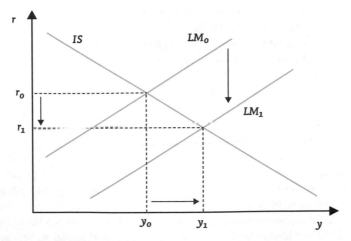

Figure 14.8: A monetary expansion.

Reality bites

As in the classical model, the interest rate that matters to firms when deciding how much to invest is the **real interest rate**. So this is the interest rate used in the IS curve. By contrast, the relationship between output and the interest rate used to derive the LM curve comes through households' preference for liquidity where the interest rate is the opportunity cost of holding money. Because this opportunity cost reflects what would be earned from holding an asset *and* losses in the value of money due to inflation, the relevant interest rate here is the **nominal interest rate**. The difference between these two interest rates is the expected rate of inflation.

When prices are assumed to be fixed, there is no inflation, so there is no difference between the real interest rate and the nominal interest rate. But when inflation is possible, the derivation of the IS-LM model presented here looks a little over-simplified. However, the problem is easily resolved by sketching the liquidity preference relationship in terms of the real interest rate and bearing in mind that a change in **inflation expectations** will be another factor that can shift the liquidity preference schedule.

Prices

So far, the analysis has been conducted with a fixed price level. It is now time to ask how the price level might affect outcomes in the IS-LM model. Look again at figure 14.5: the supply curve in the left-hand side of the diagram is the level of real money balances, the money supply divided by the general price level. A reduction in the price level will increase the supply of real money balances, and so acts just like an expansion of the money supply. Indeed the fall in prices means that the real money supply has increased. So just like in figure 14.8, the LM curve would shift downwards and output would increase as the lower interest rate stimulates investment.

So at lower price levels, output will be higher. This relationship between the price level and the level of output is referred to as the **aggregate demand** schedule. Fiscal and monetary policy can then be used to shift the aggregate demand curve to the left or right.

A monetary expansion would mean an LM curve that was shifted further down at every possible price level, and a higher level of equilibrium output in the IS-LM model at every price level, shifting the aggregate demand curve to the right.

A fiscal expansion would mean an IS curve that was shifted to the right and a higher level of equilibrium output in the IS-LM model at every price level, shifting aggregate demand to the right.

Aggregate demand is only one part of the story; the model also has to take account of how the amount of output supplied will vary with the price level – **aggregate supply**. In the classical model (see **Chapter 13**), the answer is simple – it won't. As prices increase or fall, the nominal wage will increase or fall to clear the labour market and the key determinants of output – labour; capital; and the technology to turn these inputs into output do not vary – as the price level changes.

In the Keynesian model, however, while nominal wages can adjust upwards in response to increases in the price level to keep the real wage at the market-clearing rate, they cannot adjust downwards, because workers will not consent to nominal pay cuts (see the box below). So if the price level falls:

▶ The nominal wage remains fixed and this constitutes an increase in the real wage above the market clearing level.
▶ At the higher real wage, firms will reduce their demand for labour.
▶ Using less labour, there will be less output supplied to the economy.
▶ So the aggregate supply schedule will be upwards sloping.

Prisoners bide their time

To some, the way workers resist reductions in the nominal wage sounds like irrational **nominal illusion** – the mistaking of a nominal variable for its real counterpart, the one that really matters. Keynes argued that it was nothing of the kind and saw the inflexibility of the nominal wage as a natural result of there being many different kinds of industries and workers in the economy.

"Since there is imperfect mobility of labour, and wages do not tend to an exact equality of net advantage in different occupations, an individual or group of individuals, who consent to a reduction of money-wages relatively to others, will suffer a relative reduction in real wages, which is a sufficient justification for them to resist it. On the other hand it would be impracticable to resist every reduction of real wages, due to a change in the purchasing power of money which affects all workers alike; and in fact reductions of real wages arising in this way are not, as a rule, resisted unless they proceed to an extreme degree." *The General Theory of Employment, Interest and Money*, Chapter 2.

To put this another way, workers are trapped in something like a **Prisoners' Dilemma game** (see **Chapter 8**). Full employment can be restored if everyone's money wage falls at the same time. But the privately optimal thing for individuals is to resist the fall in nominal wages in their sector and end up with a real wage advantage. So everyone resists the fall in money wages.

This is sometimes seen as an argument for allowing some inflation in the economy as the rising prices allow the real wage to fall without the nominal wage falling.

Conversely, as the price level rises, the real wage falls and more output will be supplied to the economy. As the price level continues to rise, eventually a level is reached where the price level and the stationary money wage are such that the real wage is the market-clearing real wage, and output is the most that the economy can produce with the capital, labour, and technology available to it. From this point on, if the price level were to continue to rise, the nominal wage would rise with it. Workers only resist *falls* in nominal wages: they'll happily sign up to *more* pay! So the level of output does not change and the aggregate supply schedule is vertical.

Both aggregate demand and aggregate supply are shown in figure 14.9. As explained earlier, the effect of a fiscal or monetary expansion is to shift aggregate demand out to the right. If the economy is in a recession – say income is at Y_0 in the diagram, below its full employment level – then the expansion *does* succeed in raising output and thus countering the recession. As such, the Keynesian model provides intellectual support to those who advocate a more activist government policy in times of recession. The government can engage in **active demand management** or **pump-priming** to lift the economy's output to its full employment level.

This is the core of the policy disagreement between Keynes and the classical economists: whether the government is *able*, through a combination of monetary and fiscal policy, to manage demand in an economy

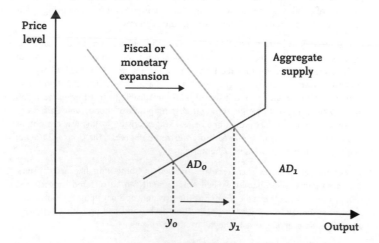

Figure 14.9: Aggregate demand and aggregate supply. The fiscal or monetary stimulus moves the economy towards full employment.

Tents to accommodate unemployed workers to be trained in forestry work as part of Roosevelt's New Deal, Illinois, circa 1935. The set of initiatives and work programmes was controversial at the time and remains so, though there is no doubt that it profoundly altered the political and economic climate in the USA.

and alleviate recessions when they occur. Keynesians believe the government can do so precisely because recessions can occur due to insufficient demand. Classical economists believe that recessions are transitory and will self-correct as prices move to clear markets which means:

▶ attempts to interfere through fiscal policy will not increase output, but simply reduce investment (so reducing the amount of capital in the economy in future periods and reducing future output).

▶ attempts to interfere through monetary policy will not increase output due to monetary neutrality, but they do risk causing inflation with potentially catastrophic consequences (see box p.268).

During the post-war years, a consensus emerged among economists and policymakers based on Keynesian theories of unemployment resulting from deficient demand. The important conclusion for policymakers was that there was a responsibility of government to ensure that the

A New Deal and a long-running argument

In 1933, Franklin D. Roosevelt became president of the United States and embarked on a programme to fight the Great Depression known as the New Deal which involved, among other things, a large increase in government spending. As the 1930s neared their end and war approached, government spending increased further as part of the necessary military preparations. Only in the 1940s did GDP in the USA return to its level prior to the crash. To some Keynesians, this is proof that demand management is a successful strategy. However, there is still some debate among historians about whether this was indeed the case. Most who question the effectiveness of the various New Deal programmes point to the persistence of high unemployment through to the late 1930s.

To any economist, there is much in the New Deal that can be criticized. For example:

▶ New taxes on businesses, encouragement of workers' collective bargaining, and government intervention in wages would have kept the real wage above the market clearing level.

▶ Jim Powell, in his book, *FDR's Folly: How Roosevelt and his New Deal Prolonged the Great Depression* (2005) points out that not only did taxes rise, but they became subject to frequent changes, which created the kind of uncertain environment likely to discourage investment.

▶ Some elements of the New Deal effectively encouraged industries to form cartels, raising prices and thus raising the cost of living. Indeed, as Jim Powell again points out, New Deal agricultural policies led to the destruction of crops and animals in order to maintain farm prices while millions of Americans were going hungry.

Defenders of the New Deal, such as Roosevelt's biographer, Conrad Black, often make two counter-arguments. First, even if the New Deal did not end the longest and deepest depression in history, the work programmes for the unemployed and the maintenance of farm prices did alleviate the suffering of the depression. Secondly, by alleviating the suffering during the depression, the New Deal showed that democratic government was not impotent and prevented Americans from turning to something more extreme as happened in other countries. While this may sound alarmist, Black points out that when Roosevelt arrived in Washington the day before his inauguration, there were guards manning machine guns around public buildings.

economy remained near full employment through careful fine-tuning of the economy using the tools of fiscal and monetary policy.

Just as the consensus around the classical model of the economy was shattered by the Great Depression, the consensus around Keynes's ideas fell victim to events. This time the events concerned the years of **stagflation**, where many economies suffered from both high unemployment and high inflation. These issues are handled in the next chapter.

Chapter 15

The Phillips curve, Friedman, and monetarism

Keynes produced a model that explained the great macroeconomic problem of his time – a depression caused by deficient aggregate demand. Keynes's model carried a prescription as well as a diagnosis – through activist monetary and fiscal policies, the government could prop up aggregate demand and restore full employment. However, by the 1970s, unemployment ceased to be *the* major macroeconomic concern. Instead, policymakers started to worry more about **inflation**.

In the post-war years, macroeconomic policy was dominated by the **Keynesian neoclassical synthesis**, a doctrine that, roughly speaking, took a Keynesian view of the economy in the short run, but believed the classical model was more accurate in the long run. At the heart of the synthesis was the **Phillips curve**, which suggested governments faced a trade-off between low unemployment and low inflation. As you might suspect, electorally vulnerable governments deemed high inflation a price worth paying for lower joblessness.

But by 1967, the synthesis came under attack from a school of thought known as **monetarism**, especially its leading light, Milton Friedman. Friedman claimed that the trade-off between unemployment and inflation suggested by the Phillips curve was a sham – and that the only responsible use of demand management was in controlling the money supply, so that inflation remained stable. If governments wanted to tackle persistent unemployment, they would have to do so directly, through **supply-side reforms**. Events in the 1970s, when Western economies suf-

The natural rate of unemployment

Full employment as economists describe it does not mean that every person in the economy is working nine to five, five days a week. As discussed in the previous chapters, it means that everyone who wants to work at the prevailing wage can do so. In other words, full employment makes allowances for **voluntary unemployment** given the prevailing wage.

Plenty of people might well be voluntarily unemployed:

▶ Students who find it better to study in order to raise their future salaries are voluntarily unemployed.
▶ Pensioners who find they have enough savings to live out their remaining years are voluntarily unemployed.
▶ Housewives or househusbands who have chosen to stay at home and bring up children are voluntarily unemployed.

There is another kind of unemployment which the concept of full employment makes allowances for: **frictional unemployment.** Even if the economy is in full employment, some workers will occasionally become separated from their jobs for a variety of reasons.

▶ It could be that their job has become obsolete. For example, the word computer originally referred to a person whose job was to perform mathematical calculations, a job that became obsolete with the advent of the electronic computer.
▶ It could be that they have decided that they are no longer suited for the job and are ready to move on to bigger and better things.

Such workers, while willing to work at the prevailing wage, will not expect to find the ideal job for them instantly. The process of matching workers to vacancies takes time. Unemployed workers waiting to be matched to a vacancy are referred to as frictionally unemployed.

The level of unemployment that persists in the economy when the labour market clears is referred to as the **natural rate of unemployment (NRU)**, and the level of output associated with this level of unemployment is referred to as the **natural level of output.**

fered both high inflation and unemployment – **stagflation** – seemed to bear out Friedman's contradiction of the Phillips curve. An even stronger repudiation of the neoclassical synthesis – Robert Lucas's (1935–) eponymous **Lucas critique** – then appeared in the 1970s, seemingly bringing the whole area of active macroeconomic policy into question.

This chapter outlines and analyses some of the intellectual evolution of macroeconomics after Keynes, setting out the ideas alongside the historical experience that informed them.

The Phillips curve

The Phillips curve takes its name from the economist who first wrote about the relationship between unemployment and inflation, William Phillips (1914–75). In his 1958 article, "The Relation between Unemployment and the Rate of Change of Money Wage Rates in the United Kingdom, 1861-1957", Phillips wrote about the relationship as a statistical trend that appeared in official data, but explaining this trend required some modifications to the Keynesian model presented in **Chapter 14**.

Long- and short-run aggregate supply

In the Keynesian model, unemployment will never fall below its natural rate (see p.258), but the trend uncovered by Phillips seemed to suggest that, with high inflation, it could. The challenge for macroeconomists was therefore to explain how, as prices increased, output could continue to rise, even beyond its natural level. The solution was to tweak the Keynesian model by distinguishing between a **short-run aggregate supply** curve and a **long-run aggregate supply** curve.

According to this tweak, the *short-run* aggregate supply curve shows output increasing as the price level rises, even beyond the natural level of output. There are numerous theoretical reasons why this might happen. One is **nominal wage illusion**, where workers know when their wage rises, but seeing as they buy such a variety of goods and services, it takes them a while to realize when the price level has increased. As a result, if both wages and prices rise by the same amount, in the short run workers will mistake their nominal wage increases for real pay rises. Firms, by contrast, are concerned with fewer prices – just the price of their output and the price of their inputs – so they will know what the real wage is.

In the event of a general price and nominal wage rise, workers are slower to cotton on to the price rise than the firms and still behave as though the price level hasn't changed. This means they will supply more work at every level of the real wage, falsely believing that every nominal wage rate represents a higher real wage rate than it actually does. There is thus an effective increase in the labour supply. So equilibrium in the labour market will occur at a higher level of employment and a lower real wage (though a higher nominal wage) than before the change in prices. Only later do workers realize that the general price level had increased too, so their nominal wage increase was just their real wage keeping pace with the price level.

Nominal wage illusion may mean these workers will take a while to realize that prices have increased, not just their wages.

When, according to this story, will there be full employment? Clearly, when workers aren't deluded about how much their wages are worth. Or, in other words, when their **price expectations** are correct. The level of output where workers correctly predict the price level is captured by the long-run aggregate supply curve, which is just a vertical line at the **natural level of output**, denoted by $\bar{Y}$ in the diagrams 15.1 and 15.2. The natural level of output is the output of the economy when unemployment is at its natural rate.

As shown in figure 15.1, this all means that the long- and short-run aggregate supply curves will intersect at the level of prices that workers expect in the short run. In the figure, this is initially P_1^e. If the price level came out at this point, then – in the short run – workers would not be led astray by nominal illusion and the labour market would clear at the natural rate of unemployment so output would come out at its natural level. However, as argued earlier:

► If the price level ends up being above P_1^e, then workers see their money wages rise and believe it represents a rise in their real wages and work more in the short run, only later realizing they are no better off.
► If the price level ends up being below P_1^e, then workers see their money wages fall and mistake it for a fall in real wages and work less in the short run, only later realizing their error.

However, once workers have seen their mistake, they reassess their price expectations, and the current price level becomes the new expectation of the price level. This means the long- and short-run aggregate supply

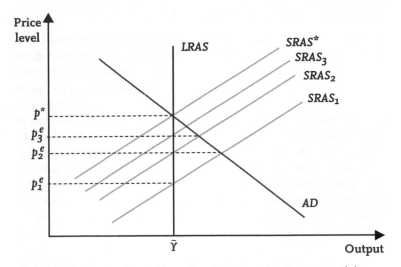

Figure 15.1: If aggregate demand is at **AD**, price expectations increase until the short-run aggregate supply has shifted sufficiently far up that expectations are fulfilled at the natural level of output, $\bar{Y}$.

curves now cross at the new price level, so the short-run aggregate supply function shifts. This process is illustrated in figure 15.1:

► Suppose that workers' price expectations are initially at P_1^e setting short-run aggregate supply at **SRAS₁** but due to high aggregate demand (**AD** on the figure), the short-run equilibrium is at a price level of P_2^e with output above its natural rate.

► But then workers adjust their price expectations to the price level that actually obtains, P_2^e, causing the short-run aggregate supply curve to shift to **SRAS₂**.

► Short run equilibrium prices are now P_3^e and output falls a bit, but is still above the natural level, because prices still end up being higher than workers expected.

► Workers revise their price expectations again and the process continues until output has returned to its natural level and workers' expectations about the price level are met. This happens when the price level reaches P^*.

Inflation and unemployment

So how does all of this relate to Phillips's observation that there is a trade-off between inflation and unemployment? Suppose that the government were to persistently shift the aggregate demand function outwards using repeated fiscal or monetary expansions (see **Chapter 14**). Then the aggregate demand curve will shift outwards every year. Of course this would get very expensive if the government did so by increasing government expenditure every year or cutting taxes every year. That would obviously be unsustainable. However, they could increase the money supply every year.

The annual increase in aggregate demand causes output to increase, the price level to rise, and the short-run aggregate supply curve would play catch-up as workers repeatedly revised their price expectations. However, because of the way workers set their price expectations (just expecting the price level to be the same as last year), the short-run aggregate supply curve will always be a step or so behind the aggregate demand curve. As a result, it's possible for the government to ensure that aggregate demand intersects the short-run aggregate supply curve at a level of output *higher* than the natural level of output *every year*.

This is illustrated in figure 15.2, where the intersection of AD_1 and $SRAS_1$ sets workers' price expectations for the next year, P_2^e, and so shifts

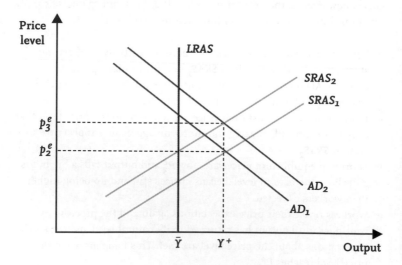

Figure 15.2: Persistently shifting up aggregate demand and short-run aggregate supply perpetually meeting at a level of output greater than the natural level.

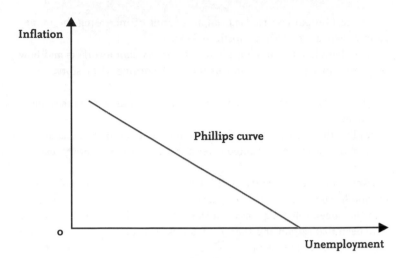

Figure 15.3: The Phillips curve, a negative relationship between inflation and unemployment.

the short-run aggregate supply schedule up to **SRAS₂**. However, when next year comes along, the government uses another monetary expansion to bump up the aggregate demand curve to **AD₂** which meets **SRAS₂** at the same higher level of output. It can repeat the same trick over and over again to keep unemployment *below* its natural rate. The cost is that aggregate demand and aggregate supply are forever shifting upwards and the equilibrium always occurs at an ever higher price level: these increasing prices constitute inflation.

But this need not be runaway inflation (see the box on p.268). In fact, since the aggregate demand curve shifts out by the same amount each year, workers' price expectations are confounded by the same amount each time and will thus be revised by the same amount each time round. This means the price level itself increases by the same amount each period. In other words, inflation will be stable. What is more, the higher output is above its natural level, the greater are the annual shifts in aggregate demand and aggregate supply, so the higher the level of inflation will be. This gives a theoretical foundation to the Phillips curve, a negative relationship between unemployment and inflation as shown in figure 15.3.

Before policymakers and economists get overenthusiastic and congratulate themselves for having violated the classical dichotomy and achieved higher real output *over the long run* as a result of increasing the money supply, there are two points worth making.

First, there is something deeply unsatisfactory about workers and how they form their expectations in this model. According to the story:

▶ workers' expectations of the price level are confounded by the same amount every year,
▶ leading them to supply the same amount of labour over and above what they would have wanted given the actual real wage every year.

Workers in this model are as gullible as a person who keeps going back for another go at "Find the Lady" absolutely certain they will manage to find the queen this time round. It doesn't matter how many times they have been that certain and turned up a jack instead. In reality, while you can fool some of the people all of the time or all of the people some of the time, you can't fool all of the people all of the time. This is why, as described below, Phillips's relationship between inflation and unemployment eventually broke down

However, there is one other point to make before considering Friedman's arguments. Suppose that this model was an accurate representation of the economy. Suppose that workers really were that dumb. Would this be an acceptable way to boost output and reduce unemployment? Remember that the increased output and reduced unemployment come about as a result of fooling workers into thinking they are getting a higher real wage than they actually receive. To put this another way, it is rather like an entrepreneur getting extra work out of their workforce by claiming they'll pay them $10 an hour, but when payday comes only giving them $5 an hour. This is an example of a policy that might increase output, but is unlikely to increase happiness.

The Keynesian–neoclassical synthesis served policymakers well through the 1950s and most of the 1960s: over this period, unemployment and inflation tended to move in opposite directions. But by the end of that decade, the theoretical shortcomings began to show. In 1966, unemployment in the USA was 3.8% and inflation was 3.5%; but by 1975, both unemployment and inflation had increased to 8.5% and 6.9% respectively. The phenomenon of high unemployment and high inflation is referred to as **stagflation**.

In the public consciousness the widespread stagflation of the early 1970s was typically put down to the 1973 oil crisis which made energy – a basic input for almost all goods and services produced in developed countries – much more expensive. However, in reality the increase in inflation and unemployment had started even before then. This was the breakdown in the Phillips curve relationship that left the Keynesian–neoclassical synthesis open to challenge.

Monetarism

In his 1967 presidential address to the American Economic Association, Milton Friedman claimed that while there might be a temporary trade-off between unemployment and inflation, there was no permanent trade-off. Friedman's point was that output and employment are maintained above the natural levels by (for example) "surprise" inflation making workers believe the real wage has risen. But workers cannot be surprised like this every year. If this year, workers are fooled into supplying more labour because they believed inflation would be 1% and in reality it was 4%, their expectations will not return to inflation being only 1% next year. Workers cannot be persistently surprised by inflation being 4% instead of 1%.

The point is that expectations are crucial to determining the position of the Phillips curve, and they are not formed in a vacuum. Friedman suggested that they are formed with reference to past inflation, a process of expectation formation called **adaptive expectations**. Workers in the Keynesian model of the Phillips curve described above had adaptive expectations of a form, but they were expectations about the price level. Adaptive expectations over the rate of inflation make a bit more sense, as inflation tends to be persistent whereas the price level itself does not.

If workers expect 1% inflation and prices do indeed rise by 1%, then output will be at the natural level of output and unemployment will be at the natural level of unemployment. However, if inflation is, for example, 4%, workers will mistake their higher nominal wage for an increase in the real wage and will supply more labour as explained above. But *next year* they will expect that inflation will be 4%. In other words, the short-run aggregate supply curve will shift even further up, so that it intersects the long-run aggregate supply curve, not at the current price level as above, but at the current price level plus 4%.

So in order to repeat the trick and obtain lower unemployment than the natural level of unemployment, the government would have to surprise workers with another additional 3% of inflation, which would mean inflation would have to be 7%. To repeat the trick the year after that, inflation would have to be 10%, and so on…

So the trade-off in the long run is not between unemployment and inflation, but between unemployment and *accelerating* inflation. Figure 15.4 shows the process of shifting Phillips curves which brings this

Milton Friedman and monetarism

Milton Friedman was awarded the Nobel Prize in Economics in 1976. Among other things, the committee cited his work on monetary theory and history. Friedman was one of the early advocates of monetarism – a belief in the potency of monetary policy, but *not* as a tool of Keynesian demand management.

For various reasons, Keynesians of Friedman's era preferred fiscal policy as a means of managing demand in the economy to monetary policy. In part, this was because of fears of a **liquidity trap**, where people do not want to hold their wealth in anything other than money. This might be the case if everyone expects the price of assets to fall (i.e. the interest rate to rise – see **Chapter 14**). If the economy is in a liquidity trap, then increasing the money supply:

▶ just increases the amount of money people hold;
▶ has no impact on the interest rate; and
▶ can't stimulate investment.

Keynesians also worried that the level of investment might be quite insensitive to the interest rate, in which case again monetary policy would not be very effective. By contrast, monetarists believed that money was always important. By the time Friedman was writing, Keynesians were already accepting that monetary policy might have advantages over fiscal policy in **fine-tuning** the economy to maintain full employment. Whereas monetary policy could be changed quickly, there were often long lags in adapting fiscal policy due to the need to pass new laws in order to change tax rates or spend more money.

But Friedman and the monetarists also rejected the goal of seeking to manage demand through policy. They saw the money supply as a poor instrument either for keeping interest rates low or for controlling unemployment. The best that could be achieved with monetary policy was to stop money itself from being a problem. In his famous presidential address, Friedman quoted from John Stuart Mill:

"There cannot be intrinsically a more insignificant thing, in the economy of society, than money; except in the character of a contrivance for sparing time and labour. It is a machine for doing quickly and commodiously, what would be done, though less quickly and commodiously, without it: and like many other kinds of machinery, it only exerts a distinct and independent influence of its own when it gets out of order". John Stuart Mill, *Principles of Political Economy with Some of their Applications to Social Philosophy* Book III Ch. 7. (1848)

With this in mind, Friedman advocated a monetary policy which would be committed to a steady and moderate expansion of the money supply designed to keep pace with the extra money that would be needed for transactions, the idea being to ensure that the money supply grew at a predictable rate.

trade-off about. If the cost of trying to maintain unemployment below its natural level is accelerating inflation, then it will not be very long before attempting to do so will lead to **hyperinflation**.

Because of the way in which inflation will accelerate when unemployment is below its

The trade-off in the long run is not between unemployment and inflation, but between unemployment and accelerating inflation.

natural rate, the natural rate of unemployment is sometimes referred to as the **non-accelerating inflation rate of unemployment** or **NAIRU** for short.

As well as the impossibility of exploiting any trade-off between inflation and unemployment over any extended period of time, Friedman's theory had another implication. Once a country had experienced inflation, it would be difficult and costly to get rid of that inflation, a process known as **disinflation**. Note that disinflation refers to reducing the rate of inflation, or slowing the rate at which prices increase, not to be confused with **deflation**, which refers to a falling price level (or negative inflation).

The reason for this is that high levels of inflation from the past will inform people's expectations of inflation for today. So once a country has had inflation at say 20%, then 20% inflation is what they will have to put up with, just to maintain the natural level of unemployment. This means that in order to reduce inflation, the government will have to induce a recession and put up with increased unemployment. Suppose inflation

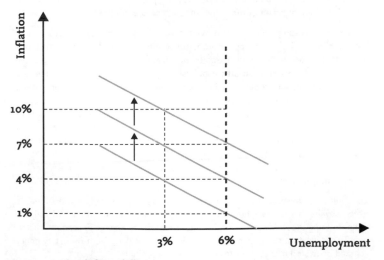

Figure 15.4: The shifting Phillips curve.

has been 20%, so workers expect 20% inflation. Any nominal wage rise less than 20% will be thought of as a real wage cut, and so workers will supply less labour. They will be surprised when inflation actually ends

Inflation – what's the big deal?

What is so bad about inflation? To an economist, the surprising answer is – not that much actually, provided the inflation is widely anticipated and moderate.

When inflation is anticipated people can incorporate it into their plans.

▶ People will be able to distinguish real interest rates from the nominal interest rate and so they will know the cost of borrowing and the rewards from lending, allowing them to make rational savings decisions.
▶ People will know how fast prices are supposed to be rising, so they will know that if the price of a particular good:
  • rises faster than average, then its relative price will have increased; and
  • if its price rises slower than average, then the relative price will have fallen.

This helps them make sensible consumption decisions.

However, if inflation is unexpected, prices stop conveying the information they are supposed to – leading agents to confound real and nominal interest rates, and relative and absolute price changes.

Moderate inflation does not prevent money from performing its central functions as a store of value, a medium of exchange, and a unit of account. But when it becomes very high – what's known as **hyperinflation** – all of these roles are compromised. It loses its value very quickly, meaning people cease to accept it as a form of payment and it becomes meaningless as a measure of prices.

The price explosions witnessed in Weimar Germany in the early 1920s, where inflation reached 29,500% per month, constitute perhaps the most (in)famous episode of hyperinflation, but it was by no means the worst. According to Steve Hanke and Alex Kwok in an article published by the Cato Institute in 2009, the worst hyper-inflation to date was in Hungary in July 1946 when inflation peaked at 41,900,000,000,000,000% per month. That is 207% inflation per day – so if a good is sold in the morning, the money received has lost more than two thirds of its value by the next morning! Under these circumstances, there is no point in using money as a medium of exchange. Any person who accepts money will race to get rid of it and exchange it for something that will hold value better. It is little wonder that in episodes of hyperinflation people tend to resort to a barter economy, or the use of another country's currency.

So while economists tend to be relaxed about moderate, expected inflation, they are keenly aware that runaway inflation can lead money to become useless, drastically undermining the ability of consumers and producers to engage in economic activity. This is what monetarists mean when they say that the goal of monetary policy should be to stop money itself from becoming a problem.

up less than 20%, and reset their expectations accordingly, so the Phillips curve will shift down.

The deeper the recession caused by reducing the money supply, the more dramatically expectations of inflation will fall. So there is a choice about how to reduce inflation: whether to try and do it with a prolonged but small increase in unemployment, or to do it with one very large recession and reset expectations. The latter approach is referred to as going **cold turkey**.

Some economists believe that prolonged periods of unemployment above the natural rate might actually increase the natural rate of unemployment. This is an effect known as **hysteresis**. If the natural rate of unemployment does suffer from hysteresis, then the cold turkey approach to reducing inflation might be preferable.

Play money not pocket money. Children use banknotes as building blocks during Weimar Germany's period of hyperinflation in the early 1920s. Other photographs from the time show people using notes for wallpaper.

On the scrap heap

Workers who have been unemployed for a long time tend to have the most difficult time getting back into employment. The longer someone spends unemployed, the more likely they are to lose skills and become discouraged – with the result that they are no longer seen as a productive worker by prospective employers. For example, an office worker who lost their job in 2000 and took three years to find a new one would have missed a significant part of the internet revolution – meaning that by 2003 his skills would be seriously out of date.

Hysteresis can make high unemployment in certain regions highly persistent: for example, many economists believe that present-day unemployment in the north of England is a hangover from the period of prolonged unemployment that followed the Thatcher reforms in the 1980s.

Monetary policy and control of the money supply

Monetarists regard the task of monetary policy as being to control the money supply and ensure it grows in a stable and predictable way. This sounds like it should be easy. Keynesians also talk of operating monetary policy by simply changing the money supply. In reality, changing the supply of money is one of those things that is easier said than done. Indeed, defining the money supply presents its own difficulty.

The simplest definition of the money supply would be that it would include all of the notes and coins in circulation in the economy. However, as a definition goes this doesn't quite work. For one thing, banks are able to effectively create money through a process known as **fractional reserve banking** (see box opposite). But even in the absence of the money created by banks, notes and coins don't really capture the idea of money in the twenty-first century. The near ubiquity of current accounts and their associated debit cards means that one doesn't actually need to have the physical cash in order to spend money and enjoy the benefits of liquidity. So deposits in many kinds of bank accounts are often included in the money supply as well. Definitions of the money supply differ in terms of whether they are **narrow** or **broad**. Narrower definitions of the money supply only include the most liquid assets that can quickly be exchanged for goods and services.

History provides several examples of how difficult it can be to control the money supply. In the UK during the early 1980s, when the government first started to try and target the money supply, the growth of the measure of the money supply they chose initially, £M3 (pronounced "sterling M3"), was persistently above target. In the USA, as Friedman pointed out in his presidential address, the US money supply actually fell by one third during the Great Depression, despite the widespread belief that the monetary authorities had been trying to increase it.

Reducing the natural rate of unemployment

Friedman's critique of the Phillips Curve shows that the only way to have unemployment below the natural rate is through accelerating inflation. And since indefinitely accelerating inflation means eventual hyperinflation, over the long run, a country must accept the natural rate of unemployment at any given level of inflation.

This gives some insight into how to tackle long-term unemployment. If policymakers believe that the natural rate of unemployment is too high,

How hard can it be to control the printing presses?

The problem is that the amount of money isn't just the number of notes and coins in circulation, and the reason for that concerns everyone's favourite industry, the banking sector.

When banks take in deposits, they don't keep *all* the money in their vaults waiting for the depositor to come and withdraw it; they lend some of it out again to an investor who needs a loan. Once the investor has spent the money purchasing the machines and plant equipment they needed the loan to finance, the people from whom they procured goods and services will deposit some of that money in their bank accounts. So some of it will be lent out again, and so on...

This is known as the **credit multiplier**, or sometimes the **money multiplier**, which means that the effective money supply is far larger than the actual number of notes that have been printed and coins that have been minted. While the government can control the amount of currency, they have little control over the size of the credit multiplier, which will be higher:

▶ the greater the proportion of their money households deposit in banks; and
▶ the greater the proportion of deposits that banks lend out again.

Deposits that banks don't lend out, they keep as reserves in case the depositors come and ask for their money back.

The government can set a minimum **reserve requirement,** for instance by requiring banks to keep at least 20% of the money people have deposited with them in reserve, but this does not allow them to control the money multiplier. Banks may independently decide to be more conservative than the reserve requirement would make them. If other factors in society are changing the money multiplier, then there may well be changes in the money supply beyond the government's control.

To take the scenarios mentioned above, after the Wall Street Crash bank failures led to a drop in public confidence in the financial system. People became less willing to trust banks with their money, so they kept more of it in cash and deposited less in the bank. As people withdrew money from banks, both reserves and deposits fall by the same absolute amount, but because reserves are smaller, the *relative* fall in reserves was greater. So in order to rebuild their reserves, banks had to cut back on the amount of money they lent out from any new deposits they might have received. Both of these trends tended to reduce the money multiplier.

In the UK in the early 1980s, at the same time as trying to control the money supply, the government was embarking on a program of **financial liberalization**. The effect of financial liberalization was to make it easier for banks and building societies to lend money. So while the government was trying to reduce the growth of the money supply, they had effectively unleashed the banks and building societies to lend a greater proportion of their deposits and thus increased the money multiplier.

they should seek to lower the natural rate of unemployment *directly*, rather than using fiscal and monetary policy to keep unemployment artificially low. Since the natural rate of unemployment is a result of frictions in the labour market, one way to reduce the natural level of unemployment is to reduce the frictions in the labour market.

Policies designed to make the labour market run more smoothly are known as **active labour market policies**, and are based around trying to make it easier for currently unemployed workers to find work. An historical example comes from when the UK's Liberal Party's president of the Board of Trade (one Mr Churchill) set up labour exchanges in the UK. These were the precursors of the modern jobcentre. They assisted in reducing unemployment simply by providing a place for workers to "meet" employers (or at least the adverts they had posted).

Modern job centres provide more in the way of active labour market intervention in terms of help constructing a CV and help to get training for people without work to increase their chances of getting a job.

The Lucas critique

The Friedmanite view of adaptive expectations envisages people basing their view of the future on whatever happened in the past. But – though this doesn't make them as gullible as the Phillips curve analysis portrayed them – this is still pretty primitive. A more sophisticated way of forming expectations is to be **forward looking**. To use an analogy from cricket or baseball, the best way to catch a ball after it's left the bat is to estimate its speed and trajectory and use your understanding of gravity to stand where you expect it to land. You don't stand where it landed the last time it was hit.

This is an example of the **Lucas critique** of basing policy on observed statistical relationships. The critique was made by the economist Robert Lucas in his essay "Econometric Policy Evaluation: A Critique", published in 1976. The critique says that policymakers should not try to exploit trade-offs implied by statistical relationships because:

▶ The statistical relationships are a result of the choices made by households and firms as part of their attempts to maximize utility or profit (see **Chapters 2** and **4**).
▶ The choices households make are going to depend on their expectations of what will happen in the future.

▶ Current policy is something that influences those expectations.

So when a policymaker attempts to exploit a trade-off implied by statistical relationships between economic variables, such as that between inflation and unemployment, they are changing policy. When policy changes, households naturally alter their expectations and, as a result, change the way they behave, and this will change the underlying statistical relationship the policymaker was attempting to exploit in the first place.

While most economists will accept that expectations are formed by people who are forward looking, the most extreme version of forward looking expectations formation, known as **rational expectations**, is more controversial. In the rational expectations world it is impossible to surprise households with inflation. People will know how quickly the money supply and the economy are growing and they know how growth of the money supply will translate into growth of the price level. Their expectations are then formed accordingly and the short-run Phillips curve will shift with their expectations.

So if a government ever pursued a policy of expanding the money supply in order to reduce the rate of unemployment below the natural level, the policy would not be successful. Households would know about the expansion, know what it would do to prices, and would not respond to any changes in the nominal wage. Inflation would increase and unemployment would remain the same. If expectations are rational, then there can be no trade-off between inflation and unemployment, even in the short run.

The rational expectations hypothesis does however hold out the possibility of painless disinflation. Recall that if expectations are formed adaptively, then the only way for a government to reduce inflation expectations is to reduce monetary growth and create a recession with less output and higher unemployment. But, if inflation expectations are formed via rational expectations, then there is no need for a recession in bringing down inflation. The monetary authority needs only to announce that they are going to reduce the growth of the money supply in order to reduce inflation and expectations will be formed on that basis. The short-run Phillips curve will immediately shift downwards so that inflation falls without the recession.

The rational expectations hypothesis is a controversial assumption within modern macroeconomics. Critics point out that since economists who spend their professional lives studying the way in which the economy works cannot agree what the full effects of things like monetary expansions will be, it seems unlikely that all households will agree. And this is

Where now for macroeconomics?

The last five chapters have covered the basic development of macroeconomics and macroeconomic theory up to the 1970s. Of course macroeconomics did not stop developing in the 1970s, but these five chapters provide the basis from which further economic theories have been developed, and provide a core understanding of how macroeconomists work. More recent research in macroeconomics seeks to provide proper **microeconomic foundations** for the core assumptions in macroeconomic models.

There is a pattern to the development of macroeconomic thought as ideas are developed and used in policy, but then challenged by events which are inconsistent with the theories. The economists then go back to their whiteboards and start again. It is entirely possible that new schools of economic thought will develop out of the financial crisis of 2007–8 and subsequent recession.

to say nothing of the superior information policymakers have compared to households over what the policy actually is. But if there's one valid point in the Lucas Critique, it's that people don't form their expectations in a policy vacuum. People are aware of the goals of policymakers and the tools policymakers will try to use to achieve them. As a consequence their expectations are as unlikely to be fully backward looking as they are to be fully rational.

There is some evidence that, once households become convinced of the direction of policy, their expectations adapt quickly and that this can make disinflations less painful than they would have been had expectations been formed adaptively. For example, the recessions in the USA and the UK that led to disinflation in the early 1980s were not as deep as adaptive expectations would suggest they needed to be. Certainly this was true towards the end of the period of disinflation, suggesting that the policy of reducing inflation gained credibility as political leaders demonstrated that they were committed to the policy and were willing to pursue it despite the recession.

Chapter 16

Open-economy macroeconomics

The previous three chapters set out conflicting views of how an economy works, but all shared the premise that the economy was **closed** – that is, that it didn't trade or invest outside its own borders. However, even the most introverted regimes – Enver Hoxha's Albania on its lone road to Stalinism and Kim-Il Sung's "self-reliant" North Korea included – have some degree of economic interaction with the rest of the world. Much as it publicly bristles against market economics, even present-day North Korea runs a lucrative export trade in methamphetamines. So just as no man is an island, no economy exists in total isolation from the wider global economic system.

This chapter considers some of the central macroeconomic concepts that arise when economies are **open** to international trade and investment, including **imports**, **exports**, the **current account**, and **exchange rates**. This makes it possible to tackle such questions as whether single currencies are a good idea, when it's sensible to run trade deficits, and how fiscal and monetary policy work in the open economy.

Sticking, as it does, to the macro perspective of the last few chapters, one thing this chapter doesn't discuss in any detail is the microeconomic rationale for international trade and investment. This is deferred to **Chapter 17**.

Income, output, and expenditure in an open economy

Chapter 13 decomposed an economy's **expenditure** into three sources: spending on consumption by households **C**, investment by firms **I**, and government spending **G**. Together, these three items make up an economy's **absorption A**, as in the following equation:

$$A = C + I + G$$

In a closed economy, this expenditure is the same as the economy's **output**, which in turn is equal to its **income** (see **Chapter 11**). But life isn't so simple with open economies.

For one thing, when the economy trades with other nations, not everything it spends will be spent on its own output. For example, China's consumers spend money on American computer games, its firms invest in German tools, and its government buys Japanese trains. In other words, a chunk of an open economy's absorption is diverted from its own output to **imports**. And by the same token, open economies also sell their output to foreigners. In the case of China, this output might be clothes to British consumers, tractors to Thai farmers, or military hardware to the Pakistani government. Whatever the source, a nation's output is bolstered by **exports**. The amount an economy exports minus whatever it imports is known as its **net exports** or **balance of trade**.

International trade means that unless imports and exports cancel each other out, there will be a difference between the economy's expenditure, given by its absorption, and its output, which as before is known as its GDP. Put in mathematical terms, an economy's output is equal to its spending plus its net exports (**NX**), as in the next equation:

$$GDP = C + I + G + NX$$

A second feature of open economies is **cross-border investment** – for example, domestic investors buying shares in foreign firms, or foreign firms constructing domestic factories. As with any form of investment, these cross-border holdings produce output wherever they are sited and this output is sold to generate income for the investor. The twist is that the output is made in one country, but the investor who receives the income from it is in another – creating a disparity between the output and income of both the economies involved. The net flow of cross-border investment income *into* an economy – that is, the income earned by the economy's foreign investments, minus the income from foreigners' investments in the domestic economy – is known as its **net foreign asset income (NY)**. (Note that this is different to its **net foreign assets**, which is just the *value* of its foreign investments minus the value of foreigner's investments in the domestic economy, recall the distinction between stocks and flows from Chapter 11).

Just as a nation's net exports make up the difference between its output and expenditure, its net foreign asset income accounts for the difference between its income and output. More precisely, income – which is known as **gross national product (GNP)** – is equal to output plus net foreign asset income:

$$GNP = C + I + G + NX + NY$$

Putting all three equations together, the difference between an economy's income and its expenditure – its GNP minus its absorption – is the sum of net exports and net foreign asset income. This difference is called the economy's **current-account balance**. A negative balance is termed a deficit and a positive balance a surplus.

External imbalances

At first sight, running a current-account deficit might seem like a rather reckless thing to do – after all, it implies a country spending more than it earns. This is the despairing view usually taken by the media: of deficit countries suffering from a form of economic decadence, living beyond their collective means. A look at the cast of leading deficit nations in the run-up to the financial crisis – the US, UK, Spain, and Greece – only serves to reinforce this impression. However, a deeper understanding of deficits suggests the "morality" of the current-account balance is far less straightforward.

For starters, it matters *who* is responsible for any deficit, *why* they take it on, and *how* they pay for it. Current-account deficits can originate in any or all of the three sources of expenditure – **consumption**, **investment**, and **government spending**. Consumers might spend more than their disposable income; firms can invest more than domestic saving; and government spending might outstrip tax receipts.

Whatever the sector, there are good and bad reasons for running a deficit. Consumers, seeing sunnier times ahead, may accumulate debt on the basis of **consumption-smoothing** (see **Chapter 10**); firms may invest heavily to exploit profitable business opportunities; or governments might run deficits as they exercise Keynesian pump-priming. In cases such as these, deficits can be sensible responses to the given economic circumstances. On the other hand, a current-account deficit may stem from consumers engaging in payday-loan fuelled shopping sprees, firms undertaking worthless projects in over-hyped sectors, or governments lacking the political spine to sort out their finances. This sort of thing doesn't look so clever. But crucially, the damage to the economy that results from an "irresponsible" deficit depends on how it is financed. If, for example, firms pay for an ill-advised investment spree by selling equity (see **Chapter 10**), the people who buy this equity incur losses and firms can continue trading. This was the typical experience of internet businesses in the aftermath of the dot com bubble of the late 1990s. If, by contrast, consumers fuel excessive consumption by taking on debts they cannot afford or secured against an overpriced asset, the bankruptcy court beckons. The proliferation of subprime mortgages in the years leading to the crisis is an example of this.

These ideas hint at a more fundamental property of the current-account balance. When a person spends more than she earns, the only way she can do this is by running down her savings or taking on debt. A country – which at some level is just a load of people – is no different. When it runs a current-account deficit, it must finance this by selling off assets (that is, selling equity) or increasing its stock of debt. This net flow of money used to finance the current account is known as the **capital account**. Any country with a current-account deficit must have a capital -account surplus of exactly the same magnitude – the two cancel each other out by definition.

This leads to the basic truth about the current account: for every country selling assets or building up debts, there must be another country buying these assets or lending money. In other words, for every dollar's worth of current-account deficit – i.e. capital-account surplus – across the globe, there must be a corresponding dollar of capital-account deficit – i.e. current-account surplus – somewhere else. Put more evocatively, *the world's current account must be in balance*. Or to put it yet another way, the world economy is a closed one.

As already mentioned, a number of countries ran very large current-account deficits in the pre-crisis years. This means that, correspondingly, there were several countries – most notably China, Germany, and Japan – that clocked up enormous surpluses. In other words, there were two groups of countries with large **external imbalances** – one earning excess income to be sent abroad, and the other drawing it in to fund domestic expenditure.

Exchange rates

So far the discussion has dealt in definitions – what is *meant* by various bits of economic jargon, such as "net exports" and the "current account". But what *determines* how large these amounts are? A variable of central importance is the **exchange rate**.

Exchange rates (or, more precisely, **nominal exchange rates**) are the prices on **foreign exchange** markets, where currencies are traded for each other. They thus give the amount of one currency needed to buy a unit of another on these markets: if, for example, it costs 0.8 euros to buy a dollar, then the euro/dollar exchange rate is 0.8. If it becomes cheaper to buy dollars using euros – say the euro/dollar rate dips to 0.6 – then the euro is said to strengthen or **appreciate** against the dollar. Likewise, if a dollar suddenly costs more in euros, the euro weakens or **depreciates** against the dollar.

Gyrations in global exchange rates can seem bewildering, but the easiest way to understand them is to remember they are nothing more than *prices* in a particular market. Just as *supply and demand* dictate the number of peanuts per pound or doughnuts per dollar, the same forces can be used to explain the number of euros per yuan or roubles per ringgit. The supply of a currency generally depends on the decisions of monetary policymakers (a topic considered shortly below) so the discussion for now treats supply as fixed and concentrates on demand.

One theory of the demand for currency has already been mentioned in **Chapter 11**. According to the theory of **purchasing power parity**, exchange rates should tend towards an equilibrium level where prices of goods are the same in all countries. The argument for this is based on a form of **arbitrage** (see **Chapter 10**). If, for example, the price of Xbox games was lower in South Korea than Japan, Japanese businessmen would be able to trade some of their yen for won, buy Xbox games from Korea at low prices, and then sell those games at a high (yen) price back home in Japan. At the end of the trade they would have more yen than they initially exchanged for won: for them, this is a won-won situation. But as they did this again and again, ever more yen would be exchanged for won on the market – meaning demand for yen would fall and demand for won would rise – so the yen would depreciate and the won appreciate. This would carry on until

America: land of the freebie?

One of the most prolific deficit nations in recent years has been the USA, where spending has exceeded income almost continuously since the early 1980s, at times by as much as 6% of GDP. As a result of this, the country's net foreign assets position has deteriorated sharply, standing at roughly minus 20% of GDP in 2012. Surely, you might think, this debt will have plunged America's net foreign asset *income* deep into the red – condemning it to lower GDP than GNP for years to come, as part of its output is used to pay off historical current-account deficits. In fact, the opposite is true: the US's net income from overseas investment has remained resolutely positive for the last three decades. How can this be?

One explanation that comes as second nature to many economists is to blame the accountants. US foreign investment often takes the form of heavily branded consumer offerings – think Disneyland Paris or McDonald's in Dubai – while flows in the other direction tend to be of a more prosaic nature. Accounting for these investments in terms of land purchases and bricks and mortar will miss the commercial edge that branding lends to US holdings, and thus understate the value of these assets. Those arches might as well be made of gold.

A second reason stems from the US dollar's position as the world's leading **reserve currency**. Most central banks, especially in the developing world, hold large stocks of assets that they can liquidate in the event of a crisis (**Chapters 18** and **19** discuss further); and the same is true of many private individuals, who will hold some investments for a rainy day. Since US-denominated assets (especially low-risk government bonds) are the easiest assets to dispose of in turbulent times, they are a natural choice for this kind of investor.

However, holding safe, liquid assets comes at a cost – in the form of a lower return (see **Chapter 10**). As a result, foreigners' investments in the US tend to bring in less income than US investments in the other direction – the difference in returns between 1973 and 2005 is estimated at a juicy 3.6% per annum. This is what the former French president Valéry Giscard D'Estaing dubbed the **"exorbitant privilege"** America enjoys from having the world's predominant currency.

So despite the fact that non-Americans own considerably more assets in the USA than Americans own abroad, the income Americans earn *from* abroad still exceeds the amount of income generated in America that gets *sent* abroad. One reason for this is that American foreign asset holdings may be undervalued in the official accounts. Another is that investment in the US is skewed towards the safest, lowest-return asset available.

equilibrium was reached when a won was worth so many yen that prices of Xbox games in South Korea and Japan were the same.

There's some evidence that the theory of purchasing power parity is good at predicting long-term trends in exchange rates. But in the short run, the argument it rests on isn't terribly convincing: transport and

Twenty-dollar bills from Puerto Rico. The dollar's status as the world's leading reserve currency gives it a certain economic "privilege".

logistical costs as well as international tariffs may all stand in the way of arbitrage. And many goods, such as a night in a hotel room or a manicure, can't be traded across borders anyway. Indeed, you don't need to look far to see evidence contradicting the theory. From backpackers taking the proceeds of a few months' bar work in the West and stretching it out to last much longer travelling in the tropics (spending much of the time the other side of the bar) to northern European retirees living it up on state pensions by the Mediterranean, it's clear that the cost of living can differ significantly from country to country (see **Chapter 11** for more on this).

What, then, does shape the demand for a currency? A surprisingly modest tweak to the argument for purchasing power parity gives an important insight. Instead of imagining businessmen arbitraging *goods*, think of investors arbitraging with *financial assets*. The force of arbitrage in asset markets means that, in equilibrium, the *returns* on equivalent assets must be the same in different countries. This is the **interest-rate parity** theory of exchange rates. Where there are tariffs or there are transport costs making it difficult to arbitrage in goods, it is relatively easy to move a promise of some kind across a border, and that is just what a financial asset is (see **Chapter 10**).

One type of asset is a **future** currency contract – an agreement to exchange given quantities of currency at some predetermined point in the future. An important feature of currency futures is that their prices reveal market **expectations** of what the exchange rate will be when the time to supply currencies comes. If, say, it's possible to take on a contract to supply a million zloty in a year's time in return for US$300,000, it must be that market participants expect the dollar/zloty exchange rate to be 0.3 a year from now – otherwise either buyers or sellers would be getting ripped off at that price. Expected exchange rates as given in futures markets are called **forward exchange rates**.

Now suppose, for example, that the Canadian/New Zealand dollar exchange rate is 1, that the one-year forward exchange rate is also 1, that the prevailing interest rate in Canada is 5%, and the interest rate in New Zealand is 10%. And imagine that you have a nest egg of C$1,000. What should you do with it? One option would be to leave it in Canada, where it would earn 5% interest, leaving you with C$1050 in a year's time. Or alternatively, you could:

▶ exchange your money into New Zealand dollars at a rate of 1:1,
▶ earn 10% interest over a year, and then
▶ expect to switch your money back at the same rate.

This would leave you with C$1,100 – an expected gain of C$50 compared to saving in Canada. What's more, if the word "expected" made you nervous, you could use the futures market to arrange in advance to change your New Zealand dollars back into Canadian at a rate of 1:1 in one year's time. This would mean you *knew* you'd end up with an extra C$50 from saving your money in New Zealand – the gain would be risk-free. To cap things off, you don't actually need to start with any Canadian dollars in order to enjoy a piece of the action. You could *borrow* C$1,000 at a rate of 5% then repeat the same trick – earning C$50 without taking on any risk or staking any of your own money.

This kind of international asset arbitrage – known as the **carry trade** – affects the demand for currencies in the following two ways:

▶ Exchanging Canadian dollars for New Zealand dollars now means less demand for Canadian and more for New Zealand dollars. So the price of Canadian dollars will go down in New Zealand dollar terms – *the C$ will depreciate against the NZ$.*
▶ Taking on contracts to swap New Zealand for Canadian dollars in one year's time will tend to push the one-year forward price of Canadian dollars up in New Zealand dollar terms – so *the future C$ appreciates against the future NZ$.*

Putting these two effects together, the carry trade creates an *expected appreciation* in the Canadian dollar versus the kiwi dollar – it starts off weaker and ends up stronger. And this affects the profitability of the carry trade itself, since it now involves holding a currency, the NZ$, that is expected to depreciate, i.e. lose its value. If things reach a point where the New Zealand dollar is expected to decline in value by 5% over the next year, that would be reflected in futures prices and any Canadian hoping to benefit from the additional 5% interest earned by New Zealand dollar holdings will see these gains cancelled out by the depreciation of the New Zealand dollar. It thus no longer makes any difference to a saver as to which currency she invests in: *the return from saving in either currency is the same.* The carry trade will carry on until this condition – known as **interest-rate parity** – is met: any more prospective arbitrage would be to get carried away.

Though there are a couple of complicating factors, most notably **capital controls**, which can prevent investors moving money across borders as in the example, interest-rate parity does seem to give a largely accurate account of how exchange rates are determined. The next section explores some of its implications for policy-making.

Macroeconomic policy in the open economy

How, then, does all this affect the mechanics of fiscal and monetary policy? As in **Chapters 12–14**, long-run models of the open economy suggest these kinds of intervention are pointless because:

▶ increases in government spending just lead to lower net exports and GDP is unchanged;
▶ increases in the money supply simply increase prices and alter the nominal (but not real) exchange rate.

So this section focuses on an extended version of the short-run IS-LM framework where they do matter. This souped-up IS-LM is known as the **Mundell-Flemming model.**

The IS–LM model of **Chapter 14** was based on the idea that prices were fixed in the short run and that the economy must be in equilibrium in two markets: the goods market (IS) and the money market (LM). The Mundell-Flemming model keeps all of this and throws in a third equilibrium condition: that, on the foreign exchange markets, nominal exchange rates are consistent with interest-rate parity. The three parts of the model are then as follows:

▶ Just as before, equilibrium in the money market implies a positive "LM" relationship between the nominal interest rate and output.
▶ And, again as before, the goods-market equilibrium means higher nominal interest rates are associated with lower levels of output (a negative "IS" relationship). *However*, in the open economy output depends not only on consumption, investment, and government spending (all as in earlier chapters) but also on net exports. And an important determinant of these is the **real exchange rate** – how expensive goods are in the home economy compared to foreign economies. If prices are fixed in the short run, the stronger a nation's currency, the dearer that economy's goods will be for foreigners, so the less they will be able to export. And, likewise, the stronger a currency, the cheaper foreign goods will be, so the more the economy will tend to import. Exchange rate appreciations thus mean declines in net exports, and depreciations lead to increases in net exports which will shift the IS curve down and up respectively.

Exchange rate appreciations ... mean declines in net exports, and exchange rate depreciations lead to increases in net exports.

▶ Finally, the interest parity condition means the economy must come to equilibrium at the global interest rate, and the exchange rate will move, shifting the IS curve, in order to make this happen. This is represented by the "BP" line on the graph (standing for "balance of payments").

The three conditions are illustrated together in figure 16.1 below.

The open-economy setting adds a couple of wrinkles to the workings of fiscal and monetary policy compared to **Chapter 14**. Consider a fiscal expansion such as an increase in government spending, which shifts out the IS curve. In the more straightforward IS-LM model, the boost in income from the fiscal stimulus is moderated by a resulting increase in interest rates, which crowds out private investment. But in the Mundell-Flemming model it is even less effective at raising output: as well as leading to crowding out, the higher interest rate sets tails wagging on the foreign exchange markets, with arbitrageurs pouring into the domestic currency. The currency appreciates, leading to a fall in net exports and a

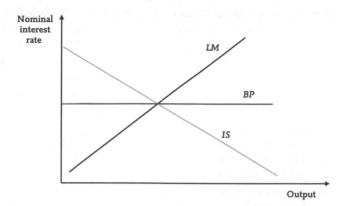

Figure 16.1: The Mundell-Flemming model.

The euro: must tri harder?

One good idea in international economic policy is to fix the exchange rate with your main trading partners – this stability will encourage international trade that can be beneficial to all (see **Chapter 17**). Another good idea is to retain control of your monetary policy – this will give you the flexibility to manage demand in case of any shocks to the economy. And finally, it's generally good to remove capital controls so investment can flow freely across borders – this ensures capital ends up getting allocated efficiently.

Alas, the Mundell-Flemming model makes it clear that it's impossible to do all of these three things at the same time – a problem known as the **trilemma** or **impossible trinity**. To see why, imagine a nation increasing the money supply while holding its exchange rate fixed: the only way it could do this would be by blocking the carry trade that would otherwise lead to a currency depreciation – in other words it would have to implement capital controls.

The decision by members of the Eurozone to form a single currency in 1999 represented a jump from one horn to another of the trilemma. Nation states that previously had the ability to set their own monetary policy relinquished this freedom in order to enjoy the benefits of a fixed exchange rate. Was this a good idea? Overall, it's difficult to say – but for each individual nation, it's a case of weighing the benefit from extra trade and the cost of losing the freedom to tailor monetary policy to individual circumstances. For the likes of Germany, which traded very intensively with the rest of the Eurozone and whose size meant it would always be a major consideration in monetary policy decisions, it was probably the right move. For countries whose economic fortunes were not well aligned with the rest of the zone – such as Ireland, whose main trading partners are the UK and USA – the decision to join has been far less happy.

partial reversal of the initial IS curve shift. Panel (a) of figure 16.2 illustrates. The net result is that, although output goes up, spending is diverted towards imports and the current account moves towards deficit.

What about monetary policy? Here, as before, a monetary expansion causes the LM curve to head out to the right, raising output and reducing interest rates. But once again, the fall in interest rates reverberates around the foreign exchange markets, with a carry trade causing a sell-off of the domestic currency. The exchange rate thus depreciates, leading to an increase in net exports and thus a further expansion of the IS curve (see panel (b) of the figure). In general, as output increases so too will imports – some of the additional spending will go on foreign goods – so the monetary stimulus induces more exports and more imports, and the overall effect on the current account is ambiguous. But the impact on output is startling. As well as the increase in investment as a result of downwards pressure on interest rates, the economy benefits from the depreciation in the exchange rate and increase in net exports.

The fact that fiscal and monetary stimuli have opposite effects on a nation's exchange rate may not seem all that stimulating in itself, but it

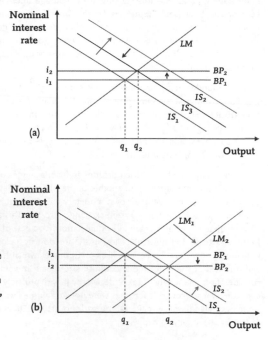

Figure 16.2. Panel (a) shows the effect of a fiscal expansion – the IS curve initially shifts out from IS1 to IS2 but the resulting upward pressure on interest rates causes the BP relationship to shift up (from BP1 to BP2), and the resulting currency appreciation shifts the IS curve back to IS3. Panel (b) illustrates a monetary expansion, with the LM curve moving from LM1 to LM2, the falling interest rate (BP1 to BP2) causing a currency depreciation, which in turn shifts out the IS curve from IS1 to IS2.

Floating currencies – more likely to sink?

The presentation of the Mundell-Flemming model given in the main text assumes the economy has a **floating** exchange rate: one that is set in the foreign exchange markets. But many countries, particularly in the developing world, operate **currency pegs**, where their exchange rate is tied to that of some other currency – usually the dollar or euro – or group of currencies. The most important peg in existence today is the Chinese renminbi, whose price is fixed relative to a basket of international currencies.

Unlike the Eurozone, whose predecessor currencies were united to promote trade (see p.285), developing countries tend to use pegs because international investors won't lend them money in their own currencies. (They aren't trusted not to wipe out their debts by creating high inflation.) The reason for this is that, if you operate a floating exchange rate, holding debts in a foreign currency can be highly risky – any depreciation of your domestic currency will make it costlier to repay your debts using this currency. And what's more, if international investors start to worry about your national solvency, they'll probably sell whatever assets they own in your currency, causing it to depreciate even more, thereby making your debts even harder to pay off. This kind of vicious cycle took hold in the Asian financial crisis of 1997, resulting in mass bankruptcy and IMF bailouts. Though currency pegs existed, governments lacked sufficient dollar reserves to buy back their currencies at the pegged rate when investors all decided to sell at once – meaning the pegs weren't credible.

What do currency pegs imply about the workings of fiscal and monetary policy? It's something of a reverse of the situation with floating rates. With a currency peg, independent monetary policy becomes impossible – assuming no capital controls, which are difficult and inefficient to sustain over the long run, the money supply has to be set in order to keep the exchange rate fixed (see p.285). Fiscal policy, by contrast, can be much more effective – as the BP rate is fixed, a fiscal expansion does not affect interest rates or (therefore) the exchange rate, so there is no crowding out.

		WE SELL	WE BUY
人民币	RMB	0.881	0.886
美國	USD	7.889	7.70
歐羅	EUR	11.20	9.80
澳洲	AUD	6.40	5.40
英國	GBP	12.80	11.20
日本	JPY	0.087	0.0755
紐西蘭	NZD	5.20	4.20
瑞士	CHF	7.40	6.20
加拿大	CAD	7.00	6.20
星架坡	SGD	5.70	4.70
馬來亞	MYR	2.55	1.90
台灣	TWD	0.26	0.21
泰國	THB	0.255	0.19
菲律賓	PHP	0.175	0.145
韓國	KRW	0.0068	0.0052

找換 牌價

人民币 卖出 881 买入 886
不收手續費
NO COMMISSION

The Chinese renminbi is pegged to a basket of international currencies

does have important implications for the way macroeconomic policy is organized internationally. The costs of a fiscal stimulus fall on the citizens of the economy that carries it out – they are the ones who will eventually have to pay for it through taxation. But because it causes an exchange rate appreciation, and thus an increase in the demand for imports produced elsewhere, the fiscal expansion has **positive spillovers** for the rest of the world, where these imports are made. This can lead to Prisoners' Dilemma-type outcomes (see **Chapter 8**) in situations like the 2008 crisis, where monetary policy had been stretched to its limits and a global fiscal expansion was acutely needed: individually, countries might find it in their interest to free ride on the spending of other countries, with the result that there is insufficient expansion overall.

On the other hand, it's possible that a monetary expansion by a country can have **negative spillovers** elsewhere, because its currency depreciates, raising its exports and reducing everyone else's. In extreme cases, this can lead to a **currency war**, where nations bombard foreign exchange markets with monetary expansions in the hope of raising their own exports at the expense of others'. The result of such wars is invariably all-round defeat, as currency fluctuations dampen all forms of global trade and aggressive monetary expansion risks long-run inflation. But nonetheless, they have been known in desperate circumstances: in the 1930s, for example, exchange-rate hostilities broke out, as governments were desperate to stimulate demand in the wake of a vast crash. If this sounds like a familiar situation to you, you're not alone – a number of pundits feared a currency war in the wake of the 2007–8 crash.

PART SIX:

Hot Topics

So far this book has set out the general perspective of the subject of economics and how this can be applied in building micro- and macro-economic models to explain all manner of phenomena. It's certainly been a lot of ground to cover. But if a lot of the earlier chapters have involved investment, **Part Six** of the book offers something by way of a return. These chapters consider some of the economic topics that crop up most frequently in heated debates over contemporary economic policy, and this part of the book introduces three of them.

First up is globalization, including the classic model of comparative advantage and more modern theories of trade based on economies of scale. These suggest the free movement of goods, capital, and people across borders can be a good thing for everyone. But they also show that, in practice, this kind of liberalization is likely to create winners and losers – which explains why free trade and immigration are so controversial, even if most economists are naturally inclined to support them. Next, **Chapter 18** introduces topics in development economics, including why some people and countries remain so abjectly poor, and what kind of policies can alleviate this poverty.

The book ends with the tale of the most important single economic event of recent decades: the financial crisis, which gripped global financial markets in 2007, cascading into the real economy in the following year. It explores how the global financial sector works and how it is regulated, before showing how a diverse set of economic trends, combined with shoddy or dim-witted behaviour by many of the most powerful actors in the economy, set the western economies on a course towards collapse.

Chapter 17

Globalization and international trade

Since the World War II, the global economy has seen ever-quickening flows of goods, services, money, and people across national borders. A process of **globalization**, driven by both technology and policy, has seemed to blur the economic frontiers that once partitioned the world. Economists are, for the most part, great cheerleaders for this, emphasizing the benefits that all nations can reap from openness to trade. But many outside the discipline remain profoundly unconvinced. They point to declining manufacturing industries in parts of Europe, increasing income inequality in the US and elsewhere, and exploitative working conditions in the developing world – and pin the blame on globalization.

This chapter takes a critical look at globalization. It begins with some historical context, arguing that globalization is neither as novel nor as inevitable a force as it is often portrayed. It then proceeds to the theories that explain its attraction: David Ricardo's (1772–1823) classic theory of **comparative advantage**; and more recent models based on **economies of scale**. The basic message is simple: free trade *can* benefit everyone involved. But the theories also offer some insights as to why putting this into practice can be complicated, both economically and politically. In this spirit, the chapter goes on to analyse measures to restrict international trade, known as **protectionism**.

Globalization through the ages

Trade between nations goes back as far as nations themselves, and goods were transported across the known globe along the Silk Road as early as the first century BC. But the first wave of true globalization is generally reckoned to have taken place in the nineteenth and early twentieth centuries. New technologies such as railways and steamships made it possible to ship large quantities of goods and people over long distances at relatively low cost, and the telegram allowed near instant communication in order to coordinate it all. Novel industrial production methods were subject to significant economies of scale (see below). And European imperial expansion across the world imposed common legal systems that facilitated cross-border commerce. All of these factors led to a rapid expansion of international trade, and by 1913 exports accounted for roughly eight percent of global GDP.

This proved to be a high-water mark. The twin traumas of World War I and the Great Depression prompted cries for protectionism that some democratic (and a few populist but despotic) Western governments were increasingly unable to resist, causing global trade to shrink as a percentage of GDP. Not only did the volume of trade stall, but it also became more concentrated within colonial blocs or spheres of influence – and so less truly "global" in nature. The *coup de grâce* was delivered by World War II, which temporarily decimated nearly all trade in many regions, and by 1950 exports amounted to little more than five percent of the planet's GDP. This was the age of **deglobalization**.

However, the post-war settlement in the Western world sowed the seeds of resurgence. Twenty-three mostly developed nations signed the General Agreement on Tariffs and Trade (GATT) in 1947, committing them to a

The World Trade Organization

The WTO came into being in 1995 as a product of the Uruguay round of GATT negotiations, which ran from 1986–1994 (the negotiators were allowed a few breaks). As well as taking over the GATT's coordinating role in future trade negotiations, the WTO acts as an arbitrator in trade disputes between members. Though it lacks the power to discipline sovereign states itself, if it finds a country "guilty" of flouting the existing treaty rules, it can officially sanction a fitting form of retribution to be carried out by the injured party.

As an example of this, in 2002 George W. Bush imposed a set of protectionist measures in the steel industry – mostly in an attempt to shore up his support in industrial swing states ahead of the 2004 presidential election. The EU complained to the WTO, won its case, and was allowed to retaliate, with seeming eccentricity, by protecting its own orange-growing and car-making industries. The main groups hurt by this were orange growers in Florida and car makers in Michigan – two key states in terms of electoral college votes needed to win the Presidency in 2004.

gradual reduction in protectionism, achieved over a series of negotiated "rounds". As well as gradually chipping away at protectionism between all of its members, the GATT made provision for the creation of regional free trade agreements, such as the European Economic Community (established in 1958 – now the EU) and the North American Free Trade Agreement (NAFTA, founded in 1994).

To begin with, this **liberalization** was largely confined to nations in the developed, Western world. But then in the 1980s and 1990s they were joined by a group of developing countries and members of the disintegrating Soviet bloc – some with debts to pay and the International Monetary Fund's (IMF) breath hot on the back of their necks. China began to liberalize in 1979, followed by India in 1991. The GATT's successor institution, the World Trade Organization (WTO – established 1995, see the box opposite), has 159 members at the time of writing, including all the major economies.

These policy decisions were one reason for increased global trade from 1980. Another was technological progress, especially in communications. This greatly reduced shipping costs (for downloaded software, music, films and e-books, these have practically disappeared) and made it possible to trade goods and services that had never previously been exchanged across long distances. For example, the "service" of listening to Americans and Britons complain about their bank account is now often **outsourced** to India, a development that would have been unthinkable two decades ago.

A Mexican farmer stands near an anti-globalization banner before a WTO meeting in Cancun. Attempts to liberalize trade in agriculture have been opposed by farmers in many countries in the developed and developing world.

After a wobble in the aftermath of the financial crisis, trade has continued to boom: exports now account for around thirty percent of world GDP and look set to rise further. The world is more globalized than it has ever been, and technologies and political institutions look sure to keep it that way, at least in the short term. However, there is nothing inevitable about continuing globalization. Some sectors, in particular agriculture, remain insulated from global trade, and many countries are erecting rather than dismantling barriers to international migration. The "Doha round" of WTO negotiations, which attempted to liberalize agriculture, collapsed in 2008 and show little sign of being resurrected at the time of writing. Indeed, the experience of the inter-war years shows that major conflagrations and recessions can put globalization sharply into reverse. There's no reason to think this can't happen again.

The Ricardian model of comparative advantage

Why have so many countries decided to open up to trade in recent decades? For the most part, nobody has forced them, so they must have seen some benefit in liberalizing. The first explanation to be considered is one of the oldest ideas still current in economics – and yet one that many journalists and politicians still seem unable to swallow. It is known as the **Ricardian model** of trade, after David Ricardo, the British economist who first set it out explicitly in 1817.

To see how the model works, imagine Argentina and Brazil can both produce two goods, wine and cars, using a single factor of production, labour. Suppose to begin with that neither country trades with each other or anyone else – they are **autarkies** that produce all of the goods they consume domestically. And suppose that Argentinian workers are more productive than Brazilians when it comes to winemaking – Argentina has an **absolute advantage** over Brazil in winemaking – but that Brazilian workers are better at making cars, so Brazil has an absolute advantage in this industry. In particular, say Argentinian workers can each produce either 100 bottles of wine or two cars per year, but Brazilians can make fifty bottles of wine or four cars. If both countries have workforces of a million, then the possible combinations of national output available to them (assuming full employment) are given by the lines in the graphs below. These lines are called **production possibility frontiers**.

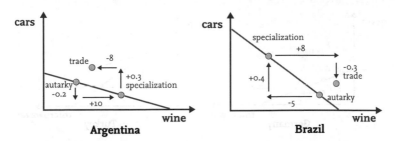

Figure 17.1: The red lines represent nations' production possibility frontiers. By specializing and then trading, both nations end up consuming more of both goods than they would under autarky. (Figures in millions of bottles or vehicles.)

In autarky, production possibility frontiers are like the macroeconomic analogues of the budget constraints used to describe consumer choice back in **Chapter 3**. They say what "bundles" of output a nation can "afford" to produce using the resources – in this case, labour supply – at its disposal. Suppose that, under autarky, each country devotes half of its workforce to each industry. This means that Argentina consumes fifty million bottles of wine and one million cars per year; and Brazil consumes twenty-five million bottles of wine and two million cars.

Sticking to the budget constraint analogy, opening to trade is like a pay rise for both nations – all of a sudden they are no longer constrained by their production possibility frontiers. The reasoning is straightforward: Argentina and Brazil are respectively better at wine- and car-making, so their combined labour resources would go further if more of Argentina's workers were devoted to making wine and Brazil's were put to work in car plants. They could then split the fruits of this extra production between them by trading.

Figure 17.1 shows what would happen if 100,000 Argentinian carmakers were dispatched to the vineyard and 100,000 Brazilian winemakers made the opposite switch. Argentina would produce 200,000 fewer cars and ten million more bottles of wine; Brazil would make 400,000 more cars and five million fewer bottles of wine. There would thus be a net increase in *both* the amount of wine (+five million bottles) and cars (+200,000) available. If Argentina were to give Brazil eight million bottles in return for 300,000 cars, Argentina would enjoy two million more bottles of wine and 100,000 more cars than it did under autarky, while Brazil would gain by three million bottles and 100,000 cars. *Salud* to that!

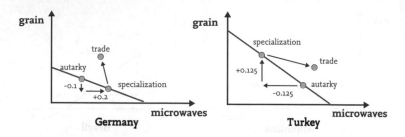

Figure 17.2: As in figure 17.1, differences in comparative advantage mean that both nations benefit from specializing and then trading. (Figures in million tonnes of grain or millions of microwaves.)

So far, perhaps, so obvious. Where each country is better at producing something different, it's clear that everyone benefits from nations concentrating on what they are good at and then trading. But the real contribution of the Ricardian model is subtler. To see this, imagine a similar example, except where Germany and Turkey use labour to produce either microwaves or grain. Once again, assume each country has a million workers but this time suppose Turkey has an absolute advantage in making *both* goods: its workers can each turn out five tonnes of grain or five microwaves per year, while Germans can only make one tonne of grain or two microwaves. The production possibility frontiers are illustrated in figure 17.2.

Surely, you might think, there is just no point in Turkey opening up to trade with Germany – whatever Germany makes, Turkey could do more efficiently. But this fails to recognize that whenever Turkey commits labour to producing microwaves, this comes at the **opportunity cost** of its not using that labour to grow grain. For Turkey, each additional microwave incurs an opportunity cost of one tonne of grain, but for Germany, making one more microwave only involves sacrificing half a tonne of grain. Even though Germany is at an *absolute disadvantage* in making both goods, Germany has a **comparative advantage** in producing microwaves – its microwave output comes at a lower opportunity cost than Turkey's. Since this must mean that Turkey's grain production incurs a lower opportunity cost in microwaves, Turkey has a comparative advantage in grain.

Ricardo's insight was that it is these differences in comparative advantage that make openness to trade mutually beneficial. If both countries commit more workers to the sectors in which they have a comparative advantage, then the opportunity cost each will incur can be more than offset by the increased production of the other nation. If making a

A shore-fire winner

Differences in comparative advantage don't just explain why different nations produce different goods. They also explain why **multinational** firms choose to locate different parts of their productive processes in different countries. For instance, many Western fashion brands locate their design operations domestically and their production lines in Asia, exploiting cost advantages that arise from variations in comparative advantage. This practice is known as **offshoring** when the company owns its foreign operations and **outsourcing** when it pays another firm to carry them out for it.

microwave costs Turkey more in grain than it does Germany, then relocating some microwave production from Turkey to Germany will mean the same number of microwaves but more grain. Once again, everyone can benefit.

The figure gives a numerical illustration. Suppose Germany were to move 100,000 workers from grain farming to microwave manufacturing and Turkey were to move 25,000 workers in the opposite direction. Germany would then turn out 200,000 more microwaves and 100,000 fewer tonnes of grain while Turkey would make 125,000 fewer microwaves and 125,000 more tonnes of grain. There would thus be 75,000 more microwaves and 25,000 more tonnes of grain on the market, so by trading both nations could end up consuming more of everything. Turkish – and German – delight.

Multiple factors of production

The Ricardian model shows how, due to differences in comparative advantage, nations can consume more of everything by trading than they would under autarky. *If* this consumption is allocated so that nobody loses out, *all* consumers will benefit from liberalization, meaning openness to trade is Pareto-improving. Unfortunately, ensuring that everyone benefits from trade will usually require the government to redistribute resources, which, as argued in **Chapter 5**, is very difficult to do effectively. This means that, in practice, trade policies invariably create winners and losers. And in the realm of political decision-making, these **distributional** effects often override the efficiency arguments in favour of openness.

One important reason for this is that making goods typically involves the use of multiple factors of production, whose productivity varies depending on how they are used. In particular, factors may be specific to

Immigration: like it or lump it?

Few topics bring tabloid blood to the boil like immigration. Though it's fair to say much of this has little to do with economics, the idea that immigrants "steal the jobs" of native workers is a surprisingly resilient one. The former UK prime minister Gordon Brown made "British jobs for British workers" a central pledge in his unsuccessful 2010 election campaign.

This is surprising because the argument involves a particularly naïve use of the **lump of labour fallacy** well known to economists. It assumes there is a set "lump" of jobs to go round, and so any job gained by an immigrant is one lost by a native. In fact, if the population of workers in a country increases, that simply means the country has more factors of production at its disposal, and so can increase its output accordingly. There's no reason why anyone need be forced out of work.

Nonetheless, immigration can have important distributional consequences. Economic migrants will tend to flow from low- to high-wage countries, increasing the supply of labour in the high-wage country and thus tending to reduce wages there, and correspondingly raising wages in the low-wage country. Unchecked, this will continue until wages are the same everywhere. This leads to an overall efficiency gain because workers are moving to a country where they can be more productive (that's why wages are so high), but there are winners and losers. Migrants and workers in the poor country obviously benefit from higher wages and so will owners of capital in the rich country – generally speaking, more labour means capital is used more intensively, driving up its return. But native workers in the rich country will suffer from falling wages, as will owners of capital in the poor economy.

In practice, the effects of immigration on wages are likely to vary according to skill level. An influx of predominantly low-skill migrants reduces the wages of low-skill natives by raising supply. But it also pushes up the return on high-skill labour, meaning skilled workers are paid more. Recent evidence from Europe and the US supports this prediction, though despite the very large inflows of migrants these regions have witnessed, most studies agree that the magnitudes of the effects on wages have been small.

Perhaps more important has been the effect of immigrants on the *efficiency* of Western labour markets. By their nature, immigrants are more flexible and mobile than most natives – so they are more likely to gravitate towards regions and sectors where there are existing labour shortages (and correspondingly high wages). Because they respond more readily to wage signals, immigrants tend to work in sectors where they are more productive than comparably skilled natives – an effect known as "greasing the wheel" of the labour market. It also explains popular stereotypes of "Polish plumbers" and "Mexican cleaners".

certain industries – that is, productive only in one sector. For instance, land might be useful only in agriculture. This would mean that if liberalization caused a country to move some of its labour force out of agriculture and into manufacturing, land would be less intensively farmed, and so landowners would be paid less for it. Unless the government could find a redistributive measure to compensate them, landowners would bitterly oppose any move towards openness. This was essentially the situation in early nineteenth-century Britain, where the protectionist Corn Laws were passed in 1815 amid much waving of pitchforks. Ricardo's model was originally stated to show the folly of the laws, which were eventually repealed in 1846.

Even without specific factors of production, the existence of multiple factors can mean liberalization causes distributional frictions. The **Hecksher-Ohlin model**, set out by the Swedish economists Eli Hecksher and Bertil Ohlin in the 1930s, highlights this. Imagine that America and China produce goods using two factors, labour and capital, and decide to open up to trade with each other. America has more capital per worker than China and thus has a comparative advantage in producing things that require large amounts of capital, such as high-tech industrial goods. These are known as **capital-intensive goods**. China, on the other hand, has less capital per worker, and thus has a comparative advantage in **labour-intensive goods**, such as agricultural produce or low-end manufactures. So when the two of them trade, China sells labour-intensive goods to America in return for capital-intensive goods.

The Hecksher-Ohlin model shows what this means for **factor prices** – the wages paid to workers and the returns paid to owners of capital. The logic works in two steps:

▶ *Trade liberalization implies that output prices are equalized in equilibrium*: the price of a traded good in America must be the same as whatever it is sold for in China. Free trade means that producers can choose where to sell their output, so if the price of any good was higher in America, nobody would want to sell it in China. This could not be the case in equilibrium, so output prices must be the same.

▶ *Output-price equalization implies factor-price equalization*, so factor prices are the same in both nations. If, say, labour was more expensive in America than in China, then China would be able to sell labour-intensive goods more cheaply than America. This means that China would shift its production further towards labour-intensive goods, while America would make more capital-intensive goods. The reduced demand for American labour would force American wages downwards, until they eventually reached Chinese levels.

One really striking thing about this argument is that factor-price equalization takes place even without any trade in factors – there's no migration of workers between China and America, but they still end up getting paid the same! The intuitive reason for this is, by trading goods, the two nations *effectively* trade factors: Chinese labour is **embodied** in the labour-intensive goods it sells to America, while American capital is embodied in the capital-intensive goods it ships over to China. Liberalization thus means that American wages will adjust downwards and Chinese wages upwards until they meet somewhere in the middle. Unless the American government can compensate its workers by redistributing some of the corresponding gains reaped by owners of capital, this is likely to be a politically fraught development.

In reality, there are a number of reasons why free trade is likely to lead to less than complete factor-price equalization. Given shipping costs, output prices won't be exactly equal, and the fact that some countries are more technologically sophisticated than others may mean they pay higher wages (see **Chapter 12**). But the model does seem consistent with recent trends in developed-country wages. In the last couple of decades, Western countries have increasingly imported goods that are intensive

Japanese food prices: a soba-ing trend

It would be natural to think that, in democracies, the prospects of liberalization depend on whether the winners outnumber the losers. Natural, but unfortunately wrong: in fact, it often works the other way round.

By way of an example, consider Japan, where less than five percent of the workforce is employed in agriculture but protectionist measures keep the local rice price up to ten times higher than the international level. For Japanese rice consumers this is a seriously sticky situation. So why don't they vote in liberalizing measures that would bring down prices?

The reason is that the large population of winners from liberalization all stand to gain relatively small amounts, so nobody has a strong individual incentive to agitate for change. (As explained in **Chapter 7**, lobbying can be thought of as a public good.) The small number of losers, by contrast, may lose their entire livelihoods under liberalization. As a result, they have formed a formidable lobby that still holds sway over trade policy.

Japan is not alone in protecting an agricultural minority at the expense of the urban majority. Both the United States and the European Union have similar protectionist policies towards their agricultural industries, which endure for similar reasons. To paraphrase Winston Churchill (who defected from the Conservatives to the Liberals over the issue of free trade), never, in the field of political lobbying, has so much been taken by so few at the expense of so many.

in low-skilled labour, such as toys and textiles, while exporting goods that are intensive in high-skilled labour, such as software and aircraft. And in accordance with the Hecksher-Ohlin model, during this period low-skilled wages have stagnated while high-skilled wages have shot up, leading to increased income inequality.

The model therefore supports the claim that globalization is responsible for growing income inequality in the Western world. But this may not be the whole story. There are other, competing explanations for increased inequality, mostly based on the pattern of technological development witnessed during the same period as globalization (as set out in **Chapter 12**). So far, the jury is out as to which is the most important.

New trade theory and economies of scale

The Ricardian model and its multiple-factor variants remain at the heart of economic thinking about international trade. But since the 1970s it's been complemented by a new set of models, collectively dubbed **new trade theory** and associated with the Nobel Prize winner Paul Krugman (1953–), which explain aspects of trade that don't seem to result from comparative advantage alone. A core theme in this body of work is the importance of **economies of scale**.

Internal economies of scale

Theories of trade based on comparative advantage predict that nations will generally export goods they can produce at low opportunity cost and import those they cannot. In these theories countries *do not* exchange different types of the *same* good, since they can't *both* have comparative advantages over each other in making it. In the jargon, trade is **inter-industry** rather than **intra-industry**.

However, you only need to take a stroll along any European street, *boulevard*, or *Straße* to notice that this doesn't reflect reality. You're likely to find a British-built Honda, French Peugeot, or German Audi on any one of them, so all three countries export and import cars to and from each other. The fact that the British-built car is made by a Japanese firm just makes things even more cosmopolitan. Trade theories based on **internal economies of scale** offer some way of understanding this.

Internal economies of scale were first encountered in **Chapter 4**, where they were just called "economies of scale". They arise within a firm whenever its average cost of production falls as its output increases. To see their relevance to trade, it's best to see how they affect a particular industry structure. So imagine an industry with significant internal economies of scale where there are **no barriers to entry or exit** and firms make **differentiated products**. The car market fits into this mould: it is possible to set up a new car-maker (and plenty have shut down in recent years); and each manufacturer is in some way distinct – so, for example, Hondas, Peugeots, and Audis each appeal to different buyers.

Because they offer differentiated products, individual firms retain some control over the price they ask for their output: in the language of microeconomics, they are **price-setters** rather than **price-takers**. However, if prices are so high that firms in the industry make positive profits, the absence of barriers to entry means new firms will spring up looking for a piece of the action; and, similarly, firms will leave if they make a loss. This kind of industry structure is known as **monopolistic competition** – "monopolistic" in that firms set their own prices but "competitive" insofar as profits tend to zero (note the difference with the *non-competitive* oligopoly models in **Chapter 8**).

To keep things simple, assume to begin with that this industry serves a fixed level of demand in an autarchic economy. The fewer firms that exist in the industry, the less intensively they'll compete against each other, so the higher prices will be (see **Chapter 8**). And the fewer firms there are, the more each will produce, so (given economies of scale) the lower average costs will be. Both of these factors mean that fewer firms equate to higher profits.

The industry is in equilibrium – there is no entry or exit – whenever profits are zero, which happens where price equals average cost (see **Chapter 4**). As panel (a) of figure 17.3 shows, this means there are n firms in equilibrium with prices set at p.

How does this change when the economy opens up to trade? Essentially, when a group of countries trade with each other, they **integrate** their markets. So the overall level of demand to be served goes up. Prices will depend on the intensity of competition in the usual way, but average costs will now be lower for any given number of firms: with a larger market, each will be making more output so they'll benefit from greater economies of scale. Panel (b) of figure 17.3 shows that, in equilibrium, this means there will be more firms serving the economy (though some of these will be foreign). All will charge a lower price.

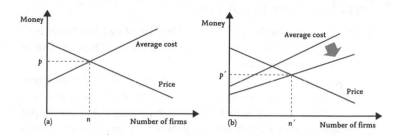

Figure 17.3: In a monopolistically competitive industry with economies of scale, costs increase and the price decreases as more firms join the industry (both are measured in "money" on the vertical axis). (The number of firms is n). Equilibrium is where these are equal so profits are zero panel [a]). Integrating markets means that a given number of firms will have more consumers, so average costs fall, meaning there are more firms charging a lower price in equilibrium (panel [b]).

For consumers, this can only be a good thing. Lower prices leave them better off and an increase in the number of firms means there are more **varieties** of the good to choose from, so they can buy a specification more closely tailored to their preferences. Some firms, on the other hand, will shut down: output per firm across the *integrated* market goes up, so if output across all markets stays the same there must be fewer firms overall. Yet those that survive will expand their output, taking on some of the workers and capital laid off by the firms that disband.

As with the Ricardian model, intra-industry trade based on internal economies of scale allows an economy to consume more of *everything*. It makes certain sectors, such as car-making, more efficient, leaving spare productive resources that can be used to make other goods – so there is a potential Pareto improvement. What's more, the distributive effects of liberalization do not seem as extreme as with inter-industry trade. Though some factors will change sectors, which can be dislocating, there isn't the wholesale economic reorientation that can arise from inter-industry trade. This perhaps explains why nations have proved far readier to liberalize trade with countries where there are no great differences in comparative advantage to be exploited (for instance, European economies forming the European Union).

> Intra-industry trade based on internal economies of scale allows an economy to consume more of *everything*.

External economies of scale

A form of economy of scale yet to be considered arises when a firm's average cost falls because the *local industry's* output increases. These are known as **external economies of scale**.

To see why external economies of scale might occur, consider the recent emergence of K-pop, a genre of music originating from Seoul and variously enjoyed and despised across the world, especially in Asia. As the size of the K-pop industry grew, it became possible for specialized suppliers to the industry – agencies, publicists, and so forth – to set up in Seoul. Similarly, with more records being made, specialist employees – session musicians, A&R men, etc – flocked to the area looking for work, making it easier for local firms to hire them, an effect known as **labour-market pooling**. Finally, as industry workers moved between firms and talked to each other about making records, local firms would learn from each

other how to improve their production techniques – in technical terms, there would be **knowledge spillovers**. All of these effects mean that the size of the recording industry in Seoul makes it cheaper for an individual label to produce a K-pop record there.

External economies of scale explain why particular countries can end up specializing in certain goods. If some industries **cluster** in particular localities and then sell to other areas, this reduces average costs in that industry, making it more efficient.

Clusters are a long-standing feature of the world economy. Nineteenth-century clusters are reflected in the nicknames of English

K-pop: by the time Psy's 2012 hit "Gangnam Style" went global the K-pop industry had already benefited from years of labour-market pooling and knowledge spillovers.

Learning the easy way

Many industries in the course of history have shown **dynamic increasing returns**, where average costs fall over time as firms gain experience of producing output more efficiently. These **learning curves** tend to be particularly pronounced in the early years of a sector's existence.

Learning curves form the basis of the **infant-industry argument** for protectionism. By temporarily sheltering firms in a nascent sector from international competition, the government gives them the chance to learn how to produce as efficiently as their foreign rivals. Once this has happened, protectionist measures can be lifted, allowing the domestic industry to compete internationally. Seemingly successful examples of this include car-making in a number of East Asian countries; and many governments today use the infant-industry argument to justify protecting their "green energy" sectors. Whether this kind of protectionism can be effective at promoting economic development will be considered in **Chapter 18**.

However, policymakers would be well advised to make the most of their own learning when it comes to coddling infant industries. The existence of learning curves does not alter the fact that protectionism is socially costly while it is in place; so the short-run costs of nurturing an industry must be outweighed by the long-run benefits. And protectionism isn't always necessary to allow an industry to grow – plenty of technology firms rely on private capital while they find their feet.

soccer teams, including Sheffield United ("the Blades" – steel), Stoke City ("the Potters" – pottery), and Wycombe Wanderers ("the Chairboys" – furniture). Well-known modern-day clusters include Silicon Valley in California, Bollywood in Mumbai, and the fashion industry in Milan. More obscurely, Hangji in China (population 35,000) has been a major centre of the dental hygiene industry for over a century, making thirty percent of the world's toothbrushes in 2009. You could call this a case of economies of scaling.

Protectionism

The previous discussion highlights various reasons why governments might want to restrict international trade, even though doing so is generally inefficient. The practice of erecting **trade barriers** in order to do this is known as **protectionism**.

One of the most commonly used trade barriers is a **tariff**. Tariffs are simply consumption taxes that are applied only to imported goods. As such, just like any other consumption tax, they drive a wedge between the price consumers pay and that producers receive. This means Pareto-improving trades between consumers and foreign firms are not exploited, and thus results in a deadweight loss. (See the argument in **Chapter 5**.) What's more, since the tariff discriminates between domestic and international firms, there's a further efficiency loss resulting from the fact that some consumers buy domestically produced goods when imports could have been supplied at a lower marginal cost.

Figure 17.4: Panel (a) shows the situation before a tariff is levied – the global shoe price is p^* and India buys q^* shoes; as many as it can supply domestically at p^* with the rest imported. Panel (b) then depicts the effect of the 500 rupee tariff. Because India buys fewer shoes, the global price falls by 250 rupees to p^*-250, but Indian consumers must pay p^*+250. Indian firms will supply more shoes at this latter price so domestic output increases, with a more than offsetting fall in imports. Finally, panel (c) illustrates the welfare implications of this from India's point of view. Area A was consumer surplus before the tariff and is Indian producer surplus after it; and B was consumer surplus before the tariff and government revenue after it. C is an efficiency loss reflecting consumers switching from cheap imports to expensive Indian shoes, and D is an efficiency loss resulting from fewer Pareto-improving trades being made. E is the terms of trade gain: increased government revenue at the expense of foreign firms, who charge less for shoes as a result of the tariff.

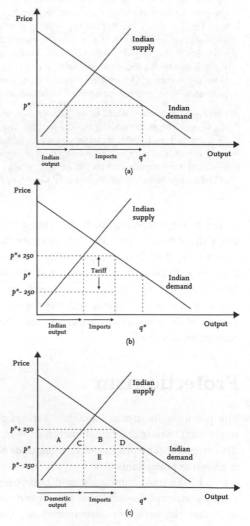

However, the fact that tariffs are applied only to foreign output complicates governments' incentives. To illustrate this, suppose India imposes a 500 rupee tariff on shoes. In the global market for imported shoes, the higher prices Indians have to pay means they will buy less, so *global* prices (i.e. not including the tariff) will fall. And since India makes up a large chunk of the global shoe market (it does, after all, have the world's second-largest population of feet), it's likely that this price change will be fairly significant, though it obviously can't be more than 500 rupees. So imagine the global shoe price falls by 250 rupees, which implies that the Indian price (the global price plus the tariff) goes *up* by 250 rupees. The effect of this on Indian welfare is illustrated in figure 17.4 opposite.

From India's point of view, evaluating the tariff involves weighing up the following changes:

▶ Indian consumers now pay 250 rupees more for their shoes, leading to a fall in consumer surplus. *Some* of this lost surplus is recovered by domestic producers, who now receive 250 rupees more for the shoes they sell; and *some* of it goes to the government in the form of tax revenue. But the remainder is an **efficiency loss** – either as a deadweight loss resulting from less trade or because consumers switch from low marginal cost imports to high marginal cost domestic output.

▶ However, by slapping on the tariff, the government reduces the price of imported shoes by 250 rupees. This benefits the Indian government at the expense of foreign firms. Because India now pays less for its imports, it benefits from a **terms of trade gain**.

This leads to an intriguing conclusion: if the terms of trade gain is larger than the efficiency loss, India itself benefits overall from imposing the tariff. This is a central plank of what is called a **mercantilist** or **beggar-thy-neighbour** trade policy – where protectionism is used to promote individual countries' interests at the expense of others. The result of widespread mercantilism can be a **Prisoners' Dilemma** (see **Chapter 8**) where all countries make the individually rational choice to impose tariffs on imports, even though everyone would benefit if they all agreed to remove them.

Note, however, that the terms of trade gain arises only because India's tariff affects the price it pays for imported shoes. This happens only when India makes up a significant part of global shoe demand: a reduction in the number of shoes it imports will cause the global price to fall. If, by contrast, a small country such as Bhutan imposed the same measure, there

Creative diversion

Much of the world's trade takes place within regional blocs where internal barriers to trade are largely eliminated. Examples of such groupings include the EU, NAFTA, ASEAN in southeast Asia, and Mercosur in Latin America. They are known as **free-trade areas** when each member can set barriers to external trade independently (as in NAFTA) and **customs unions** where all members set common external barriers (as in the EU).

Given the inherent difficulties of getting countries to agree to global free trade, you might think regional free-trade agreements are a reasonable step in the right direction – allowing some, but not all, efficiency-enhancing international trade to take place. Unfortunately, the reality isn't so simple. By dismantling internal barriers to trade, these agreements are responsible for **trade creation** between their members – efficient trade that would not have been possible if the barriers had been present. But they can also lead to inefficient **trade diversion**, where efficient trade with non-members is replaced by less efficient trade with members because non-members face trade barriers while members do not.

would be a minimal impact on the global shoe price, so the terms of trade gain would be negligible. Small countries therefore have a much weaker incentive to impose tariffs than large ones.

Other forms of protectionism shift the balance of domestic and international production in a similar fashion to tariffs. **Quotas** are simple restrictions on the amount of a good a country can import – in their most extreme form, where the quota is set at zero, they are known as **embargoes**. And **export subsidies**, of which the EU's Common Agricultural Policy is an egregious example, boost exports by lowering the price foreign countries pay for them (note that this involves a terms of trade loss!).

More subtle protectionist measures involve setting regulatory standards that are easier for domestic producers to meet than their foreign rivals. Examples include the US's federally mandated "dolphin-safe" standards for tuna, which are more stringent in waters fished by Mexican boats than those plied by American boats. These were ruled discriminatory by the WTO in 2012.

However, distinguishing this kind of protectionism from more enlightened social policy can be difficult. For instance, the EU's regulation of genetically modified food is far tighter than the US's, and this has the effect of making it difficult for US farmers to export to Europe. Do the regulations spring from genuine environmental concern in the EU or a cynical desire to protect farmers? Or maybe a bit of both?

Chapter 18

Development economics

The world is a richer, healthier, more educated, and freer place than it ever has been. According to the IMF, the *world's* GDP per capita currently stands at more than $12,000 – comfortably above the subsistence levels seen globally until the Industrial Revolution. But not everywhere has shared in this prosperity. One billion people still scrape by on less than $1.25 per day, facing a degree of deprivation unimaginable to anyone in the West. **Development economics** is the economic study of such poverty and the countries in which it is prevalent.

At first sight, it might seem puzzling that development warrants its own "subfield" in economics. Why can't poor people and poor countries be analysed using the same tools as everyone else, as in earlier chapters? The answer is that they can and are, but extreme poverty also introduces exceptional problems – in particular **poverty traps** – and the experience of global development raises questions that are important in themselves: why is it that some countries are poor while others are rich, for example. What's more, the sheer destitution of extreme poverty introduces moral considerations that affect policy choices – nobody's likely to suggest sending aid to Japan, just because its growth performance has been a bit rocky of late, though they might make this argument for Somalia.

This chapter offers a basic overview of the field of development economics. It begins from a microeconomic perspective, looking more closely at what poverty is and how it affects people, before turning to macroeconomic explanations of why some countries have remained poor. Finally, it looks to solutions, including aid and trade, and asks what can be gleaned from the seeming success of countries such as China in growing rich and reducing poverty.

Poverty and poverty traps

Chapter 11 argued that measuring a nation's wellbeing is a difficult problem to which GDP per capita is a deeply flawed solution. The task of measuring **poverty** throws up similar difficulties. Just as "wellbeing" is understood in broad terms, most people would agree that someone is in poverty whenever he is unable to attain some minimal acceptable standard of living. But translating this into a precise measure of the level of poverty in an economy is fraught with difficulties.

To start with, using a country's per capita GDP to measure poverty is obviously misguided, since this only gives the *average* income per person in an economy, while the amount of poverty will also depend on how equitably this income is *distributed*. For example, at the time of writing, India's GDP per capita is approximately 30% higher than Pakistan's, but whereas around 20% of Pakistanis subsist on less than $1.25 per day, as many as a third of Indians do.

For this reason, poverty is generally measured with reference to a **poverty line** – a level of income or consumption below which a person is said to be **poor** – such as the $1.25 level cited above. These thresholds may be **absolute** – specifying a fixed level of income or consumption to apply to all nations in all years – or **relative** – where the line varies according to place and time. "Poverty" in most developed countries is used in a relative sense – in the UK, for example, it is set at 60% of the median income, adjusted for household size. Such measures can give off strange readings: for example, the 2008 recession "lifted" thousands of British people out of poverty because the median income on which the poverty line was based fell significantly. But they do capture the idea that what counts as an "acceptable" standard of living may vary with the economic context, perhaps because such a lifestyle involves a degree of integration with the rest of society.

Whether absolute or relative, measuring poverty by tallying up the percentage of a country's population with income or consumption below a given line – calculating the **headcount ratio** – is still a crude way of gauging deprivation. For one thing, it takes no account of the *depth* of poverty – a person whose income is half of the poverty line is counted just the same as someone whose income is one cent below it. And for another, the line itself is bound to be arbitrary – a life on $1.26 per day is unlikely to differ much from one lived on $1.24 per day. And finally, any measure of poverty based solely on economic variables omits a range of other factors, such as health, education, and the environment, which can also have a decisive impact on a person's wellbeing.

Plenty of alternatives to the headcount ratio have been put forward that address these and other issues, but for the purposes of understanding poverty, it's more enlightening to think about *why* poverty is significant rather than how to measure it. For some, poverty represents a degree of deprivation that is *morally* unacceptable in itself, possibly justifying special interventions. This suggests the poverty line has to be deduced, somehow, from ethical principles. For others, poverty is unacceptable primarily because of the impact it has on an individual's freedom to better herself, because **poverty traps** make it self-perpetuating. The rest of this section takes a quick look at how these vicious cycles might work.

Perhaps the most straightforward poverty trap involves **nutrition**. A person with a very low income may be unable to afford enough calories to sustain her through a day's work – especially if this involves physically arduous tasks such as agricultural or construction work. As a result, her capacity to do work is limited, which drags down her potential income. She thus remains poor, succumbing to a vicious cycle of poverty and malnutrition.

Microfinance: too small to succeed?

The **microfinance** industry specializes in providing access to credit and other financial services to poor people in developing countries. One of its leading lights is the Bangladeshi economist Mohammed Yunus, who set up Grameen Bank in 1976 with a mission to open up credit markets to those in poverty, especially women. Yunus's insight was that, although poor borrowers may be unable to post collateral – leading to moral hazard – their low wages also mean it is relatively cheap (in terms of the opportunity cost of time) for them to **monitor** each other's behaviour, which can mitigate the problem.

Grameen Bank exploited this by adopting a policy of **group lending**: instead of doling out loans to individual borrowers as most banks do, it lends to groups of five or more; and if any one member of the group defaults on her loan, *everyone* in the group is denied access to future credit. This kind of structure may seem bizarre, but it gives the group members strong incentives to make sure everyone else works hard to repay their loans. And this takes the edge off the moral hazard problem. By 2011, it had $1bn of loans outstanding, 97% to women, with a rate of default of only 3%.

Critics of microfinance point to the high costs of making large numbers of small loans – noting that Grameen Bank can only afford to offer reasonable terms of credit due to the subsidies it receives from the Bangladeshi government and international donors. But by offering poor borrowers a self-directed route out of poverty, Grameen Bank may be a rare case of a bank that taxpayers should feel good about propping up. Yunus was awarded the Nobel Peace Prize in 2006 for his work in establishing it.

The microfinance institution Grameen Bank specializes in loans for small business and helping workers, especially women, become self-employed: a rice farmer in Dhaka using the scheme tends her paddy field.

Another trap has to do with finance. An obvious escape route from the nutrition trap described above would be for the malnourished individual to borrow some money, agreeing to pay it back from her enhanced earnings once she has built up her strength. But this kind of loan is not invested in any asset that the lender could seize in case of a default and, being poor, it's unlikely that the borrower has anything else she can post as **collateral**. So repayment of the loan becomes less credible, creating **moral hazard** and potentially causing the loan to be withdrawn (see **Chapter 9**). One ingenious solution to this is described in the box on p.311.

A final, subtler potential trap, emphasized by Abhijit Banerjee and Esther Duflo of MIT, arises because of an interaction between poverty and aspiration. Life in poverty is a degrading, demoralizing experience that drains the motivation of those who suffer it, often to the point of clinical depression. Lacking hope, they are less prone to invest in their own future, and lacking motivation, they are less effective, less reliable workers. Unfortunately, these are precisely the qualities that make them much more likely to remain poor.

Economic growth in poor countries

Poverty traps show how poor individuals can get stuck at low levels of income. But what about whole economies? In 2012, the average per capita GDP of the developed countries that make up the OECD stood at around $36,000, while the equivalent figure for sub-Saharan Africa was $1,500 – less than five per cent of the OECD figure. The model of economic growth described in **Chapter 12** suggested that economies should **converge** to similar levels of incomes – but there has been no discernible trend for poor African countries to catch up with the rich world over the last fifty years. So what is going on? This section investigates some of the most widely cited explanations, involving coordination failures and institutions.

Coordination failures

Imagine you live in a large village where everyone needs to communicate with each other and there are two technologies available for doing this – email and carrier pigeon. Carrier pigeons are free but it takes time to send a message and occasionally birds go astray, while email is efficient and failsafe but costly to set up. Which technology should you adopt?

The answer is that it depends on what everyone else in the village is doing. If they're all on email, it's well worth the cost of getting yourself online; but if everyone uses pigeons, setting up e-mail would be both expensive and futile, since nobody would be able to receive any of your messages. The same reasoning applies to everyone else in the village – they would like to do what everyone else does. And so there are two possible equilibria: one where all of the villagers correspond via email and another where they "tweet" by carrier pigeon. In the language of **Chapter 8**, this is a **coordination game**, where the players are the villagers. Everyone would be better off at the equilibrium where the whole village used email, but if nobody has the technology, no single villager will find it in their interest to install it, so using pigeons is also an equilibrium.

The first explanation of global income disparities, set out by Paul Rosenstein-Rodan in 1943, is that the respective plights of rich and poor countries are analogous to those of emailing and pigeon-using villages: being rich is preferable to being poor, but both are equilibria, so without some form of intervention there will be no tendency for poor countries to become rich. Low levels of development can thus arise due to **coordination failures** where everyone plays the "wrong" equilibrium.

How might this analogy work? The critical concept is **increasing returns to scale** or **economies of scale** (see **Chapter 4**), where average production costs decrease as output becomes large. Most "primitive" production technologies don't involve increasing returns to scale. Think of traditional labour-intensive methods in sectors such as textiles, agriculture, mining, or construction – for most of these, in order to double output one would have to double the number of suitably equipped workers, so costs increase in proportion to output. However, "advanced" production techniques often do feature significant increasing returns. This is because they usually involve large fixed costs – for instance, buying tractors, cranes, or other machinery – that mean average costs are high for small levels of output, but come down quickly as more is produced. As a result, for small levels of output, it's often cheaper to stick to traditional production methods, but when output is large it's more efficient to embrace modern technology. Which approach each sector chooses will depend on how much demand it faces is.

This gives a basis for coordination failures. Suppose every sector in an economy opts for low-scale production using traditional methods. Then output and hence income will be low across the economy. And *this* means all sectors will face low demands for their goods – certainly not high enough for any one of them to justify upgrading to more advanced technology. So one equilibrium involves low incomes and primitive production techniques.

But what if all the sectors in the economy were simultaneously to ramp up their output using high-tech production methods? Then the contrary reasoning applies: economy-wide output and income will be high, so the demand for each sector's output will be high enough to make deploying modern technology worthwhile. No single sector wishes to switch back to the old ways of doing things, so there's also a high-income, high-technology equilibrium. Whether a country is rich or poor can thus depend on which equilibrium they find themselves locked into.

The idea that coordination failures lie behind global income disparities is hard to take seriously at face value, since the problem seems so easy to overcome. In Rosenstein-Rodan's terminology, a **big push** of government-directed investment could shunt any poor economy into the prosperous equilibrium. Or, even easier, by joining a regional trade bloc or the World Trade Organization, firms in the economy could access global demand, giving them incentives to raise production to exploit increasing returns to scale. (The next section revisits these ideas in more detail.) But on the other hand, it is clear that many developing countries do typically use inefficient technologies in many sectors, just as in a coordination failure. And for some, such as landlocked countries in Africa or Central Asia with ineffectual governments, neither a big push nor openness to trade may be viable.

Culture and institutions

Coordination problems can mean poor countries end up stuck at a low-income equilibrium while rich countries forge ahead. But what if there's something dysfunctional about poor nations that means they'll be poorer *even if* they coordinate effectively? In terms of the **Solow-Swan model** of **Chapter 12**: what if, for some reason, investment is less productive in poor countries, so they have a lower steady-state level of income per head?

One potential factor, once widely believed to be decisive to economic performance, is "**culture**". The Europeans who colonized the world were similar in race, religion, and custom, while other nations tended to be quite different. In particular, the most successful economies at the turn of the twentieth century – Britain and her colonial offshoots in North America and Australasia – were, relatively speaking, culturally highly homogenous. The German sociologist Max Weber (1864-1920) suggested these societies all shared a **Protestant work ethic**, where hard work and financial success were held in high religious esteem. Capital would thus be put to more productive use in these countries, raising the return on investment and thereby increasing the steady-state level of income.

However, today this story is extremely unconvincing. Many of the richest economies in the world, including Japan, Singapore, and Hong Kong, are culturally non-European, while the US is now highly mixed. And there are examples – North and South Korea being the most striking – of countries that began from identical cultural starting points but ended up economically far apart. Though there may be certain cultural practices such as excluding women from the workforce that are harmful to a nation's economic prospects, the proposition that culture is *the primary* factor behind today's global income disparities is hard to sustain.

A far more promising explanation is based on **institutions**. As **Chapter 12** argued, the economic and political "rules of the game" – especially concerning markets, contracts, and property rights – can have a profound impact on how much investment takes place and how efficient it is. And poor countries monopolize the wrong end of international rankings on the strength and independence of political and legal institutions. Recent econometric studies in this area seem to confirm the central role of institutions in holding the poorest countries back.

The wrong place at the wrong time?

Thanks to path dependence, European colonialism has left an indelible mark on the institutions of the countries it touched. Many nations' current legal and political systems – even their religions and languages – bear the imprint of a former colonial master. But whereas for some, such as Canada and Australia, this inheritance has been a healthy one, for others, such as the Democratic Republic of Congo and Angola, it has been toxic. Why such a difference?

One answer, suggested by Daron Acemoglu, Simon Johnson, and James Robinson in a 2001 paper, is that Europeans' approach to colonialism was partly dictated by **geography**. In subtropical regions, where they were ill-adapted to the climate and vulnerable to diseases such as malaria and yellow fever, settling down was unattractive. This meant that their colonial rule was based on extracting as many resources as possible with minimal involvement – so they established the repressive, authoritarian institutions best suited to this. Unfortunately, for the most part, these have been inherited by the countries' present rulers.

In temperate regions, by contrast, the climate was familiar and the disease burden modest, so Europeans tended to settle down – meaning they had to live under whatever institutions they imposed. This gave them an incentive to set up institutions that favoured general prosperity – largely founded on stable property rights, democracy, and the rule of law. As a result, there remains a very strong correlation between a nation's income per head and its distance from the equator.

This, however, raises the question – if institutions are so important, why don't countries with bad ones just "upgrade" them? Though some countries have succeeded in reforming, unfortunately it's usually very difficult to supplant existing institutions. Those who benefit most from the prevailing institutional structures will invariably be those who have the most wealth and political power – and this creates a powerful (though not always irresistible) force against wholesale change. Institutional arrangements are thus **path dependent**: how they function today is strongly influenced by how they worked in the past. As the box above argues, this means institutional differences can persist over centuries.

A similarly intractable problem is caused by **corruption**, where the institutional rules of the game simply aren't observed by the most important "players" – civil servants, businessmen, politicians, and the like. When corruption is endemic, those with the most power will usually be those with the strongest incentives to keep it that way. What's more, they can use their power – perhaps through promoting corrupt deputies or sacking whistle-blowers – to ensure that this happens. As a result, tackling corruption effectively can require drastic measures, such as Georgia's 2005 decision to

Harassed by the law

A particularly prominent form of corruption in many countries is **harassment bribery**, where an official demands a bribe in order to give someone something they are legally entitled to anyway, such as a tax rebate or smooth passage through a checkpoint. Pondering the issue in 2011, the Indian economist Kaushik Basu caused a stir by suggesting the best way to solve the problem would be to legalize it.

Basu's insight is that where harassment bribery is illegal, the rational thing for an ordinary citizen is to pay the bribe and keep quiet. Not paying the bribe means that they do not, for example, get their income tax refund, which would be larger than the bribe they are being asked for. And once they have paid the bribe, they have committed a crime and so would only incriminate themselves if they complained to the police.

Legalizing the *payment* – but not receipt – of harassment bribes would change these incentives. The citizen would still find it in their interest to pay the bribe if asked, but having done so they could then report the bribe to the authorities without landing themselves in trouble – potentially even recovering some or all of their money. So bribe takers would be more likely to get caught, and so would be far less likely to demand bribes in the first place.

fire all 16,000 of its traffic police officers. And this requires political will, likely to be lacking if the top people also have their snouts in the trough.

Becoming prosperous

So far the focus has been on why individuals and countries may be poor. The chapter now concludes on a more constructive note, examining what can be done to address this problem.

Aid

The most straightforward way of raising the income of a person or a country is to send them more resources. This could be through a simple cash transfer or a loan made on favourable terms, or less directly via some form of investment that makes workers more productive – perhaps in education, health, or access to clean water. It may even be as a gift of goods or services – sending over food parcels or teachers. This is the approach of **aid**.

Much of the discussion so far suggests a rationale for aid. Individuals may be unable to borrow if they are trapped in poverty; economies may be marooned in a poor **equilibrium** where no individual household or firm has an incentive to invest but everyone would benefit if they did; and governments may be incapable of supplying the investment themselves – or at least untrusted by the markets to do so effectively. In situations such as these, investment in an economy *can* be efficient, but its households, firms, and government are unable or unwilling to raise the necessary funds. Through aid, international donors step in to fill the gap.

It all sounds so easy, but the track record of aid has been disappointing. Despite flows from Western governments to Africa currently standing at over $50 billion per year, the evidence that this has made *any* difference to its growth rate is at best mixed. How could this be so? One theory is that the level of aid – around 3% of GDP for Africa – isn't sufficient to effect a **big push** into prosperity. If this is true then the obvious solution is to pour more aid in, though this is likely to meet resistance among sceptical donors.

Other explanations of aid's seeming impotence stress the motivations of donors and recipients. Most obviously, aid isn't provided solely for the alleviation of poverty. The US has historically furthered its own interests by channelling development support to strategic allies such as Egypt and Pakistan – much of this was then "invested" in military hardware. France has similarly tended to use aid to maintain colonial ties, devoting much of its aid budget to francophone Africa.

Even with the purest of intentions, the mechanism of aid offers weak incentives for successful outcomes. Compare investment in the stock market, where shareholders, eager to earn a return on their investment, attempt to provide managers with sharp incentives to carry out their wishes. **Chapter 9** showed that this solution to the **principal–agent problem** is often imperfect, but with aid things can be much worse. Donors are often content to be seen to be "doing something", so fail to pay adequate regard to how their money is spent (look at how frequently donor countries stress how much they are spending, rather than what they are achieving). Recipients – especially corrupt governments – may then divert whatever is given to further their own ends rather than investing it efficiently. Even if the money is earmarked for a specific purpose – say $100m for education – the donation is **fungible**: the recipient can put "this" $100m towards its education budget, but then move "another" $100m from education into a different department.

This suggests that donors, if they really want to make a difference, should attach more strings to the aid they send out. This approach is known as **conditionality**: providing aid only on the condition that it is used as intended and that the recipient acts responsibly. But conditionality is hard to implement: it requires donors to monitor the actions of recipients, which is costly. And it often lacks credibility: will future aid really be withdrawn if the recipient misbehaves? If not, then there's little point in complying with the conditions. In an article published in 2000, Ravi Kanbur of Cornell University recalls how Ghana received large sums from international donors in the early 1990s on the basis of its "good behaviour" in implementing reforms asked of it by the IMF. But then in 1992 it reneged spectacularly on a commitment to budgetary responsibility – awarding a backdated 80% pay rise to the civil service and military personnel. The aid, however, continued to flow – stopping it would have been too disruptive to the Ghanaian economy (not to mention the development organizations now based there).

A deeper, and perhaps more disturbing problem with aid is how little is known about how best to spend it. In his 2007 pamphlet, *Making Aid Work*, Abhijit Banerjee decries the lack of **randomized field trials** in development economics. These are the kind of tests used by pharmaceutical companies to establish whether a new drug is safe and effective. They take a group of subjects and give the drug to some randomly chosen sub-group, before recording any significant difference between the people who take the drug and those who don't. Provided the groups are large enough, this difference will indicate the effect of treating people with the drug.

These trials can be useful in the field of development because there are often many plausible "treatments" for any particular malaise. To promote primary school enrolment, for instance, aid could be used to fund free school meals, it might go towards extra welfare payments for parents whose children attend regularly, or it could be spent on one of many other reasonable-sounding measures. Without any rigorous evidence on which policy offers the best value for money, it's likely that the wrong one will be prescribed.

Trade

A route to development long favoured by international organizations such as the World Bank and IMF is **trade liberalization**. The reasons for this include all the arguments for free trade presented in **Chapter 17** based on **comparative advantage** and **economies of scale**. Indeed, for developing countries, economies of scale could be particularly beneficial if they are stuck at a low level of income due to low domestic demand (see above). Studies of the data largely confirm that openness to trade is good for developing countries' growth performance.

A further, more indirect way in which trade can help with development is through **technology transfers**, where technological know-how spreads from one country to another. As **Chapter 12** showed, improvements in technology drive long-run economic growth – so by "importing" technology from the rich world, developing countries can enjoy **catch-up growth**, where they converge to developed-nation income levels. The most straightforward way in which trade promotes technology transfers is in allowing low-income countries to buy advanced capital equipment from the West. Perhaps more potent, however, is **foreign direct investment (FDI)**, where a firm sets up factories outside its home market. FDI can mean both cutting-edge capital *and* the knowledge of how to use it flows into developing countries, and then percolates through their economies as workers at foreign-owned factories move jobs.

However, as with the general argument for liberalization in **Chapter 17**, this comes with a couple of caveats. As was stressed in the last chapter, though liberalization improves **efficiency**, it may be harmful to **equity**. And if the poorest people in a developing country are already living in poverty, any policy that could make them even poorer should be thought through carefully. However, in practice, most developing countries will have a comparative advantage in sectors that make heavy use of unskilled workers – meaning the poorest are likely to gain most from liberalization.

A more influential case against liberalization is based on the **infant-industry argument** given in **Chapter 17**. Developing countries may lack a comparative advantage in sectors where specialist workers are paid highly, but that's not to say they could never develop one. The problem with liberalization is that, because it leads economies to focus on their *current* areas of comparative advantage, it can mean they never progress along the **learning curve** of more advanced sectors, as they need to in order to become competitive in them. Temporary **protectionism** allows them to nurture these industries before they compete on the global market.

The infant-industry argument lies behind two seemingly divergent approaches to development. **Import substitution**, where measures such as tariffs and quotas allow locally produced goods to compete with imports, was popular up until the 1980s. It is best suited to large economies, where the domestic market is big enough for firms to exploit economies of scale, and so was primarily used to protect industrial sectors in countries such as India and Brazil. The policy, however, failed to achieve the learning effects it promised – instead creating a powerful lobby for the indefinite protection of inefficient industries. It was only abandoned at the behest of the

The dragon roars

China offers the most remarkable tale of development in recent years, lifting 680 million of its citizens out of poverty between 1981 and 2010. What has been the recipe for its roaring success?

The most fundamental ingredient has undoubtedly been the institution of **markets,** which it began to embrace from 1978. But, though China has become markedly more capitalistic in the last 35 years, nobody could accuse the Communist Party of operating a nightwatchman politburo. The government has played a central, though sometimes dubious, role in its economic rise.

A common misperception is that China owes its prosperity to exports, through some regime of **export orientation.** In fact, **investment** is the central plank of China's growth model. By keeping its currency cheap – thus ensuring imported consumer goods are expensive – and offering very weak social protection, it encourages extremely high rates of savings: more than 50% of national income in 2011. This means it has a correspondingly sky-high level of investment, much of which is funnelled through state-owned enterprises.

There are pros and cons to the state's control of China's investment. The negatives are that it is often squandered – most glaringly on building cities where few people want to live or palatial government offices in its remotest provinces. But on the other hand, a large portion of it has been devoted to **infrastructure** that has positive externalities for the economy's productivity – including the world's largest high-speed rail network.

The state has also been canny in using its bargaining power to extract technology transfers from developed countries. It lures in Western investors with the promise of its large and growing market, but then requires them to invest in **joint ventures** with local firms, ensuring that advanced production methods spread around the economy. As a result, an economy regarded as primitive a generation ago now boasts some of the world's leading technology firms, such as Huawei, the telecoms giant.

IMF when the economies using it ran into debt crises and needed bailing out (much of Latin America in the early 1980s; India in the early 1990s).

Export orientation, by contrast, relies on protectionist measures such as export subsidies to promote an economy's industries in global markets. It potentially suffers from the same drawbacks as import-orientation – plus the fiscal cost of the subsidies – though by integrating the economy's domestic industries with global markets, it ensures that all economies of scale can be exploited. Many economists attribute South Korea's rise from the 1960s up to the 1990s to a successful policy of export orientation, though it was combined with a strong dose of liberalization.

Chapter 19

The financial crisis of 2007–8

This *Rough Guide* now concludes with the story of the economic event of our times: the financial crisis that began in 2007. Understanding the crisis requires a sure footing in both micro- and macroeconomics, so it's a logical – not to mention climactic – topic to end with.

Telling the story requires a clear understanding of banks' balance sheets, so the chapter begins with an explanation of how these work, showing why banks are regulated and how this is done. In the years before the crisis, regulation became more lax and new practices such as **securitization** and **off-balance sheet leverage** spread around the system. The general feeling was that this had allowed banks to better allocate risks between investors, spurring investment and thereby firing economic growth.

However, though few noticed it at the time, almost the entire financial sector was building up a huge exposure to the American housing market through mortgages to subprime borrowers. When house prices fell in the United States, the same practices that were meant to have made banks more efficient left the financial system stricken and caused huge collateral damage to the rest of the economy.

With many countries reeling from the effects of the crisis – and some set to suffer for years to come – it's perhaps unsurprising that the clamour of blame for it still echoes around the media. Among those routinely singled out for responsibility are bankers, governments, China, and – yes – economists. As it goes along, this chapter will consider how culpable these and other groups were for the crisis and the economic carnage it wrought.

Banks and financial regulation

By channelling savings into investment efficiently, banks are one of the critical **institutions** that promote economic growth (see **Chapter 12**). However, they are also inherently unstable entities. This section describes how they work and how governments try to contain their instability.

The balance sheet

In order to understand how banks work and what went wrong in the crisis, it is necessary first to understand banks' balance sheets. A balance sheet consists of **assets** and **liabilities**. For a bank:

▶ Assets are the things a bank owns that generate its income. For example, a mortgage generates income for the bank in the form of the monthly repayments.
▶ Liabilities are the claims that other people can make on that flow of income. For example, the money customers have deposited with the bank and the money shareholders have invested in the bank.

By definition, the value of the cashflows generated by a bank's assets must be the same as the value of the claims on these cashflows. So it must be that the value of its assets is equal to the value of its liabilities. This is the **balance-sheet identity**.

The balance sheet of a bank might look something like that shown in table 19.1. The left-hand side of the table gives the bank's assets. Some of these assets, such as mortgage loans, will be relatively difficult for it to sell should the need arise – they are not **liquid assets**. Other assets, including any cash the banks hold, are classed as liquid. All banks have an account at

Assets	Liabilities
$80m of loans and other earning assets $20m of liquid assets (cash and central bank reserves) **Total: $100m**	$85m of debt in customers' deposits and other instruments. $15m of equity **Total: $100m**

Table 19.1: A bank's balance sheet.

the central bank where they hold some of their reserves; this offers a very convenient way to settle payments between banks as they can just transfer funds across the books of the central bank. As a result, these reserves are highly liquid.

On the other side of the balance sheet, the bank's liabilities can also be broadly divided between equity and debt. Debts consist of the loans the bank has taken from the general public in the form of customers' deposits, as well as any loans the bank has taken out with other banks (this is known as **wholesale lending** and takes place in the **interbank market**). The equity of the bank is the value of whatever is left once the bank's debts have been paid off; it's the value of actually owning the bank, given by the value of all of the shares in the bank.

Generally speaking, banks are vulnerable to two kinds of threat to their balance sheet, known as **solvency shocks** and **liquidity shocks**, and they faced both during the financial crisis.

Solvency shocks occur when the loans the bank has made in the past suddenly look less likely to be repaid. As a result, the bank's assets become less valuable. This means that, once all of the debts have been repaid, there's less left over as equity – so the fall in the value of the bank's assets is "absorbed" by a fall in its equity value. After a solvency shock, the bank's balance sheet might look like that in table 19.2.

A solvency shock can be dangerous because the equity of the bank cannot go negative. Once the equity hits zero, the bank is **insolvent** and must cease trading and declare bankruptcy. Nobody, apart from lawyers and accountants, benefits from this; selling off all of the bank's assets is a costly and time-consuming process, usually followed by much legal wrangling over who is entitled to the proceeds. Once it's complete, the holders of the bank's debt will end up with less than they lent it and the equity will be wiped out.

Assets	Liabilities
$70m of loans and other earning assets $20m of liquid assets (cash and central bank reserves) **Total: $90m**	$85m of debt in customers' deposits and other instruments $5m of equity **Total: $90m**

Table 19.2: A bank's balance sheet after a reduction in the value of its loan book leads to a reduction in the equity of the bank.

Assets	Liabilities
$70m of loans and other earning assets	$70m of debt in customers'
$5m of liquid assets (cash and central	deposits and other instruments.
bank reserves)	$5m of equity
Total: $75m	**Total: $75m**

Table 19.3: A bank's balance sheet after it is unable to roll over a large amount of debt.

Liquidity shocks occur when the bank's stock of liquid assets suddenly needs to be used up. Suppose that, for some reason, the interbank borrowing market freezes up and the bank is unable to renew various borrowing agreements with other banks. Instead it must pay off these outstanding debts using its cash. As a result, on the liabilities side of the balance sheet, there will be a fall in the bank's debts, while on the assets side of the balance sheet there will be a fall in the bank's liquid reserves. After such an event, the bank's balance sheet might look something like that shown in table 19.3.

Banks need liquidity to function from day to day. Extending loans to households or businesses and paying back depositors or debt holders all requires access to ready money. If their reserves of liquidity become seriously depleted, they may need to top them up by holding a **fire sale** of their less liquid assets here they allow discounts on market value in order to effect a quick sale.

Each kind of shock can cause the other. A solvency shock can lead to a loss in confidence in the bank's ability to repay its debts. Depositors respond by withdrawing their money and it becomes harder to borrow in interbank markets, leading to a liquidity shock. And liquidity shocks can cause solvency shocks if the bank is forced to accept large discounts when selling assets in a fire sale. The potential for a vicious cycle of solvency and liquidity shocks only serves to magnify the general instability of banks.

Leverage and bank regulation

Like any other business, a bank must decide how to finance itself – that is, how to divide its liabilities between debt and equity. The higher the proportion of debt in its liabilities, the more **leveraged** it is said to be. In principle, since the value of a bank's assets always equals the value of its liabilities, its choice of leverage shouldn't have any impact on how much its liabilities are worth: its assets are the same regardless of its leverage. This was a central insight of one of the seminal papers in financial economics, "The Cost of Capital, Corporation Finance and the Theory of Investment", published by Franco Modigliani and Merton Miller in the *American Economic Review* in 1958.

However, as the discussion above suggests, there are a couple of wrinkles that make a bank's leverage decision more important than the **Modigliani-Miller theorem** suggests. First, should the bank become insolvent, it would have to carry out a fire sale of its assets, receiving a lower price for them as a result, and incur all sorts of legal and accounting fees as its creditors fight over who is entitled to what. Even coming close to bankruptcy can be costly, as suppliers start to demand payment up front and fearful creditors call in their loans – putting stress on the bank's stock of liquid assets. These **costs of financial distress** suggest that any firm would like to avoid any prospect of bankruptcy, giving it a definite preference for low levels of leverage.

However, debt has its attractions. Most importantly, while firms have to pay tax on their profits before they hand them over to shareholders as dividends, debt repayments are deductible pre-tax. This **tax shield** for debt repayments means highly leveraged firms pay less tax, and are therefore more valuable. For firms in general, the decision of how much leverage to take on involves balancing the advantage of the tax shield and the disadvantage of the costs of financial distress.

But banks are different. If a bank becomes insolvent, this can have serious ramifications for the broader economy. Its customers, including firms and consumers, will no longer be able to rely on it for overdrafts or short-term credit. So the insolvency of a bank may force other people and businesses into bankruptcy. What's more, this wave of bankruptcy will spark a solvency shock to other banks, who are owed money by the insolvent bank through the interbank market and its customers through normal lending. This process of **contagion** may bring them down too. The failure of a single bank thus risks causing the whole financial system to unravel, with catastrophic economic consequences. For this reason, governments offer banks an **implicit guarantee**: if they come under serious risk of insolvency, the government will step in with extra funding to bail them out. When they accept this cash, banks' holdings of assets increase, causing their equity to rise in value, thus fending off insolvency.

The implicit guarantee may be a sensible way of ensuring economic stability, but it introduces **moral hazard** (see **Chapter 9**). In a stroke, it all but eliminates the potential costs of financial distress to the bank, giving it a strong incentive to take on leverage. But the costs of financial distress haven't disappeared: they are transferred to the taxpayer.

As a quid pro quo, governments impose **regulations** on banks that ensure they do not run excessive risks of insolvency. The most important of these is the **capital adequacy ratio**, which requires banks to rein in their leverage: their equity must not fall below a certain level relative to the value of their assets, where these assets are weighted according to their riskiness. The rationale for this is that the riskier a bank's asset holdings are, the higher the chance it will face a solvency shock that threatens to wipe out its equity. This is why capital adequacy ratios use a bank's **risk-weighted assets**: banks must hold more equity against a risky asset such as a personal loan than they do against a "safe" asset such as a government bond.

The NICE old days

So much for the theory of bank regulation. In practice, during the two decades leading up to 2007, a number of trends combined to leave banks acutely vulnerable to destabilizing shocks. This section reviews the most important contributing factors.

The calm before the storm

From a post-crisis vantage point, much of the Western world from the mid-1990s to 2007 looks economically idyllic. Unemployment and inflation were relatively low, growth respectable, and cheap imports from Asia meant households' incomes could fund ever more consumption. Not everything in the garden was rosy – the US hiccupped in the wake of the dotcom crash, while Japan and parts of Europe faltered – but it was a lot brighter than what was to come. The then governor of the Bank of England, Sir Mervyn King, could have been speaking about much of the developed world when, in 2003, he proclaimed the UK's "Non-Inflationary, Continuously Expansionary" – or NICE – decade.

Where were the signs of impending trouble? Leaving aside the inner workings of the financial services industry for now, a couple of things seem amiss in retrospect. First, in the five years running up to the crisis, interest rates in the US were significantly lower than they had been under similar economic conditions in the past. This was partly down to policy decisions – the **Federal Reserve** operated an unusually loose monetary policy in this period. And it was partly a result of a "savings glut", where foreigners (especially the Chinese – see box below) invested heavily in American assets, raising their prices and therefore pushing down their returns (see **Chapter 10**). Low interest rates gave American firms and consumers a strong incentive to take on debt, which they did – particularly by taking out mortgages, the stock of which rose from $4.9tn to $14.1tn from 1997 to 2007. This rising demand for real estate pushed up house prices by more than 90% over the same period.

The second problem was that economic success bred complacency, with many investors concluding that NICE economic weather was here to stay. In particular, as well as *expecting* good economic performance, they also perceived very little *risk* in this level of performance. One reason for this was that the global economy appeared to operate in a more secure way than it had before: new approaches to demand management (see **Chapter 15**) looked successful, while new practices in finance seemed to make that

Chasing the dragon... blaming China

For Western leaders, China is a politically convenient villain of the piece. As noted in **Chapter 18**, China has sustained a gargantuan rate of investment in recent decades, not only matched but also *exceeded* by its rate of savings. These extra savings were largely ploughed (by the Chinese authorities) into US government bonds, reducing the returns on these securities. And this led investors to look elsewhere for returns, so they bought up alternative assets and returns fell across the board – including on mortgage credit. The actions of the Chinese state thus contributed to the availability of cheap credit in the West that was at the root of the crisis. Western critics of China argue that no democratic country would ever have pumped so much money into US government bonds – more than $1.3tn as of 2013 – when it could have been used for much-needed social services.

However, this reading of the crisis is far too charitable to Westerners. For one thing, China did have good reasons for building up a large stock of **official reserves** in US debt – it meant it could credibly intervene in the foreign exchange market to maintain its currency peg (see **Chapter 16**) – though it's dubious that it needed to acquire quite so much. And for another, Chinese activity was only one factor behind the cheap credit – the others being loose monetary policy and delusional behaviour by investors.

Fundamentally, blaming China for the crisis is akin to an obese person blaming low prices at McDonald's for their predicament. China may have provided the funds, however irrationally, that guaranteed low interest rates in developed economies, but it is the people in these economies who made the truly wayward investment decisions that led to the crisis.

sector both more profitable and robust (of which more later). Another possible reason for confidence was that investors placed too much weight on the *recent* past in forming their expectations about the future. This is a well-known psychological bias (an example of what behavioural economists call **the law of small numbers**) and it was encoded throughout the financial system in the computer models used by the financial sector to assess risks. Whatever the rationale, the fact was that investors saw future economic growth as a safe bet, and this made them more willing to lend out money at low interest rates.

Light-touch regulation and off-balance sheet leverage

As emphasized above, banks are one of the critical institutions in promoting economic growth. Imposing regulatory constraints on them, though necessary to preserve the safety of the system, can thus be a drag on economic performance. Regulators and politicians therefore have a natural eagerness to reduce the burden of regulation that banks bear. With lower costs of regulatory compliance, banks are free to innovate and create new financial instruments to use capital more efficiently. The fewer people whose permission banks have to seek beforehand, the more innovative they can be. Though there may have been other reasons for it (see the box on p.330), this was the intellectual case for **light-touch regulation**, adopted gradually throughout the West from the 1980s up to 2007.

As it was practised, light-touch regulation essentially involved placing a great deal of trust in banks to ensure they met the regulatory standards they faced. For example, calculations of risk-weighted capital were based on the banks' own models of how risky their assets were. While the models did have to be approved by regulators in order to prevent banks gaming the system, the regulatory reliance on banks' own models was representative of the faith placed in the sector.

One consequence of light-touch regulation was that banks could get away with activities that, though not contrary to the letter of the law, certainly contravened its spirit. Regulators, avowedly leaving banks to manage their own affairs within the law, were none the wiser. An important example of this was the increasing use by banks of **off-balance sheet vehicles**, effectively mini-banks that were controlled by the banks, but whose assets stayed off the parent banks' balance sheets. These vehicles could thus be used by banks to pile on extra leverage without contravening capital adequacy regulations.

Sweet FSA... blaming regulators

There's no doubt that better regulation could have made the financial sector more robust and prevented the financial crisis. It's unsurprising, therefore, that much of the blame has been directed to the various agencies in charge of this, including the UK's Financial Services Authority (FSA) and the Securities and Exchange Commission (SEC) in the US.

But regulators are only there to enforce the rules and the rules were for the most part adhered to. It's true that, as people who should be highly attuned to risks in the financial sector, the regulators failed to raise the alarm before it was too late. But the same criticism applies equally to economists and bankers. And in the realm of setting the rules, regulators had only limited influence, with much of the debate dominated by bankers, economists, and politicians.

Regulators were also subject to severe internal and external pressure. Internally, they were acutely vulnerable to **regulatory capture** (see **Chapter 7**) – as banks could offer pliant regulators the prospect of much more lucrative career options. Indeed, salaries were so much higher at the banks than at the regulators, it was inevitable that many of those best qualified to police finance ended up working in it.

Externally, the newly globalized nature of finance gave banks significant bargaining power over regulators: banks could now choose where to base their activities, and so they tended to gravitate to the places where regulation was least onerous. The practice of choosing where to locate business on the basis of the regulatory regime is known as **regulatory arbitrage**, and in many economies was a hugely potent force behind deregulation. According to the UK's Office of Budget Responsibility, financial services contributed around seven percent of UK tax receipts in the years before the crisis, so anything that the government did that made the sector up sticks to a different jurisdiction could have left a serious hole in the public finances. Indeed, regulatory arbitrage gave financial centres strong incentives to deregulate *competitively*, in the hope of capturing business from each other. The result was a **Prisoners' Dilemma** (see **Chapter 8**) type of situation, where jurisdictions would deregulate to steal business off each other, leading to an equilibrium where there was little net gain to any particular jurisdiction, but the system was much less safe.

One way banks could get away with this was by supporting their off-balance sheet offspring with **credit lines**. A credit line is rather like an overdraft facility, a promise to lend up to a certain amount of money, but it only shows up as an earning asset with a risk weighting on a bank's balance sheet if it is drawn down. So banks were able to use these off balance sheet vehicles to increase the leverage in their businesses without violating capital adequacy regulations. The end result was a banking sector much more highly leveraged than the regulators envisaged.

Securitization

As **Chapter 10** showed, any uncertain stream of cashflows has asome given value. So if Maria is entitled to such a stream, she can cash in on its value immediately by issuing a security that entitles the bearer to the stream of cashflows and selling it on to Avin. In doing so she **securitizes** the cashflow; literally, she turns it into a security. Securitization was widely practised in the NICE era. David Bowie even securitized the future royalties from his album sales in 1997, raising $55m.

A particular form of securitization that emerged during these years involved mortgages. Banks would combine several mortgages that were assets on their balance sheets – in fact, usually thousands of them – and then sell the rights to some percentage of the returns generated by this pool of assets. So, for example, a bank might sell a security that entitles the holder to 0.01% of the returns generated by a group of 4500 mortgages. This kind of security is known as a **collateralized debt obligation (CDO)**. CDOs usually come in **tranches**, where if some of the mortgages underpinning the CDO go into default, the holders of the bottom tranches are

Singer David Bowie in the year that he securitized future royalties from his album sales.

those who lose their money first. The higher or "senior" tranched CDOs were thus safer than those in the lower tranches.

In principle, CDOs were a sensible idea. For one thing, they made it possible for smaller investors to buy mortgage-based securities in an efficient way. The combining of many mortgages together is a kind of risk pooling which should make a CDO a safer asset than a mortgage loan provided the risk on the different mortgages is not too strongly correlated (see **Chapter 10**). And thanks to the way CDOs were tranched, they allowed investors to choose a CDO that offered the level of risk and return best suited to their requirements. CDOs thus promised to make the mortgage market more efficient, allowing more people to own their own home in a financially sustainable way – surely, an unalloyed social good. In the US, birthplace of the CDO, millions of people on low incomes became home-owners for the first time. This was the **subprime mortgage** sector.

For banks, there was another benefit. Consider the position of a bank that is hard up against its capital adequacy ratio, but knows of a lot of customers they believe would be good credit risks and wants to extend a mortgage to them. Making the loans is a profitable business opportunity, but would put the bank on the wrong side of their capital adequacy requirement. One option is to direct the customers to another bank. For obvious reasons, that is not such an exciting option for the bank. Another option is to securitize some of the existing mortgages it holds (earning a profit in the process), turning these risky, illiquid assets into cash that can be lent out to the new customers. And then it can repeat this process again and again.

This was the **originate-to-distribute model** of conducting business for lenders, where the monthly repayments are no longer the incentive to sell mortgages. Instead, banks started making money from the fees they could charge for arranging the mortgage, and the ability to package mortgages into CDOs and sell them on.

Mortgage securitization thus seemed to benefit banks, investors, and homeowners alike. What could possibly go wrong? First, the originate-to-distribute model relied on everyone having a clear understanding of the risks involved, so CDOs were easy to price and sell. But these risks became very complicated. Assumptions were needed on the rate of default for each individual mortgage, and how defaults were correlated with each other. Investors came to rely on the intellectual firepower of the **ratings agencies** (see the box below) to understand these risks, rather than coming to their own assessments.

Second, and relatedly, the verdicts of these agencies gave banks a strong incentive to buy back the CDOs they had sold. A lot of CDOs were given the highest rating of AAA by the agencies – as safe as sovereign debt! This meant that they had a very low rating in the calculation of risk-weighted capital, even lower than that given to mortgages. The result was that banks could package up their mortgages into CDOs, sell them, and then use the proceeds to buy mortgage backed CDOs. In the process, their risk-weighted assets fell, but the assets under their control grew and their exposure to the housing market increased! Regulators could have stepped in to prevent this increase in exposure, but in the climate of light-touch regulation there was little prospect of this kind of intervention.

Getting Moody... blaming the rating agencies

Rating agencies are certainly a big part of the story of the financial crisis. What made them so important was that banks were restricted, for certain kinds of investments, to purchasing only financial instruments which had received an "investment grade" assessment from one of the ratings agencies. And not just any ratings agency, but one that had been approved by the Securities and Exchange Commission, of which there were just Moody's, Standard and Poor, and Fitch in the run-up to the crisis.

One problem was with the business model pursued by these agencies. They were hired by the firm issuing the debt instrument that was to be rated, which gave them an obvious incentive to give their clients the ratings they wanted. The belief at the time was that reputational concerns would be enough to keep the ratings agencies on the straight and narrow. If they got a reputation for pandering to their clients and describing debt as being safer than it was, then no one would find their investment grade ratings reassuring. If the investment grade ratings don't reassure investors, then there is no reason for debt issuers to ask for a rating (aside from any regulatory requirements).

But another problem came from the complexity of the CDOs and the computer modelling to assess how risky they were. As the products themselves were complex, the computer modelling had to become equally complex. The problem with greater complexity in modelling is that fewer and fewer people then understand how the models work and how potentially flawed assumptions about risks and correlations can give a misleading rating. Eventually a point was reached where the only people who understood the models were the people at the agencies who worked on them. The investors who made decisions on the basis of the ratings given by these models had only a superficial understanding of what the models' conclusion meant.

Bankers' bonuses

If regulation looked ropey, the ratings agencies compromised, and securitization and off-balance sheet leverage dangerous, luckily there was a safety valve. The financial sector was one of the leading areas of the economy to make use of performance-related pay (see **Chapter 9**), thus aligning the incentives of bankers with those of the bank's shareholders, so even if the regulations were inadequate, this would mean bankers themselves would want to keep their houses in order... right? Well, sadly, no. Bankers' bonuses are now seen as having provided **perverse incentives** to the people making decisions. How did performance-related pay end up incentivizing the utterly abject performance of the financial sector in 2007?

For one thing, as already mentioned, the looming possibility of bailouts meant that what was good for the banks was not generally good for society. Banks had an in-built incentive to take on too much risk.

But bankers' bonuses may even have made things worse. First, performance-related pay in the financial sector is often a "one-way street". Bosses and workers will get bonuses when they perform well and raise profits. However, their actions might also result in substantial losses, and when this happens they do not take a similar hit. So the rewards and penalties of the bonus structure are skewed, with employees sharing in the profits when their business strategy pays off, but sharing none of the losses when it goes horribly wrong. This makes risky business strategies *even more* attractive to the bankers than they would otherwise be. Technically, employees who really screw up can be fired, but if the mistake they made was exactly the same as the one everyone else in the industry was making, this is unlikely (another example of **rational herding** – see **Chapter 10**).

The second problem with bonuses as actually practised is to do with time horizons. A decision to issue a load of short-term debt and purchase CDOs backed by mortgages might have looked like a very good one in 2005. So to the extent that it boosted the profits of a financial institution the people who made that decision would get rewarded with a higher bonus. However, it was that same decision which in 2007–8 meant that some banks collapsed. The problem is, of course, that the 2005 bonus has already been paid. This is why some people think that bonuses should only be paid out after some time has elapsed, or should be paid in shares rather than cash (ideally shares which cannot be sold until after some time has elapsed).

Banksterism... blaming bankers

With all the moving parts in place, the next section shows how the machine drove itself into destruction in 2007–8. In a nutshell, weak regulatory oversight and flawed practice by the rating agencies allowed banks to exploit securitization and off-balance sheet leverage to take on too much risk. So when those risks blew up, so did the banks, and then so did everyone else. But unlike the regulators and the ratings agencies – not to mention the politicians who set the rules and the economists who informed them – bankers just did what they were meant to: they followed their incentives. So according to one school of thought particularly prominent in Wall Street and the City of London, bankers do not deserve the tabloid scorn heaped upon them – the crisis wasn't their fault; *it was the system*.

But hang on. These are masters of the universe, not beasts of the field. Senior bankers, like doctors, lawyers, politicians, and academics, occupy privileged, societally important positions. We rightly expect them to act out of a wider sense of professional responsibility, rather than a narrow focus on their bank balance.

▶ *They could* have asked regulators to close the loopholes they were exploiting rather than cynically playing them off against each other in a game of regulatory arbitrage.

▶ *They could* have questioned the logic behind the balance-sheet contortions they carried out, urging constructive reform rather than engaging in short-term profiteering.

▶ *They could* have set bonuses so that their employees' incentives were better rather than worse aligned with their shareholders' interests.

And let's be clear: *none did*.

Had the CEO of a bank done any of these things, it would have left his bank at no disadvantage to its competitors since better regulation would have applied to all major banks. All it would have required was a smidgen of courage to stick his neck out and a willingness to make himself, personally, less spectacularly wealthy.

Bankers who emphasize defective incentives fail to appreciate their own absolutely central role in setting those incentives. This is why they do deserve widespread public opprobrium. And as John Lanchester concludes in *Whoops!*, hatred of bankers is bad for the economy. At the time of writing, widespread loathing of bankers means another round of bailouts would be politically impossible. But it might become economically necessary.

Crisis

Low interest rates and hubris from the NICE era created a fertile market for investment. And, thanks to lax regulation and questionable modelling by the ratings agencies, banks were free and more than happy to facilitate this investment, especially in mortgages. As many have noted, banks and other financial institutions traded around mortgage-backed securities like a game of pass-the-parcel. Unfortunately, nobody noticed the parcel was ticking.

Practices in the financial sector had increased the level of risk to which the banking sector as a whole was exposed. But what ended up making this much worse was the *complexity* of CDOs: as the crisis unfolded, it became very hard to work out the total exposure of any given bank to any given mortgage. This lack of transparency was a crucial problem as the crisis developed.

The crisis started in the American housing market, but the problems quickly spread from there to the banks, and from the financial sector to the rest of the economy.

The US housing market

Mortgages are generally seen as fairly safe loans. Even if it turns out that the borrower can't afford the repayments, the bank can seize the house as collateral and sell that to recoup its money. Since the borrowers involved were on low incomes, everyone knew subprime mortgages were a bit riskier than standard mortgages. But a couple of features of the way subprime mortgages were structured made them much more dangerous than people realized:

► The mortgages had high-loan-to value ratios (the ratio of the loan amount to the price of the house) of 90% or 95% or even in excess of 100%.
► The mortgages were structured so that the interest rate was fixed at a low rate for the first two to three years of the mortgage, but would then jump up. The idea was that borrowers would refinance their loans before these interest-rate hikes kicked in (paying their mortgage broker a fat fee for the privilege).

In a world where house prices were always increasing, there was no problem with extending credit at generous loan-to-value ratios: the price of the house was likely to rise anyway... or so everyone thought. In 2007, house prices in the United States began to fall. All of a sudden, a lot of subprime borrowers found themselves in **negative equity** – their houses were worth less than the outstanding mortgage on them, so they couldn't sell their houses to repay their debts. It also meant they were unable to refinance their mortgage; a house that will only sell for $75,000 cannot be used as collateral on a $100,000 loan.

In principle, even this shouldn't have been a problem as the borrowers should have been able to continue paying their monthly repayments on their mortgages. But this is where that second feature of subprime mortgages became relevant. Many of these mortgages were coming to the end of their fixed rate period, so the interest rate and monthly payments were about to rise. With every other avenue closed, and monthly repayments rising to a level subprime borrowers would never be able to keep up, there was only one avenue left – default. Foreclosures – known as repossessions in the UK – skyrocketed from just over 800,000 in 2005 to more than two million by 2007.

This was only the beginning of a vicious cycle. As banks foreclosed on subprime mortgages in default, they sold the houses that formed the collateral as quickly as possible. This led to an increase in the supply of houses and a further fall in house prices, which led more subprime borrowers into negative equity and default. By 2011, foreclosures were close to four million.

The way the fall in house prices led to widespread default across so many subprime mortgage borrowers demonstrates that one of the assumptions that led people to see CDOs as safer than mortgages was false. The risks of the mortgages that went into CDOs were in fact much

CDOs: safe as houses they were not. This residence in Queens, New York was boarded up by an activist group to discourage a bank from reclaiming the house, throwing out the owner and selling it by auction.

larger and more strongly *correlated* than the financial modellers had realized. Defaults by some borrowers caused prices to fall, triggering a spiral of further defaults and falling house prices.

As Keynes once observed, "owe your banker £1,000, and you are at his mercy; owe him £1 million and the position is reversed". Each individual subprime borrower owed the bank enough money that they were in trouble; collectively they owed the banks enough money that the banks were in trouble.

In terms of banks' balance sheets, this was a massive solvency shock as the value of many banks' assets in mortgages and CDOs fell dramatically overnight. As described earlier, such a shock must be matched on the liability side by a squeeze on the banks' equity. Needing to meet capital adequacy ratios, banks were now faced with an urgent need to either increase their equity or reduce their risk-weighted assets by selling assets and keeping hold of the cash that came their way. It was this behaviour on the part of so many banks which was partly responsible for the ensuing credit crunch.

The credit crunch

All banks knew that they were facing huge losses as a result of the wave of subprime defaults, but it was very difficult to work out exactly how much. The CDOs were too complicated in their structure, especially when talking about CDOs made up of other CDOs and CDOs on top of that. The CDOs became virtually impossible to value and price, and so while they had been very easy to trade before the wave of defaults, after the crisis hit no one wanted to buy them. So a large proportion of the assets that banks owned which had been purchased as liquid, safe assets now looked decidedly illiquid and risky! And then things got worse...

Banks knew they were going to take large losses as a result of the position they had taken, effectively gambling that house prices would never fall. They also knew that other banks would take similar – maybe larger– losses for the same reasons. What if they lent money to another bank, and that bank turned out to have an even worse exposure to the housing market, and collapsed? They'd never see that money again. The possibility of default by a financial entity that owes you money is known as **counterparty risk** and, as a result of it, in the summer of 2007 banks stopped lending to each other at low interest rates. Up until this point, **interbank lending** had been a vital source of short-term funding for banks – if they suddenly needed funds to pay out to depositors, they'd usually rely on lending from each other. So banks now suffered a liquidity shock, as they

RIP Northern Rock

Northern Rock was a high-profile victim of the credit crunch. They had embraced the originate-to-distribute business model, borrowing heavily in interbank markets to raise the funds to offer to customers as mortgages, and then securitized the mortgages to pay back other banks so they could do it all again. As discussed above, all banks knew that they and all other banks would take huge losses from the write-downs in the value of CDOs. Northern Rock looked particularly vulnerable and so other banks, suspicious of its true level of exposure, shunned it en masse.

In September 2007, Northern Rock was forced to approach the Bank of England as lender of last resort. When news of this got out, it caused panic among Northern Rock's depositors. The result was the first bank run in Britain for where depositors rushed to withdraw their money, causing a sharp, sudden liquidity shock.

To stem the panic, the government moved very quickly to raise the limit on personal deposits guaranteed by the Financial Services Compensation Scheme and to guarantee all the deposits in Northern Rock, but it was too late. Efforts to find a private buyer willing to take on Northern Rock came to nothing, and so, in February 2008, the British government nationalized the bank. Once in government hands, the bank could be recapitalized by bailout money, with any profits from selling it on coming back to the public purse.

were unable to rollover the debts they had been using to lend out money. This was the **credit crunch**.

If banks' finances had been clearly understood by everyone involved, the credit crunch would have been far less severe. Banks would have been able to make a rational assessment of each other's financial health and been able to lend to each other at appropriate rates. But the complexity of the CDOs in which mortgages had been bundled meant banks had a great deal of difficulty working out how much money other banks might lose as a result of problems in the US housing market. This lack of transparency was only compounded by the way in which a lot of the potential exposure to the housing market was kept off the balance sheet.

As a result banks had little idea how large each other's exposure was to the problem. Indeed, they barely understood *their own* exposures. Interbank lending simply dried up. This threatened the liquidity of banks that relied on it, forcing them to sell off assets in fire sales to pay their debts. But this would reduce asset prices, threatening the solvency of banks regardless of their liquidity problems. And so the stability of the entire financial sector became imperilled. As the box overleaf explains, this eventually necessitated a vast global bailout

RIP Lehman Brothers

Before the financial crisis, Lehman Brothers was the fourth largest investment bank in the United States. At 1.45 in the morning on 15 September 2008, Lehman Brothers declared itself bankrupt.

Lehman and its various **off-balance sheet vehicles** had been heavily exposed to the American subprime housing disaster. As a result, it was simply unable to absorb its losses from **subprime mortgages** with its small equity base. In the weeks prior to Lehman's bankruptcy, there had been a desperate search for a buyer with interest from the Korea Development Bank, Bank of America, and Barclays, but to no avail.

For Lehman Brothers, there was no bailout, and so it was forced to declare bankruptcy. This shocked global markets, causing widespread turmoil. First, there was counterparty risk involving Lehman itself. Although no one had deposits with Lehman Brothers, it was a massive international investment bank and many other banks had lent money to it or borrowed money from it, depositing assets as collateral. It was going to take a long time to work out which of Lehman's creditors would get what. So uncertainty was going to persist for a long time as to how large other banks' losses would be as a result of Lehman's bankruptcy, and whether it would take other banks with it.

But second, and more importantly, the failure of the authorities to bail out Lehman Brothers suddenly made the other banks look a lot riskier. If Lehman wasn't too big to fail, who was? A collapse in confidence in the financial sector put the entire system at risk. Governments across the world had no option but to intervene and bail out their banks.

From crisis to collapse

The crisis originated in – and initially afflicted – the decidedly surreal world of international finance. But it wasn't long before its effects extended to the rest of the global economy – the parts journalists like to call the *real* economy. If the losses to banks had been vast – by April 2009, the IMF put them at $4.1tn – the cost to the wider economy would be devastating. All major developed economies suffered steep recessions. Indeed, the *world's* GDP per capita fell more sharply in 2009 than it had in any previous recession since World War II. This **Great Recession** had socially disastrous consequences for the developed world. In Spain, for example, unemployment rose by more than ten percentage points between 2007 and 2011.

How did the crisis spread out from Wall Street to Main Street? Broadly speaking, there were two processes involved. First, as many of the previously safe, liquid assets banks held became worthless and impossible to

The fault, dear Brutus, lies not in our stars but in ourselves... blaming governments

When it comes to assigning blame, we can bash the bankers all we like, but few of them crossed the line into illegality. We can blame the regulators, but they just enforced the rules: they didn't make them. A big part of the problem was the rules themselves, and the people with ultimate responsibility for the rules were the politicians. In the years before the crisis, almost all politicians, those in government and those in opposition, were climbing over each other to say how they would reduce the "burden" of regulation on the financial sector. Nobody in the mainstream was calling for tighter regulation.

So why did politicians deregulate the financial sector and fail to see the coming storm? First, remember that politicians (with one or two exceptions) tend not to have any expertise in economics, so they are somewhat reliant on the advice they receive. Part of the problem was that faith in the model of **light-touch regulation** followed the same path as the financial bubble itself. In every year that the financial sector produced astonishing profits (and astonishing tax revenues), the advisors to politicians (many of them bankers) saying the financial sector represented a new paradigm of wealth creation looked a little more credible and the advisors urging caution looked a little less credible. This process continued throughout the NICE era, leading to further deregulation in order to stimulate further financial innovation.

What happened then was a case of **regulatory capture** (see **Chapter 7**) that went to the heart of government. But it is worth asking to what extent politicians were responsible for having been "captured" in this way. They were neither economic nor financial experts in most cases, and so their only sources of information were the ones that fell into their laps – in most cases coming from economists, regulators, and the financial sector. However, we should also consider whether we are entitled to expect slightly more of our politicians. It doesn't take a huge amount of financial expertise to ask questions, and politicians should always be a bit wary of their sources of information.

sell, the asset side of banks' balance sheets fell. This meant the liabilities side had to fall as well, through their shareholders' equity. And this put banks in the position of needing to raise their ratio of equity to the value of their loans in order to meet capital adequacy requirements. There were two ways of doing this: either raising more equity from private investors or public-sector bailout funds; or reducing the amount of loans they made. And pushed to the very limits of solvency, banks had to do both.

However, by cutting back so drastically on lending, they threatened the solvency of all manner of businesses that relied on lending for their operations. Some businesses worked on the basis that they could raise short-term credit should they need it; others assumed they'd be able to raise new debt to pay off old debt when it reached its maturity. All of a sudden, these business models were no longer viable, and previously healthy firms went to the wall. The credit crunch had hit the real economy.

The second process was more general. As described earlier, one of the less stable features of the NICE era was an under-appreciation by investors of the risks facing global economic growth. The crisis prompted a sudden revision of this view. Perceiving greater risks all over the economy, they ceased to invest widely and retreated to a few safe havens, notably gold and American and German government bonds. Instead of investing,

The Eurozone: lacking peripheral vision

In some ways, the Eurozone crisis that began in 2009 is a microcosm of the wider global economic turmoil that sparked it. Its sources were very similar: a banking crisis, which hit Spain and Ireland particularly hard, requiring gargantuan government bailouts; and a simultaneous reassessment of risk, with investors shunning the debt of poorly managed economies such as Greece and Italy. The result was that the governments of many of the Eurozone's "peripheral" economies were suddenly unable to borrow money at low interest rates, calling their solvency into question. What had started as a private debt crisis with subprime borrowers in the United States defaulting on loans became a **sovereign debt crisis** in Europe.

When a country cannot borrow more money, it becomes very difficult to find the money for ordinary government expenditure and for servicing the debt the government has issued historically. Default beckons. This is problematic enough on its own, but being in a single currency area makes it even more so. An individual country might be able to default, their currency depreciate as a result, and then export their way to economic growth on the basis of the more competitive exchange rate. But being in the Eurozone closed off this path to the likes of Greece.

However, the single currency also meant that other European countries had a strong interest in ensuring that the periphery pulled through the crisis. Broadly speaking there were two reasons. First, countries can suffer from contagion in much the same way as banks, and while a default by Greece might not be hugely expensive for the richer eurozone economies, a default by a larger southern eurozone country, such as Italy, would be much more expensive. So there is a hope that by bailing out Greece, lenders will be reassured and other countries will not suffer from a similar crisis of confidence in their debt. The second and related issue concerns the debt holders, who include many Northern European banks who might then need a bail out themselves in the event of all-out Greek default. But bailing out "feckless Mediterraneans" proved just as unpopular with taxpayers as picking up the tab for greedy bankers; and the Eurozone's distinctly unwieldy decision-making process made it difficult to agree the terms of any deal.

firms and households stashed their money in safe assets to protect themselves from future calamities and the economy suffered.

A problem with both of these processes was that the rational responses of individual banks, firms, and households to them, when taken by everyone, tended to make the problem worse. If all banks decide to lend less, many firms will be forced out of business, meaning banks' loans are less likely to be repaid and so they should reduce their lending even more to meet capital adequacy ratios. And if firms and households hoard cash to protect themselves, the resulting fall in investment makes the economy more vulnerable – meaning they should save even more. It was an example of animal spirits turning beastly (see **Chapter 14**).

With a terrifying meltdown in the offing, governments and central banks responded with extraordinary fiscal and monetary stimulus measures. Budget deficits exploded – topping ten percent of GDP in both the US and UK – and with official interest rates close to zero, monetary authorities launched successive rounds of **quantitative easing**, where central banks purchased long term government bonds and other safe assets from banks in order to reduce their returns and thus encourage investors to switch to lending to firms and consumers.

If quantitative easing looked a lot like more bailout money, that was because, in part, it was. Governments faced the dilemma that, in order to revive the financial sector, banks needed to rebuild their balance sheets by curtailing lending; but that, in order to stimulate the economy, banks needed to support business by increasing lending. The only way to achieve both aims was to offer the banks massive public-sector support.

At the time of writing, recovery in the developed world has been underwhelming, with America faring reasonably well, but the UK, Japan, and – especially – the Eurozone (see box opposite) disappointing. Though economists disagree on the best way forward, one thing understanding the crisis tells us is that an essential ingredient of a sustained recovery is a healthy banking sector.

And finally, blaming...

Economists were certainly caught by surprise by the credit crunch and ensuing Great Recession. To make matters worse, some of them were cheerleaders for the securitization and off balance-sheet accounting measures that we now know helped to cause the crisis. This failure did not escape Queen Elizabeth II of the UK, who couldn't resist raising the subject during a visit to the London School of Economics, asking why the crisis had not been foreseen. This prompted perhaps one of the more surreal moments of the whole story when the great and the good among the British Academy felt the need to answer the Queen in an open letter.

They highlighted the difference between the risk to a specific institution or financial instrument and the risk to the financial system as a whole. In essence, their argument was that while plenty of people were trying to look at the risk to institutions, no one was considering the system-wide risks that resulted from securitization and bank leverage.

There is a sense in which this is a poor excuse. The privilege of an academic life is to be able to ask the questions no one has thought of yet. So among all academics, such a failure of collective imagination should not really have happened and someone *should have* realized that such systemic risks posed a question that was both interesting and important. Was there some sort of bias in the discipline against doom-mongering? Were economists too beholden to the consultancy fees they could earn from the finance industry to question their practices? These are all questions worthy of serious consideration.

But does the failure of economists to predict and prevent the financial crisis somehow debunk the whole enterprise of economics, or show that the way it is practised is fundamentally misguided? Your authors sincerely hope that, having reached the end of this book, you don't think so. The economist's box of tools is fashioned for an eccentric blueprint of the way people behave and the global economic system functions. Economists failed to use this toolkit to fix global finance before the crisis, and they will doubtless fail again in other ways. But though the tools are imperfect, they have developed a body of knowledge that explains a staggering amount: how individual producers and consumers determine supply and demand; how markets work and how they can fail; how prosperity can develop and spread; and how government policy can manage the ebb and flow of economic activity. The toolkit can even explain, albeit with hindsight, what happened in the world of finance in 2007–8 and how it affected everyone else. Of course there's much more work to be done, but without economics we would be, both intellectually and financially, all the poorer.

PART SEVEN:

Resources

Books

Economics books don't often compete with fiction titles on bestsellers lists. The majority of economics volumes published are mainly destined for a dusty corner of a university library. This short list unapologetically opts for the more entertaining reading in the field with a nod to more specialist texts that have been useful to the authors in developing their wider understanding of the subject.

General reading

Tim Harford, *The Undercover Economist* (2006) and *The Logic of Life* (2008). One reviewer (David Bodanis) described reading *The Undercover Economist* as like spending an ordinary day wearing x-ray goggles. The book takes a number of oddities we observe in everyday life (and many we don't necessarily observe) and explains the economics behind them. It also explains how the economist's toolkit and a keen awareness of incentives can be used to solve various policy problems. *The Logic of Life* focuses on several decisions that seem, on the face of it irrational, and goes on to show how, given the incentives faced by the protagonists, they are, in fact, rational.

Steven E. Landsburg, *The Armchair Economist* (1993) and *More Sex is Safer Sex* (2007). Consists of a series of short, entertaining essays contemplating some problem or issue. These pieces demonstrate and explain the economist's way of thinking about almost any problem whatsoever, and do so with a level of wit that is sometimes cutting, such as: "A fiasco of this magnitude merits wider recognition. We learn from the mistakes of others, so it is a stroke of fortune to find so many mistakes gathered in a single place." *More*

Sex is Safer Sex was written with the express purpose of challenging the preconceptions that come from "common sense". Here, Landsburg uses economic logic to propose new and surprising ways of thinking about problems and their equally surprising solutions. The problems covered illustrate the wide range of issues to which economic thinking can be applied, from the spread of sexually transmitted diseases to the differences in the price of insurance in different cities.

Steven Levitt & Stephen Dubner, *Freakonomics* (2005). In the first of the bestselling *Freakonomics* sequence of books the authors use the economic methods of considering incentives to answer questions that economists are not normally thought of as asking. Such questions include: why do drug dealers tend to live with their parents; why was there a drop in crime in the USA in the late 1990s; and how can we spot teachers cheating on tests on behalf of their students? The answers are often surprising.

Paul Krugman, *The Accidental Theorist* (1999). This is a collection of short essays by Paul Krugman, usually written in response to some (at that point) current issue in the news and published in *Slate* or *The New York Times*. This makes it relatively easy to dip in and out of the book and enjoy each essay in isolation. Krugman's aim is to dispel many economic fallacies and misconceptions frequently encountered in newspaper commentary and policy circles.

Tyler Cowen, *Discover Your Inner Economist* (2007). This has been described as an economics self-help book, but don't expect to read it and then be able to play the markets like Gordon Gekko. This book is about how you can use incentives to improve things in your everyday life and get more of what you want. One of the key points made is that not all incentives are monetary, and there are times when monetary incentives will undermine other, more efficient, incentives.

Dan Ariely, *Predictably Irrational* (2009). In this book, behavioural economist Dan Ariely describes some of the ways in which human beings fall short of the perfectly rational ideal of *homo economicus*. The book contains lots of examples of the experiments used to prove that these shortfalls in rationality exist. The emphasis is on the way in which these biases are not random, but systematic, and the way in which they are able to persist despite the presence of market forces. Hence the title, *predictably* irrational.

Joseph Stiglitz, *Globalization and its Discontents* (2002). Stiglitz wrote this book based on his experiences since leaving academia, first to work as an economic advisor to the Clinton administration and then to work at the World Bank. Stiglitz believes that globalization certainly has the potential to be a force for good which will lift people out of poverty, but that the global institutions that manage international financial crises are too dogmatic and that the policies they insist on in return for relief are not always appropriate. Stiglitz argues that he great potential of globalization to raise living standards is being missed.

Richard Layard, *Happiness* (2005). This is the book in which Richard Layard sets out his argument that although we are getting richer, we are not getting any happier. He proceeds to examine what causes happiness and what governments might be able to do to make their citizens happier.

The classics

You might actually be surprised at how few economists have read the classic texts most often associated with economics. A straw and entirely unscientific poll conducted among your authors' contemporaries at graduate school was startling: fewer than twenty percent had read at least one out of the two classics.

However, it is worth asking why we find this so surprising. The ideas expressed in these books are hardly at the cutting edge of modern research; they are now the basics. The technology of communicating ideas has advanced since these books were written so these ideas will be grasped more quickly if a student consults a modern textbook rather than the original texts. Anyone who does not appreciate the benefits of grasping the basic ideas more quickly does not have the appreciation of efficiency that will make for a good economist. Nevertheless two books stand out.

Adam Smith, *An Inquiry into the Nature and Causes of the Wealth of Nations* (1776). Widely regarded as the first book on economics, it has certainly been influential. It was not long after publication that the book was being referred to in political debates. It is also the source of the oft-cited economic analogy of the "invisible hand" which guides people, when seeking to act in their own interest, to promote the public interest as well.

John Maynard Keynes, *The General Theory of Employment, Interest, and Money* (1936). This was Keynes' attack on the classical economic model. In it he advocated a new way of thinking about the economy which could allow for the possibility of recessions caused by insufficient aggregate demand. This model also meant that there was room for government action to increase demand during a recession.

More technical books

The list below includes textbooks in both microeconomics and macroeconomics, which are frequently used in university courses and thus usually regularly updated. These are typically the books the authors have found most helpful when learning about economics themselves and which they use in teaching.

Robert H. Frank, *Microeconomics and Behavior* (2009)

Hal R. Varian, *Intermediate Microeconomics: A Modern Approach* (2009)

N. Gregory Mankiw, *Macroeconomics* (2012)

Wendy Carlin & David Soskice, *Macroeconomics: Imperfections, Institutions, and Policies* (2006)

Joshua D. Angrist & Jörn-Steffen Pischke *Mostly Harmless Econometrics.* (2008) The empirical side of economics, finding the relationships that will prove or disprove economic theories is known as econometrics. This book provides a good introduction to the most commonly used econometric methods for distinguishing between true relationships and mere tricks of randomness. While it is written in an accessible style, some background in statistics is required.

Websites

There is no shortage of websites with reference to general economic principles and recent information, from Wikipedia (though be careful) to *The Economist* magazine. Our list highlights the voices of individual contemporary economists and two leading online resources. A dedicated companion website to this book maintained by the authors with topical links and further resources can be found at www.theeconomicsguide.com

Blogs

Many economists have taken to the events of the internet revolution with gusto, and blog and tweet with an economic perspective on the issues of the day. Economics blog posts come in two broad types. Some will contain in-depth analysis of some current issue or a link to a newspaper comment piece where the blogger previously wrote their analysis; others will operate by providing links to other people's analysis of some issue which the blogger found interesting.

Both of your authors blog:

Oliver Walker
oliwalkerecon.wordpress.com

Andrew Mell
econspective.blogspot.co.uk

Some excellent examples of other economics blogs are:

N. Gregory Mankiw
gregmankiw.blogspot.co.uk

Paul Krugman
krugman.blogs.nytimes.com

Tyler Cowen and **Alex Tabarrok**
marginalrevolution.com

Steven Landsburg
www.thebigquestions.com

Tim Harford timharford.com

Freakonomics freakonomics.com/blog

Other online resources

One standout online resource for anyone who wants to learn more about economics is Jodi Beggs' website: economistsdoit-withmodels.com. The web address is an indication of the kind of humour to expect. The website contains educational materials in the form of video lectures and economics problems (and solutions) as well as blog posts by the author on current issues.

The founders of the **Marginal Revolution** blog have also founded the Marginal Revolution University (mruniversity.com) with free to watch videos explaining economic ideas and economic concepts. It is also possible to enrol for a course online, taking a final exam and gaining a certificate upon completion.

Index